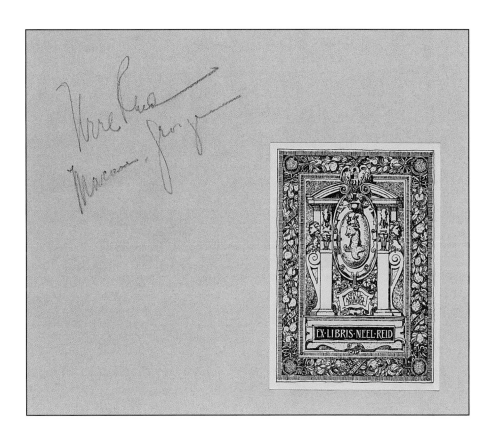

EX·LIBRIS·NEEL·REID

J. NEEL REID
ARCHITECT

of

Hentz, Reid & Adler

and

the Georgia School of Classicists

William R. Mitchell Jr. (signature)

WILLIAM R. MITCHELL, JR.

PHOTOGRAPHY BY JAMES R. LOCKHART

A GOLDEN COAST BOOK
for
THE GEORGIA TRUST FOR HISTORIC PRESERVATION

The Georgia Trust for Historic Preservation, chartered in 1973, is the country's largest statewide,
non-profit preservation organization with more than 9,500 members. Committed to preserving and enhancing
Georgia's communities and their diverse historic resources for the education and enjoyment of all, the Georgia Trust
markets endangered properties through its Revolving Fund, provides design assistance to Georgia Main Street
communities, connects Georgia's educators and students with their local historic resources in Georgia counties,
and advocates for funding and laws aiding preservation efforts.

For information on the Georgia Trust, write to:
Department Manager, Communications
Georgia Trust for Historic Preservation
1516 Peachtree Street, NW
Atlanta, GA 30309-2916

This project was conceived and initiated by William R. Mitchell, Jr.,
The History Business, Inc., Atlanta.

Designed and produced by Van Jones Martin,
Golden Coast Publishing Company, Savannah.
Edited by Jane Powers Weldon and William R. Mitchell, Jr.
Illustration research assistance: Michael Rose and Bill Hull, Atlanta History Center,
Kathryn S. Brackney, Architecture Library, Georgia Tech.
Color Separations by Digital Pre-Press International, San Francisco, California.
Printed in Hong Kong through Asia Pacific Offset

2nd Printing 2003

Dedicated to
E. Meredith Reid and Neel W. Reid

FOREWORD AND LIST OF DONORS

The Neel Reid Educational Fund of the Georgia Trust for Historic Preservation was established in 1993 to publish this book, the Georgia Trust's first major publication. As the Trust nears its twenty-fifth anniversary and ten-thousandth member, we are pleased to publish the work of a well-known Georgia writer-historian and preservationist. Proceeds from the book sales will be used for educational and preservation purposes.

The Neel Reid Committee of the Georgia Trust for Historic Preservation happily presents this scholarly volume, which is beautiful and complete in the manner of Neel Reid's designs. With it the Trust hopes to encourage the preservation of Reid's authentic early twentieth-century contributions to the architecture of the South. For all of their work, we wish to thank William R. Mitchell, Jr., and his associates on this project, James R. Lockhart and Van Jones Martin, and the Georgia Trust staff. As we celebrate, we recognize and thank all whose generosity has made this important publication possible.

Gregory B. Paxton, President
Georgia Trust for Historic Preservation

Mr. W. Moses Bond, Cochair
Neel Reid Committee

Mrs. Frank C. Jones, Cochair
Neel Reid Committee

NEEL REID CIRCLE

Anonymous Friend
Margaret Davison Block
Mrs. Alice Hand Callaway
Katherine John Murphy Foundation
Mr. and Mrs. Samuel B. Kellett
Mr. and Mrs. Arthur L. Montgomery
Amy and Harry Norman
Mrs. D. Williams Parker
H. English and Ermine Cater Robinson Foundation
Mrs. Thomas L. Williams, Jr.

CORINTHIAN ORDER

Neel W. Reid
Mrs. Deen Day Smith

IONIC ORDER

Cherokee Garden Club
Mrs. Hugh M. Dorsey, Jr.
Mrs. Edward P. Ellis
Mr. and Mrs. Frank C. Jones
Kilpatrick Stockton LLP
Mr. and Mrs. John R. McDonald
Peachtree Garden Club
Mr. and Mrs. Richard Rawlins
Mr. T. Marion Slaton

SUBSCRIBER

Constance Spalding Anderson,
    in memory of Hal F. Hentz
Mr. and Mrs. Byron Attridge
Mr. William N. Banks
Mr. and Mrs. Griffin Bell
Jean Robitscher Bergmark
Mrs. Joseph E. Birnie
Mr. and Mrs. W. Moses Bond
Mr. David Richmond Byers III
Mr. and Mrs. John H. Cheatham Jr.
Mrs. George S. Cobb Jr.
Mr. and Mrs. Thomas G. Cousins
Mary Jane Hill Crayton
Mrs. Elizabeth Hay Curtis
Mrs. Julius B. Dodd
Mr. and Mrs. Jerry A. Dubrof
Anne Smith Florance
Mr. James R. Gamble Jr.
Mrs. John T. Godwin

Mr. and Mrs. Bernard Gray
Mr. and Mrs. Robert H. Gunn Jr.
Mr. and Mrs. Sheffield Hale
Anne and Bradley Hale
Dr. and Mrs. William M. Harper IV
Mr. and Mrs. Neil H. Hightower
Mr. and Mrs. Robert P. Hodges
Mr. C. Ralph Hodges Jr.
Dr. and Mrs. Peter O. Holliday III
Mr. and Mrs. Fred A. Hoyt Jr.
Ms. C. Randolph Jones
Mr. and Mrs. C. Dexter Jordan Jr.
Mr. and Mrs. Robert A. Keller
Mr. and Mrs. Austin P. Kelley
Mrs. E. Buford King Jr.
Dr. and Mrs. James F. Kirkpatrick
Mr. and Mrs. William Lanham
Mr. George H. Lanier
Mrs. John Lowenberg

Mr. and Mrs. Roy Mann Jr.
Mr. and Mrs. Harold F. McCart Jr.
Anne Morgan Moore
Mrs. O. Ray Moore
Carolyn Reynolds Parker
Mr. and Mrs. Frank A. Player
Mr. and Mrs. S. DuBose Porter
E. Meredith Reid
Mr. and Mrs. Clayton E. Rich
Mr. and Mrs. Hugh Rickenbaker Jr.
Mr. and Mrs. Roby Robinson Jr.
Mary Rose and Mack Taylor
Mr. and Mrs. Wesley Rhodes
    Vawter III
Phil and Peggy Walden
Mrs. Wayne Watson
Jane Bradley Wheeler
Mr. Tom B. Wight

FRIEND

Jennie Lee Lehman Acree
Mrs. Halstead T. Anderson
Mr. Norman Davenport Askins, P.C.
Lillian A. Balentine
Virginia Shankle Bales
Mr. and Mrs. James J. W. Biggers Jr.
Mr. and Mrs. Gene Brown
Dr. and Mrs. James C. Bryant Jr.
Miss Patricia Stewart Burgess
Mr. and Mrs. Franklin Burke
Mr. and Mrs. C. Merrell Calhoun,
    in memory of Hal F. Hentz
Dr. and Mrs. F. Phinizy Calhoun Jr.
    (Dr. Calhoun is deceased)
Dr. and Mrs. James E. Clark
Mr. and Mrs. Thomas Hal Clarke
Mr. and Mrs. R. Barksdale Collins
Mr. and Mrs. Charles S. Conklin II
Mr. F. H. Boyd Coons
Martha F. Crabtree
John D. Currie Jr.
Mr. and Mrs. Jarrett L. Davis
Mr. and Mrs. W. M. Dickey
Mr. and Mrs. Robert L. Dickey
Mr. and Mrs. Clare H. Draper IV
Mrs. Beverly DuBose Jr.
Mr. and Mrs. J. Joseph Edwards
Mr. and Mrs. H. Alan Elsas
Mr. and Mrs. Freddie W. Evans Jr.
Federated Garden Clubs of Macon, Inc.
Cathy Mitchell Fiebelkorn
Mr. and Mrs. James R. Fortune Jr.
Mr. and Mrs. Holcombe T. Green Jr.
Mrs. Mary Guy Robinson Gunn
Mr. and Mrs. John C. Hagler III

Mr. and Mrs. C. Edward Hansell
Elizabeth Warner Harbin
Mr. and Mrs. Jack H. Harmon
Mr. and Mrs. Byron Harris
Mr. Richard E. Hatfield and
    Mr. Timothy R. Thomas
Mrs. Nathan V. Hendricks III
Marian and Benjamin Hill
Dr. and Mrs. Jasper T. Hogan Jr.
Mr. and Mrs. Howell Hollis III
Stephanie and Henry Howell
Mrs. Lowry W. Hunt
Intown Macon Neighborhood Association
Mr. and Mrs. E. Neville Isdell
David H. Jenkins
Anne and Jim Kelley
F. Clason Kyle
Mr. and Mrs. Cody Laird III
Mr. and Mrs. J. Hicks Lanier II
Mr. and Mrs. William F. Law Jr.
Mr. and Mrs. Tony Long
Elaine and Jerry Luxemburger
Miss Isabella T. Lynn
Elizabeth A. Lyon
Mr. and Mrs. William Jay MacKenna
Macon Heritage Foundation
Mrs. Katie Dickey Marbut
Dr. and Mrs. Sanford Matthews
Ruth Johnson McDaniel
Mr. and Mrs. Clinton McKellar Jr.
Mr. and Mrs. John Hays Mershon
Middle Georgia Historical Society
Mrs. William R. Minnich
Joseph Henry Hightower Moore
Mr. Dudley L. Moore Jr.

Mr. and Mrs. Frederick L. Muller
Anne and Flew Murphey
Mr. and Mrs. C. V. Nalley III
Mr. and Mrs. Bert R. Oastler
Mr. and Mrs. Wiley S. Obenshain Jr.
Mr. and Mrs. George J. Polatty
Mrs. Catherine T. Porter
Blanche Neel Redding
Charles E. Roberts Jr.
Mrs. Peyton Robinson
Phillip R. Rogers
Mr. William E. Rudolph (Deceased)
Susanne and Roger Schlaifer
Ms. Frances Schultz
Val and Mary Sheridan
Mrs. William P. Simmons
Stephen K. Simpson
Jeffie Tyson Smith
Dean DuBose Smith
Mr. and Mrs. Hughes Spalding Jr.
Jim Speake
Laura Smith Spearman
Joyce Milner Sterling
Mr. and Mrs. John P. Stevens
Dollie Cardwell Swanson
Betty Talmadge
Mr. and Mrs. Marion L. Talmadge
Mr. and Mrs. John H. Terrell Jr.
Bruce H. Thompson
Mr. and Mrs. Hugh B. Williamson III
Mr. and Mrs. Thomas M. Willingham
Susan B. Withers
Mr. and Mrs. E. Howard Young
Mr. and Mrs. W. D. Young

CONTENTS

PREFACE AND ACKNOWLEDGMENTS

Background for this undertaking, and acknowledgment of help received, must begin long before 1993 when the project began. My interest in the architecture, career, and mystique of Neel Reid and his era began in the 1950s when I was a student at Atlanta's Westminster Schools. Two influential books published then, one scholarly and the other journalistic, piqued my interest: Frederick Doveton Nichols's *The Early Architecture of Georgia* and Medora Field Perkerson's *White Columns in Georgia.* Seeming to speak directly to me as an Atlantan in the early stages of an architectural history hobby, which in time became my career, Nichols wrote, "So great, indeed, was the classical fashion that it dominated the architecture of Georgia, except for the later years of the nineteenth century, and the first part of the twentieth when it was revived in the wide practice of Neel Reid, Hentz, Adler & Shutze, Henry Toombs and others" (p. 139).

My parents gave me a Christmas copy of Nichols's book, and that statement about Neel Reid jumped out from the early history. Reid's revived classicism was all around me to study in Atlanta, but most examples of nineteenth-century classical revival were located elsewhere in the state. Card games on a classic Reid side porch at the home of a classmate's parents on Habersham Road, in the midst of "Reid country," made Reid a familiar and friendly presence and his work more accessible than Greek Revival and other early buildings miles away.

In those days, I was becoming aware that Reid's beaux arts classicism and eclecticism could produce congenial places for living and visiting, places which had an all-around beauty, including intimate formal gardens, that I did not find in modernist designs or in more modest schemes. (I pondered why Georgia produced Neel Reid and his compatriots, and Chicago, Louis Sullivan and Frank Lloyd Wright.) About the same time, I had read the several mentions of Neel Reid in Perkerson's *White Columns,* especially that knowledgeable journalist's account of Reid's purchase of Mimosa Hall, an antebellum classical house north of Atlanta in Roswell, as his home, which he proceeded to landscape and renovate much as it is today. Perkerson wrote: "One of the South's most gifted architects . . . the late Neel Reid [who] designed many of the houses which have won Atlanta its reputation as a city of beautiful homes . . . chose an old house . . . for himself" (p. 176).

During current research, I found that Medora Perkerson had done a similar article for the *Atlanta Journal Magazine,* October 20, 1946. Written to coincide with the establishment of the Peachtree Garden Club's Neel Reid landscape architecture scholarship at the University of Georgia, it was entitled "He Made Atlanta Beautiful." Such popular sources allowed the general public, of which I was an eager young member, some knowledge of what Perkerson called Reid's "creative genius"; that evaluation has been canonical in Georgia since Reid's early death from a brain tumor, February 14, 1926, in the prime of his career.

Nichols's and Perkerson's statements pointed to a possible relationship between historic architecture and the architects who design new buildings, hinted at historic preservation such as that of Mimosa Hall, and celebrated Neel Reid as a seminal figure of genius, all of which must be acknowledged as fundamental background for my work on the book in hand. Although this is first and foremost a book of documentary research, the romance and mystique of Reid's celebrated name, as well as nostalgia for the nearly vanished era from which he came, were inevitably influential. Ralph McGill, the noted *Atlanta Constitution* editor whom I grew up reading, once wrote about the South in *Vogue:* "And while the legend remains and the myth remains, there is a reality which in time may win, keeping only what was real and good in the legend" (1942). My research has only corroborated the popular view of Reid's importance, allowing me to keep what is "real and good" in the legend.

Neel Reid and his partner, Hal Hentz, and their later partner, Rudolph Sartorius Adler, were all "Southern boys," and by the time the Hentz, Reid & Adler partnership was formed in 1916, all three were living in Atlanta, although only Adler was a native. (Adler was not born in Germany, as one writer guessed.) Their geographic roots and the context in which they designed certainly help explain the devotion they held for classicism and the lasting respect they have received in their home region, enduring even through the fashionable phase of modernism. In mid-twentieth-century America, particularly in architecture and graduate schools, classicism was dismissed as irrelevant to the modern world. Statements from an American history textbook published in 1961 remind us that "The New York firm of McKim, Mead & White, which endeavored to revive the classical style by fitting it to American needs, however large its talents, was essentially imitative and derivative. These men copied and adapted European forms, and their designs had little relevance to the facts of American life and little vitality for the needs of the American scene, especially for the growing urban centers" (Current, pp. 580–81).

Academic opinion today has turned back 180 degrees from its mid-century condemnation to a point of renewed appreciation approximating the popular acclaim of Reid's era. To cite an example, University of Delaware Art History Professor Wayne Craven, writing in his 1994 college textbook *American Art, History and Culture*, contradicts with praise the interpretation of thirty years earlier: "The firm of McKim, Mead & White rose to the challenge of creating urban dignity and grandeur through a classical style that equaled the emerging American megalopolis in scale, organization and expressiveness. . . . They did this by adapting the architectural theories of the Ecole des Beaux Arts. . . . McKim, Mead & White infused the cities with a sense of order, humane sophistication, and exquisite taste" (page 293).

Through modernism's hegemony, appreciation of Neel Reid's wide variety of traditional work—both urban and suburban—survived in the more conservative, preservation-minded, traditionalist South, which never fully embraced the post–World War II anticlassical cause. In 1973, before the academic critics began to rediscover classicism's virtues, a celebration of Reid's work was sponsored by a group of people who had grown up, lived in, and socialized in his houses. Members of the Peachtree and Cherokee Garden Clubs, the oldest and next-oldest organizations of that kind in Atlanta, formed a trust to publish *Architecture of Neel Reid in Georgia* by James Grady (1907–92), a Georgia Tech professor of architecture. A few years before his death, Jim Grady inscribed for me my battered copy of this valuable and worthy production. He wrote, "For former student, fellow historian, with best wishes." We had known each other for many years; evidently, the emeritus professor believed by then that I had been a student of his, but I had never attended Georgia

Tech, although I appreciated his confidence. (Neel Reid is considered a founder of the Peachtree Garden Club and his mother, Mrs. John W. [Bessie Adams] Reid was a member.)

Professor Grady began his preface: "Architecture is so dependent on fashion that only recently have eclectic buildings of the late nineteenth and early twentieth centuries been considered suitable for preservation as examples of an important sequence in the . . . rapidly changing modes. . . . It is possible now to study them for their architectural qualities rather than as survivors of a decadent period when architects copied past styles to produce buildings without significance for their time" (p. viii).

Grady regretted that his book could not include "a complete catalogue of the firm's designs." For reasons discussed in the bibliography, this study is based on and includes a more complete and corrected catalogue, which is derived from the firm's actual buildings list beginning with its first jobs, c. 1909, a copy of which Grady did not have. The annotation of this lengthy list was one of the most time-consuming aspects of the research, as was the study, both on microfilm and in hard copy, of the working drawings and blueprints filed at the Atlanta History Center and Georgia Tech. (See bibliography and Appendix 3.) Designs were not confined to Georgia or even the South, nor only to domestic architecture, although that was Reid's first love. I have studied many of the firm's works *in situ*, especially those photographed for this book. Where feasible I have provided addresses, present conditions, and illustrations. There are wonderful discoveries and some lingering questions and uncertainties.

Knowledge, like gold, is where you find it. During research, I uncovered an *Atlanta Journal* lead editorial from February 16, 1926, two days after Reid's death, which eulogized him as "A Poet in Architecture." The editorial began: "'He created more beauty for others to live in than any other artist-architect, from the beginning of our city till now.' So writes one who watched the career and judged the genius of Neel Reid. Happier praise no man could have earned; better service no man could have rendered. Called hence in the full tide of his dream and doing, that rare young designer of stateliness and charm has left his memorial in the homes, the hearts, the lives of a people." It was lengthy and continued:

What a community likes not only reveals, but also largely determines what it is and shall become. To quicken its desire for things beautiful, fostering the while good taste and artistic judgement, is to enrich its soul and heighten its destiny. This was Neel Reid's contribution to Atlanta and to many another city of the South. In architecture he was a poet, born with an eye for harmony and proportion and with a deft creativeness that could translate his vision into form and fact. Fortunately, too, his gift was cultivated by study under masters in America and abroad. His years in Paris at L'Ecole des Beaux Arts and in leisurely travel through Europe were invaluable in maturing and refining his powers. He dedicated all to the land of his birth and upbringing.

A staff writer for the *Macon Telegraph* echoed this lyrical and laudatory approach about two years later, on August 5, 1928, with "Neel Reid, Poet in Architecture." Fortunately, that Macon writer's biographical facts can hardly be improved upon, as they were based on interviews with well-informed Reid family members and check out now as quite accurate. (Present members of the Reid family are acknowledged below.)

Warm eulogies, obituaries, and front-page articles at his death expressed the regard with which Reid and his work were held in his time, and it is essentially true that the beauty, status, and impact of his work had introduced architecture to the general public as a fine art worthy of practice, emulation, preservation, and poetic celebration in a way not quite done before (or since) in Georgia. With this book, perhaps that approach can be revived.

Although this is a history, a presentation of research about a career that ended a dozen years before I was born, there has been nothing dull about the research, protracted though it may have seemed. There has been an excitement in discovery—discovery that proves the reality of what was real and good in the legend. For example, I have passed and admired the handsome two-story brick house at 132 Peachtree Circle in the Atlanta neighborhood known as Ansley Park thousands of times during my many years of residence there, never knowing until this research that it was a "Neel Reid." On the firm's jobs list housed at the Atlanta History Center this structure is listed as "Number 134, the Misses

Nagle, Atlanta." The jobs are not dated and are listed in that simple way. The context indicated a date of about 1911–12. That was all I knew until, in the process of reviewing all of the hundreds of Hentz, Reid & Adler drawings that are filed and microfilmed at the history center, I recognized my old neighbor, and the Misses Nagle appeared in the 1913 city directory at that address. (Hal Hentz contributed these drawings and blueprints just before his death in 1972.) That Ansley Park house is only one of many discoveries published here. There are many in Druid Hills. (See Appendix 3.)

I must acknowledge the encouragement and support I have received all along the way from the 1950s—from family and friends, teachers, professors, and colleagues, all of whom have helped to make possible such works as this. Each of my already-published books, a dozen in all, has contributed to the ongoing process of acquiring knowledge and scholarly perspective, and most have had at least one mention of Reid or Hentz, Reid & Adler.

Professor Grady's book, by the way, long out of print, which sold for $30 in 1973, now trades for $300 and up, depending upon condition. It is an invaluable source, especially for illustrations of buildings that are now altered or demolished.

The monetary value of Neel Reid houses has also appreciated. One sold on Atlanta's Cherokee Road in 1980 for $740,000 and the same place for $3,500,000 in 1987. Both were the largest sales of record up to that time. But unlike the books, condition made little difference: that multi-million-dollar house needed a new slate roof.

The owner of the Cherokee Road "Neel Reid" and many other owners have helped and must be thanked for their cooperation as research and photography proceeded. Many of these have also contributed to the Neel Reid Educational Fund of the Georgia Trust for Historic Preservation. We established this tax-deductible fund in 1993–94 with inaugural contributions from the Peachtree Garden Club, Julie and Arthur Montgomery, and Marion Slaton of Atlanta; from Marguerite Williams of Thomasville, Georgia; and from surviving members of the Reid family in Baltimore—Joseph Neel Reid's niece and nephew (children of his brother, John Jr.), Meredith Reid and Neel W. Reid, who is sometimes called Neel Reid II in honor of his uncle. Meredith and

Neel remember their uncle at Mimosa Hall when they were small children visiting their grandmother, Bessie Adams Reid, who was originally of Jacksonville, Alabama. Their aunt Louise, who also resided at Mimosa Hall and who, like her brother Neel, never married, became their benefactor after their parents died when the children were teenagers. From Louise they inherited many valuable Need Reid–connected things from Mimosa Hall which had been packed away for years and have never been published. (See p. 189.) Three times I visited Meredith and Neel in Baltimore where they moved many years ago with their mother. In July 1996, the last visit, I was joined by the photographer Jim Lockhart, who cheerfully and professionally copied the numerous archival and other items, including furnishings, that were needed for the book. Among the memorabilia was Reid's diary from 1907 when he traveled in England and Europe, with accompanying colored pen-and-ink sketches that give a vivid idea of Reid's exceptional artistry. Also copied was Neel Reid's Columbia University yearbook when he was a special architectural student (1905–7) and for which he was the art editor and illustrator.

For this book project with the Georgia Trust for Historic Preservation, of which I had been an incorporating trustee in 1973, my title is author-consultant, and I have been involved in all phases with the trustees, the trust staff, and the Neel Reid Committee. Special thanks to W. Moses Bond of Atlanta, cochair with Mrs. Frank C. (Annie Anderson) Jones of Atlanta and Macon, and the committee members, who are listed below. Special thanks, also, to trust staff members who have contributed, as have the committee members, in ways too numerous to detail; this book is the evidence of all of their assistance.

Artistic collaboration was the mark of early twentieth-century American architectural classicists. Firms such as Hentz, Reid & Adler in Atlanta and McKim, Mead & White in New York practiced in what were essentially atelier offices based upon an American adaptation of the French Ecole des Beaux-Arts system of architectural education and practice, whereby apprentices assisted and learned from seasoned practitioners and the entire office learned from each other. Similarly, this book has also been a work of collaboration between me, as author-consultant, and others, including Jim Lockhart as photographer.

Also Van Jones Martin of Savannah, producer-editor-artist-photographer and publisher, joined the project to help realize and refine the conception I had been evolving over several years.

The magic of Neel Reid's legendary mystique opened many doors for us seventy years after his death. To all of those who opened theirs to us, "much obliged." Already acknowledged here are some who undoubtedly succumbed more to the legendary Reid than to me. In the bibliography are listed some who helped during research, and here are some others whom I want to thank as we turn to the prelude: Miriam H. Mitchell; Rebecca H. King; Baxter P. Jones, Esq.; George Owens Haskell III, Esq.; F. Sheffield Hale, Esq.; and Joseph M. Beck, Esq.; Hugh K. Rickenbaker Jr.; Jane Powers Weldon; Lynne Smith, Atlanta Document Services; Minuteman Press, 1421 Peachtree; Emily Gordy Dolvin; Mr. and Mrs. Lawson Yow; Mr. and Mrs. John McDonald; Mr. and Mrs. Leland Jackson; Margaret Davison Block. Also see people acknowledged in the bibliography.

The Neel Reid Committee of the Georgia Trust for Historic Preservation: W. Moses Bond and Mrs. Frank C. Jones, cochairs; Mrs. Julian S. Carr, Mrs. Joseph R. Curtis, W. M. Dickey Jr. (Macon chairman), Mrs. Hugh M. Dorsey Jr., Mrs. Edward P. Ellis, Mrs. Anne Gray, Howell Hollis III, Henry L. Howell, C. Randolph Jones, George H. Lanier, Mrs. Arthur L. Montgomery, Hugh K. Rickenbaker Jr., Mrs. Peyton Robinson, T. Marion Slaton, Mrs. Fluffy Tambke, Mrs. Susan Branch Withers, and Mrs. Thomas Lyle Williams Jr. Since the Reid book project began in 1993, two Georgia Trust chairmen have completed their terms, W. Moses Bond and T. Marion Slaton. At the time of publication, Mrs. J. Joseph Edwards is chairman. Much appreciation to them, their fellow trustees, and the Georgia Trust staff.

William R. Mitchell, Jr.

Note: Arranged by locale, sections after the prelude and introduction are somewhat self-contained and may be studied separately. The list of jobs in Appendix 3 contains significant descriptive information and is fundamental as an index to the jobs of the several partnerships for which Neel Reid was the principal designer. Due to new research and archival sources, this history may challenge some long-held misconceptions about Reid, his colleagues, and their works.

PRELUDE / *Esquisse*

Esquisse is the French word for sketch. It was used in the beaux arts
ateliers in a specific sense and means a preliminary sketch showing
the main ideas of a solution to a design problem.

For Neel Reid and this book we must think back seventy years and more, to another time—of porte cocheres and sleeping porches, French doors and parterre gardens, trellises and pergolas, porticoes and fanlights, summerhouses and servants' quarters—a time of classic but not antebellum columns, before the Great Depression and World War II.

We must look back through the latticework of time into the 1920s and earlier, prior to World War I, when Hentz, Reid & Adler came into being during the revived classicism of the beaux arts. It was the period of the Colonial Revival and the American Renaissance, that celebration of history, nationalism, and the City Beautiful—monumentally Roman in scale—which had received its impetus in the gilded days of the 1890s at the World's Columbian Exposi-

(12.1)

Above: Reid's esquisse of house for W. Emmett Small, Macon, 1908.
Opposite page: Neel Reid at Mimosa Hall, c. 1924–25, in his late thirties..

tion in Chicago. We must recall the days of McKim, Mead & White, the architects who helped New York City rival London and Paris as capitals of the Western world—the New York where, in the first decade of the twentieth century, three Atlantans, Hal Hentz (1883–1972), Neel Reid (1885–1926), and Rudolph Adler (1889–1945), studied architecture at Columbia University when Charles McKim's influence was pervasive.

We must envision an (always) ambitious, growing Atlanta, but with a much smaller population than today; with new, not-so-tall skyscrapers in a bustling downtown, when the genteel, green suburbs of Ansley Park, Druid Hills, Brookwood, and Buckhead were still being built, and local real estate fortunes were being assembled. We must envision a time before urban sprawl, superhighways, and jet aircraft; before air-conditioning, television, and shopping malls. But not before Coca-Cola! (One of Hentz & Reid's earliest jobs, before Adler became a partner in 1916, was a Coca-Cola Company factory in Atlanta about 1910.) It was a time of train stations, downtown department stores and movie palaces, swank apartment houses, and smart social clubs.

Let us remember those days when the Atlanta golf champion

(13.1)

Bobby Jones was a national hero, but had not yet won the Grand Slam (1930); when *Gone with the Wind* was only a gleam in its author's eyes, and Peachtree Street north of Ponce de Leon Avenue was largely residential. Let us recall the short-lived Florida boom of the early 1920s, when Hentz, Reid & Adler maintained a Tampa office, providing stylish "Mediterranean" buildings with tile roofs shimmering among newly planted palm trees. (Hal Hentz was originally from Florida and returned there to retire in 1943.) We should remember too, the Georgia towns that were also beginning to grow—among them Macon, in middle Georgia, where Reid was reared and where he started his youthful design practice, and where he and Hentz early on had a busy branch office.

Let us picture this world that Neel Reid helped to build and to give form and style. And let us imagine a rare thing—a Southern cultural hero—yes, and a Southern gentleman as well, handsome and social (a popular bachelor), but a genius who was first and foremost an artist and tastemaker, not yet forty-one years of age when a brain tumor took him away: loved, celebrated, mourned, and seldom forgotten.

Let us reacquaint ourselves with this champion of architecture, gardens, and interior decoration, of fine arts and antiques, a leader of charm and style who helped to establish architecture and landscape architecture as professions in his region. And let us be aware that he and his partners and staff of interns and draftsmen from their Candler Building (beaux arts atelier) office/studio founded a Georgia school of classicists, spawned numerous careers and other firms, and set lasting professional and aesthetic standards.

We must celebrate again these men from three generations ago who fostered the architecture department at the Georgia Institute of Technology, acted as teachers and design critics, and gave students part-time employment. At the same time they helped to start a chapter of the American Institute of Architects and encouraged the drafting of a state law for the registration of architects, a law that is still essentially intact.

We recall and celebrate these achievements, especially this legacy of the artistic leader and legendary hero of the Georgia school of classicists, Joseph Neel Reid, known as Neel. His Southern genius for the classical tradition shines in this book. May it long survive in the handsomely proportioned pediments and elegant but fragile fanlights from his drawings and designs—beautiful and abiding manifestations of American civilization from the first quarter of this century, providing inspiration for new schools of classicists in centuries to come.

Gentle reader, ladies and gentlemen, we present J. Neel Reid of Hentz, Reid & Adler, and the Georgia school of classicists.

INTRODUCTION / *Parti*

Parti is the French term used in the beaux arts ateliers for essential approach or scheme chosen for the solution to a design problem.

(14.1)

A public exhibition of architectural drawings held in downtown Atlanta during ten days of early May 1910 is where we begin. The exhibit was mounted in the club rooms of the Architectural Arts League at 130 ¹/₂ Peachtree Street. For the newly organized league (1909), it was a first annual exhibition in conjunction with the almost equally new Atlanta Chapter of the American Institute of Architects (1906). (For Atlanta of May 1910, a mixed architectural and theatrical metaphor is highly appropriate: Enrico Caruso and Geraldine Farrar and the Metropolitan Opera were in town from New York for the inaugural season of Opera Week, and the newspapers reported with civic pride on the architectural exhibit and grand opera; they were cited as evidence that the Georgia capital had fully recovered from the Civil War and was at center stage, which it then and evermore has sought.) Preserved at the Atlanta History Center is a fragile copy of the handsome hard-bound catalogue for the long-ago exhibit in which works by Neel Reid and his partner Hal Hentz and future part-

ner Rudolph Adler were displayed. This precious relic was dedicated to "the honored memory of Charles Follen McKim, Architect," and sets the stage for our history, for represented at this exhibition are many of our book's cast of characters, and here the plot was foreshadowed for what we are constructing—the foundation and ground plan.

Charles McKim, who had died the year before the exhibit, was the great beaux arts classicist of the renowned New York firm McKim, Mead & White. Mentor to a generation of architects, McKim influenced others by his teaching and exemplary professionalism and by his scholarly and restrained interpretations of splendid antique Roman and Renaissance precedents. His office nickname was Bramante, after the Italian Renaissance architect of genius, and he designed much of the Morningside Heights campus of New York's Columbia University in the Renaissance mode. He was also known for respecting American classical traditions and landmarks, and he was honored for the institutions he

GA · LIFE · INSVRANCE · CO. · BVILDING ·

Opposite page: Cover design for the catalogue for the Architectural Arts League exhibit, 1910.
Above: Rendering from the exhibit of the Georgia Life Insurance Building in Macon, job number 101.

fostered (in addition to Columbia), such as the still-thriving American Academy at Rome, Italy.

J. Neel Reid and Hal Fitzgerald Hentz, who became acquainted in Atlanta in 1905, had come under Charles McKim's direct influence while he was a professor and atelier head at the Columbia University School of Architecture—Reid, without other college experience, was a special student, a formal category at Columbia, for two years from 1905 to 1907; Hentz was a candidate for another bachelor's degree as he had already graduated from Emory College at Oxford, Georgia, in 1904. Both men had acquired practical experience as apprentices in architectural firms prior to going to New York and had traveled abroad for further study after their Columbia tenure. As members of the Arts League and the AIA (Hentz was secretary), Reid and Hentz were exhibitors at the 1910 show. Also exhibited were drawings by the late Gottfried L. Norrman (1856–1909), who had been Hentz and Reid's partner for less than a year when he died in the autumn of 1909; the short-lived partnership was styled Norrman, Hentz & Reid, in order of seniority. Represented also was a student drawing by Rudolph Sartorius Adler, another Atlantan who was then studying architecture at Columbia, where the three young Southerners had been acquainted; Adler had even joined the Southern Club there. His drawing for "A Monument to Robert Fulton" came from a group sent to the exhibit from the New York Society of Beaux-Arts Architects.

Among others whose work was exhibited are names familiar in the architectural history of Atlanta: Haralson Bleckley (1870–1933), who was the first Atlantan to study for a time in Paris at L'Ecole des Beaux-Arts; A. Ten Eyck Brown (1878–1940); W. T. Downing (1865–1918); Henrietta C. Dozier (1872–1947); Thomas Henry Morgan (1857–1940); and Francis Palmer Smith (1886–1971), who headed the department of architecture at Georgia Tech. Smith was its first professor; the department was started in 1908. The acknowledged student founder of that program, Ernest D. (Ed) Ivey (1887–1966), exhibited "A Country Home" and "End Pavilion of a Public Building." Another student in that department, and later a leading Georgia classicist, Philip T. Shutze (1890–1982), exhibited "A French Window and Balcony" and "A Fountain of a Formal Garden." Shutze would follow the pattern and also study at

Columbia. Both Ivey and Shutze would work with Neel Reid, Hal Hentz, and Rudolph Adler; Ivey formed his own firm in 1923 with Lewis Edmund Crook Jr. (1898–1967), another Hentz, Reid & Adler alumnus, and after Reid's tragic early death from brain cancer in 1926, Shutze would become Hentz and Adler's partner in the new firm of Hentz, Adler & Shutze (1927).

A dozen drawings were shown by "Hentz & Reid, Candler Building, Atlanta, Georgia," a large number for so young a firm, but prophetic of its output, success, and range of building types:

1. Building for Georgia Life Insurance Company, Macon, Georgia
2. Coca-Cola Building, Atlanta
3. Residence for Mrs. Helen Logan, Macon
4. Residence for Mr. T. C. Johnson, Atlanta
5. Residence for J. N. Neel, Macon [Joseph Neel, Reid family friend and business associate, gave Neel Reid his name, financial assistance, and patronage.]
6. Residence for Dr. E. G. Ballenger, Atlanta
7. Residence for Mrs. L. P. Hillyer, Macon
8. Residence for Thomas Hall, Macon
9. European Sketches by J. Neel Reid
10. European Sketches by Hal F. Hentz
11. Country Club, Spartanburg, South Carolina
12. Rendered Drawing of Capital by J. Neel Reid (This student *analytique* color rendering has survived and is displayed at the University of Georgia, School of Environmental Design, where there is a Neel Reid Scholarship for European travel. See 200.1.) Illustrations of some of these were included in the catalogue, illustrations of almost all exist, and most of the actual buildings survive, especially the residences in Macon, Georgia.

Among well-known exhibitors from out of the region were Charles A. Platt (1861–1933) of New York, whom Reid admired perhaps even more that he did Charles McKim. Platt exhibited eight drawings, including one of his influential Colonial Revival designs for a residence in the art colony at Cornish, New Hampshire. There were six entries from James Knox Taylor, Supervising Architect of the Treasury, among them the new Federal Building in Atlanta, completed in 1911 at 56 Forsyth Street, now the U. S. Court of Appeals. There were designs for murals, mosaics, stained-glass windows, and other aspects of interior decoration, including schemes for wallpaper and rugs.

No part of this rare catalogue and groundbreaking exhibition is without interest as entree into Neel Reid's world. At the very back is a double-page advertisement featuring "The Wonders of the Pennsylvania Station" at Thirty-second Street, New York City, from the firm of McKim, Mead & White; McKim was the principal designer of the station that was completed in 1910. Here spread out for all to emulate was a stunning example of McKim's restrained but monumental classicism combined with rational planning and functional technology, which had become the model for cities desiring to be beautiful and harmonious, civilized and up-to-date, as American cities grew by boundless leaps in the first years of this century. As we proceed we shall see that among the most symbolic links to the beaux arts tradition Neel Reid helped bring South is a perfectly scaled and proportioned small pavilion of a classical railroad depot, the Southern Railway Peachtree Station at Brookwood; today it is part of the Amtrak network and is the only remaining railway passenger station in Atlanta. Reid and his partners perfectly transposed their lessons from McKim's classicism for the smaller scale of suburban Atlanta and its Peachtree Street site. Happily, this station remains generally in its original condition, unlike the now-demolished Penn Station advertised in the 1910 catalogue.

In decades of the late nineteenth and early twentieth centuries, as Atlanta began to assert its position as the leading city of the New South, the day was clearly at hand for the beaux arts in America. Both Hentz and Reid had studied for a time in Paris at L'Ecole des Beaux-Arts, Hentz formally and Reid less so. It was rare then for sons of the South to venture to that ancient school of architecture and fine arts. (It predated the United States.) There they were exposed firsthand to the principles and techniques of design originating in the Italian and French Renaissance, which McKim had taught in his atelier at Columbia in modified form. McKim's American Renaissance was a neoclassical revival that aspired to rival and emulate that of Thomas Jefferson in the early American republic. In 1901 McKim had led the revival of L'Enfant's grand plan for Washington, D.C., and directed renovations of the White House in 1902 to accord with the original style and character begun in George Washington's day. Not long after returning from Europe, Neel Reid and Hal Hentz brought McKim, Mead & White's beaux arts classicism to a Deep South that had barely recovered from the Civil War, leaving a beautiful legacy, indeed.

In the beaux arts tradition, knowledge of the scale and proportions of classical models was of primary importance. In *Architecture of Neel Reid in Georgia*, Professor James Grady's oft-quoted opinion was that "Reid was a master of scale; it is the indefinable essence of his style." Scale *is* a definable characteristic of Reid's work, however, traceable to his innate artistic gifts and taste and to his beaux arts training, in which the smallest detail must be proportionally related to a vision of the whole. Reid's study and use of the classical orders and human scale—as interrelated phenomena—was one of the most fundamental aspects of the beaux arts method, and Reid was a consummate artist-architect in the manner of that era; his beautifully drafted compositions and carefully crafted buildings and settings were scaled to human beings and pursuits; they reveal a sure hand at transforming historical precedents into fresh new designs appropriate for his clients and modern conditions.

In a letter written at the death of James Means in 1979, Philip Shutze recalled the functions and duties at Hentz, Reid & Adler: "Neel was responsible for all design output from the office" (just as Shutze would become in 1927). Responsible, of course, is the operative word, for in such firms, no one person drew every line or supervised every brick. But one person was responsible for seeing that "the vision of the whole" was realized throughout. And if, as Reid often did, the scale of a part was increased to give it visual and ceremonial importance, Reid knew what a happy effect the over-scaled element would achieve.

Reid designed in the light of historical precedent, but rarely with archaeological precision, because even though his beaux arts training included archaeological projects, he was not a copyist. The prose of architecture was not his calling, which is why at his death a newspaper editorial headlined him as "a poet in architecture." (Beaux arts, after all, means beautiful, or fine, arts.) He was the office design genius until death took him away in February 1926. This his partners, other associates, and clients understood and this study confirms.

(18.1)

Above: College Street, Macon, c. 1905. Below: The Georgia Life Building, 1911.

Georgia and the deep South were in Neel Reid's blood. His father, John Whitfield Reid, was born in Troup County, Georgia, at the Reid plantation near LaGrange, and his mother, Elizabeth Adams Reid, was born in Jacksonville, Alabama, in the northern sector not far from the Georgia border. Elizabeth Reed traveled back to the Adams family farm from Atlanta to give birth to Neel, whom the Reids named for Joseph N. Neel, a close family friend and later one of Neel's benefactors and first clients. In 1890, when Neel was five years old, the Reids (with older sister Louise and younger brother John Jr.) moved the eighty-five miles south from Atlanta to Macon to go into business and to be near Joe Neel. The Neels lived in the College Hill and Saint Paul's Episcopal Church neighborhood, and the Reids settled nearby at the northeast corner of Forsyth Street and Arlington Place. John W. Reid died in 1901, but Mrs. Reid continued to live in Macon until 1915, when she

(18.2)

moved to Atlanta to be with Neel. Macon would remain an important place for Reid for the length of his brief life. There he was a grammar and high school student, attended church and was a choir boy, made many lifelong friends, began his career, found his first clients, and designed his earliest and many more buildings; and there he rests at Rose Hill Cemetery with family members, the plot appropriately marked by a large classical urn.

In 1890 the central Georgia town of Macon was about sixty-five years old, the seat of Bibb County, with about twenty-three-thousand inhabitants. (The capital city of Atlanta was about forty thousand larger in population.) At that time, Macon, the birthplace of poet and musician Sidney Lanier (1842–81), was a major cotton market and a main depot on the Central of Georgia Railroad between Atlanta and Savannah. In 1823 the state legislature had located the town at the shoals of the Ocmulgee River—the fall line where the hilly

(19.2)

(19.3)

Above: The Reid home at Forsyth Street and Arlington Place, Macon. Right: John Whitfield Reid and Elizabeth Adams Reid. Below right: John Jr., Louise, and Joseph Neel Reid. Bottom right: Reid Shoe Company, Macon.

piedmont plateau meets the sandy coastal plain. This location gives flat as well as elevated building sites: the best early suburban residential sites, such as College Hill, overlooked the river plain, where the business district and near-town residential area was laid out in a generous grid pattern punctuated with wide streets and medians and large parks and squares on the western bank of the river. For Mulberry Street downtown, Reid and his partner Hal Hentz would design their first skyscraper, the ten-story Georgia Life Building. Listed as job number 101, it was completed in 1911 for Reid's friend and client W. Emmett Small, for whom Reid had already, in 1908, designed and built a charming cottage set in an extensive garden on a hill in suburban north Macon.

(19.4)

Architecture has been perhaps the most important of the fine arts in Macon beginning in the founding antebellum period when the classical revival and Italianate styles prevailed there as they did throughout the South. These antebellum styles dotted the hills and plateaus above the town in the College Hill neighborhood where the Neels and Reids lived, adjacent to Saint Paul's Church, where the Reids were members, and Wesleyan Female College, which gave its name to the hill and its main east-west street. A similar Victorian period architectural style was shared by the (still-surviving) church

(19.5)

(20.2)

(20.1)

Neel Reid was named for Joseph N. Neel (above, with his wife Blanche). The Neels were close friends of the Reids and would become one of Neel Reid's early clients. The house Reid designed for the Neels was job number 105. The interior elevations are dated February 24, 1910, and signed by Neel Reid (JNR) and Harry Lindley (HEL).

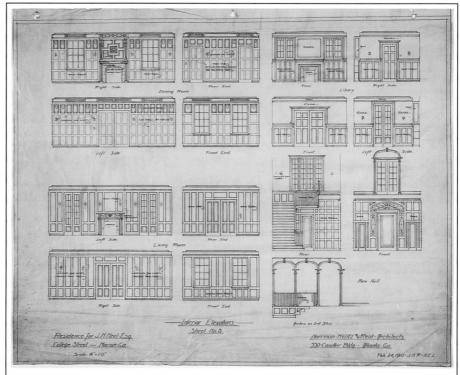

(20.3)

(20.4)   (20.5)

(21.1)

(21.2)

(21.3)

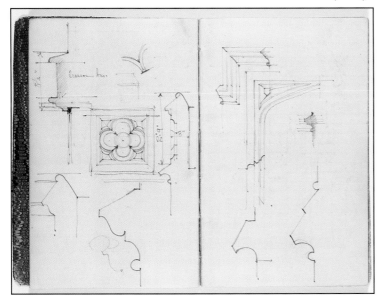

Reid's travels in England, as revealed in his diary and sketches (left), and the architectural context of the College Hill neighborhood and elsewhere in Macon encouraged references to the English Gothic revival in several designs, such as those for J. W. BATES (above), job number 92, 1909, and C. E. ROBERTS (top left), job number 149, 1911.

(1883–85) and the (now-demolished) college (founded 1836, main building built in 1839, remodeled in 1881, college relocated to the new suburban Rivoli campus in 1928, and old main building burned in 1965). The church is, and the college was, a fine example of red-brown brick English Gothic revival. Reid would respect and complement this style with nearby house designs subtly compatible because of their half-timbered, medieval details, multi-gabled forms, and somber color schemes.

The intersection of Forysth Street and College Avenue, where Saint Paul's stands, and the nearby intersection of Georgia Avenue and College, where the Wesleyan College structure stood until 1965,

were the centers of a neighborhood that Reid made his own as he grew up, began his architectural apprenticeship, and built some of his earliest designs. Here is an unusually large selection of "Neel Reid houses," c. 1910–c. 1915, at least a dozen, as well as the Massee Apartments at 347 College (1924–25), built much later in his career. This monumental, eight-story, Georgian revival brick structure, with Baroque limestone details, adds a note of urban sophistication to the residential heights near the college and above the downtown. Together, these certainly qualify as a very special early twentieth-century aspect of the College Hill part of the nationally registered Macon Historic District. Neel

Neel Reid, c. 1900.

(22.1)

(22.2)

Above: Wesleyan College, near the Reids' house.
Below: Post card to Neel Reid while he was
with Willis Denny's office in 1905.

(22.3)

Reid's well-designed and well-preserved examples of period eclecticism harmonize with the decidedly nineteenth-century styles from about 1840 to 1900 that more often than Reid's early works are featured in Macon historical tours and historic preservation plans and chamber of commerce brochures.

An academic education in architecture was not available in Georgia and the South in 1901 when Neel Reid was graduated from Macon's John J. Gresham High School at age sixteen. (That same year his father died.) At that time, entrance into the profession was largely through apprenticeship with practicing architects, and office training often began at an early age. For example, James Means (1904–1979), a Georgia native who would learn architecture from Neel Reid and his partners in the era of World War I, started as an office boy and became an accomplished draftsman and residential designer in his own right, with only a bare minimum of academic education.

Somewhat in the same manner, Neel Reid started his career as a teenage beginner in the office of architect Curran R. Ellis, a Macon associate of Willis F. Denny (1872–1905) of Atlanta. Denny was a Louisville, Georgia, native who practiced in Atlanta and was the architect of the Amos G. Rhodes house (1904) on Peachtree Street in Ansley Park, now the headquarters of the Georgia Trust for Historic Preservation. During this period Reid met his future partner Hal Hentz, who had just graduated in the class of 1904 from Emory College at Oxford, Georgia.

In the fall of 1905, after two years as an apprentice with Denny & Ellis, both in Macon and Atlanta, Reid left Georgia with his friend Hal Hentz to attend Columbia University in New York City, Reid as a special student. This two-year category for non-degree candidates was inaugurated that year. He stayed for much of the two years, electing courses which would be his academic training, except for a short time spent in 1907 at the Ecole des Beaux-Arts in Paris. Reid and Hentz also traveled to England and Italy (financed by a $1,400 grant from Joseph N. Neel) as part of their associated study of architecture. His travel diary from that summer abroad has survived, as well as associated sketches. And from that stint at Columbia University is an *analytique rendu* now at the University of Georgia; a Columbia University annual, of which he was art editor and principal illustrator (1906–7); and a scrapbook con-

(23.1)

"An artist in more ways than one."

JOSEPH NEEL REID, Macon, Ga.
Σ A E; Columbian Board; Architectural Society (2, 3);
Beaum Arts Society (2, 3).

(23.2)

(23.3)

FRESHMAN ATHLETICS

Images from the Columbia University annual, 1907. Above left: Neel Reid is standing in the back row on the right in this photograph of "The Columbian Board of Editors." Left: Reid's class photograph with caption. Above: Reid was the art editor and principal illustrator and executed a number of illustrations for the annual, including this for "Freshman Athletics."

(23.4)

taining clippings from magazine illustrations of New York buildings. More than a few of these were in the beaux arts classical manner from the firm of McKim, Mead & White. The scrapbook, signed "Joseph Neel Reid," also contains a number of pencil sketches and studies of architectural projects and details with a strong flavor of the *esquisses,* or sketches in the approved beaux arts manner. (These have been preserved because his family and others have treasured everything Neel Reid's talented hands ever touched.)

The Columbia University architecture program was begun in 1881. From the first, it was an American adaptation of the French beaux arts system. Students were instructed by means of design projects with solutions based on historical precedents, within a logical step-by-step technique that began with the first *esquisse* and ended with the final renderings and plans. Definite influences were felt from practicing architects, such as Charles McKim, acting as critics and jurors in the atelier, or studio, approach which approximated office conditions. Drawing and drafting were paramount skills, and designers were king in that rarefied world, which is why Neel Reid's natural gifts as an artist allowed

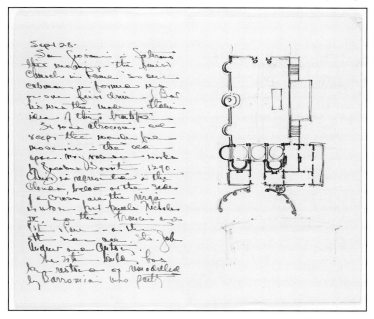

Reid's travel diary from 1907 is filled with plans for his itinerary; objective, sometimes wry, observations; and sketches of details, floor plans, and elevations. Shown above is Reid's sketch of the ground plan for the Villa Madama, Rome, Italy.

(24.1)

Neel Reid kept a scrapbook during his years in New York and filled it with magazine photographs of designs for buildings, houses, and gardens he admired. This scrapbook, which also contained some Reid sketches, has survived as a remarkable document of Reid's dedication to his art.

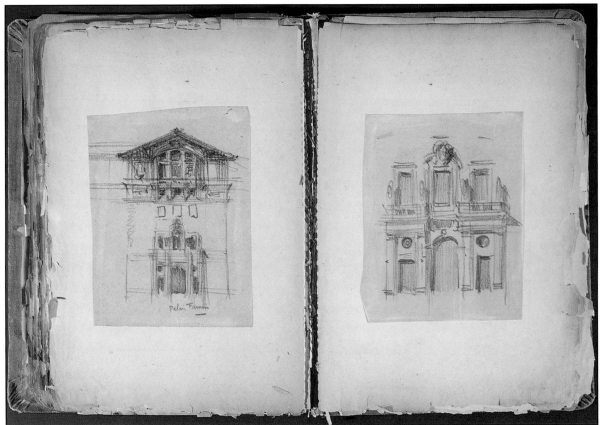

(24.2)

(25.1)

(25.4)

(25.5)

(25.2)

(25.3)

Pages from Neel Reid's sketch book from his travels in England and Europe, 1907.

(26.1)

Sketches by Hal Hentz from his tour of Europe, 1908. Hentz was a talented artist-architect who always praised the talents of others above his own. Above: Detail of a balcony at Assizi. This kind of baroque doorway became a favorite motif of Hentz, Reid & Adler. Right: Sketch of S. Maria Della Consolazione at Todi, Italy.

(26.2)

Lion of Lucerne, Switzerland.

(26.3)

his entry. In 1905, when Reid began at Columbia, the atelier system was becoming even more pronounced, and McKim led the movement as a visiting professor and atelier head with special emphasis on the Italian Renaissance as the basis of American Renaissance or beaux arts classicism. (Neel Reid and Hal Hentz would later play similar roles as jurors and critics in the new architecture department of Georgia Tech.)

The school of architecture at Alabama Polytechnic Institute in Auburn, Alabama (Auburn University since 1960), was the oldest program in the South, but it was not established until 1907. Not until the fall of the year following was Georgia Tech's department begun, the state's first. In 1905 Reid and Hentz had no option for architectural study but to leave the South. In the four-year bachelor of science program at Georgia Tech the first graduates were not produced until 1911. The first architecture school in the United States was founded in 1865, only forty years before Reid attended Columbia, at the Massachusetts Institute of Technology. Neel Reid and Hal Hentz were among the very first sons of the South to follow the academic path into architecture and then to return home to practice. (Both H. H. Richardson [1838–86], originally of Louisiana, and John Wellborn Root [1850–91], born in Lumpkin, Georgia, studied abroad, but neither returned to their native region to live and practice.)

When Neel Reid went back to Macon in the summer of 1908, he applied his taste, learning, and

(27.1)

(27.2)

(27.3)

training to the design of a cottage for suburban Macon set in a large garden for his friends the W. Emmett Smalls. No longer standing, it sat far back from the road in the midst of a twenty-four-acre estate fronting on what later became Riverside Drive. In 1919 he and his partners added to and altered it for the Smalls, but it burned to the ground Christmas night of 1949, when it belonged to the H. E. Papes, who, like the Smalls, called it Hill House.

The first commission Neel Reid received when he returned to Macon in 1908 was a cottage design for the W. EMMETT SMALLS. This project, called "Hill House" by its owners, is no longer standing, but several photographs from the Reid family scrapbook illustrate its charm. The top photograph was taken during construction. Top right: A young Neel Reid relaxing under the Small garden pergola. Above: Garden view. Mr. Small was Reid's client for the Georgia Life Building (18.2).

(28.1)

(28.2)

The combined garden house–art studio in the rear garden survived the fire, and the widowed Mr. Pape adapted it and continued to live there for many years, but it, too, has disappeared.

The letterhead of the firm of Hentz & Reid, Architects, read "Atlanta and Macon" from 1909 until 1915. The manager of the Macon office was Harry E. Lindley (who signed his working drawings HEL). The office was in Suite 417 of the Georgia Life Building designed by the firm. An eyewitness account of an encounter with Neel Reid in that building has survived with a granddaughter of the gentleman who originally told it. Dr. Joseph Walter Rogers practiced medicine in the Georgia Life Building, and his daughter, who became Mrs. Harry E. Pape and later lived at Hill House, happened upon Neel Reid there in passing. The young lady told her father the

(28.3)

doctor, "Mr. Reid is the most beautiful man I have ever seen." Dr. Rogers replied, "No, my dear, the handsomest. One doesn't call a man beautiful."

It was often said that this handsome man "made Atlanta beautiful," but the same may be said for what he did for his childhood hometown. For sites all along suburban Vineville Avenue and its cross streets and in the nearby Cherokee Heights area, Reid designed a series of American Georgian, Colonial Revival, and Italian Renaissance derivations in the years before World War I. Other architects, such as W. Elliott Dunwody, emulated these livable, elegant houses. Together, almost all of these have survived and are cherished as beautiful survivors of a simpler era of sleeping porches, garden houses, and graceful gardens approached through French doors—before air conditioning seduced everyone inside, into the comfortable but less social seclusions of the Sunbelt South. Macon without Neel Reid's classic eclecticism would not be the same middle Georgia city. His beaux arts architecture brought early twentieth-century American Renaissance style to the long-appreciated antebellum Greek Revival and Italianate charms of this beautiful and cultured city. To its reputation as the birthplace of a great Southern poet, Sidney Lanier (who also died young), should be added its early role in the life and career, and the final resting place, of a great Southern architect, Joseph Neel Reid.

The classic eclecticism of Neel Reid, Hal Hentz, and their firm (Norrman, Hentz & Reid; Hentz & Reid; and Hentz, Reid & Adler) had a lasting effect on Reid's childhood hometown. In addition to the English Gothic-inspired residences in the College Hill area were a variety of styles they created throughout the Macon landscape—from the Colonial Revival of job number 91 for HELEN LOGAN in 1908 (opposite page, far left),to the Italianate villa for the L. P. HILLYERS (opposite page, near left, job 100) and the fashionable neoclassical interior remodeling of his Victorian family home (right, job 108) both in 1910, to the Georgian Revival MASSEE APARTMENTS (below, job number 534) of 1924.

(29.1)

(29.2)

(30.1)

(30.2)

HOUSE FOR DR. THOMAS H. HALL,
job number 80, 1909. Below left: Elevations. Below right: Floor plan.

(30.3)

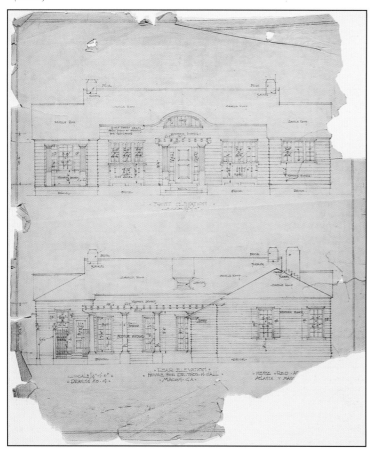

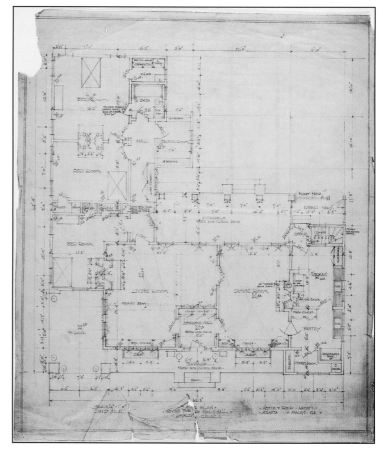

(31.1)

Above: ALTERATIONS FOR MRS. ROBERT LAWSON BROWN, job number 81, 1910.
Below: HOUSE FOR W. P. COLEMAN, job number 82, 1910.

(31.2)

(32.1)

HOUSE FOR JOSEPH NEEL,
job number 105, 1910. Below: Dining room with furniture designed by Reid for this room.

(32.2)

(33.1)

Above: View of the Forsyth Street, Jefferson Terrace, and College Street area, showing a number of Reid designs. From the lower left, the light blue house on Jefferson Terrace is job number 144, 1911, for MR. HUGUENIN; to its right is 180, built in 1912 for MRS. I. N. MCNAIR; and next to it is job number 110, 1910–11, for WALTER JOHNSON (also below). The gray house at the far right is a remodeling, number 146, 1911, for MRS. J. W. SHINHOLSER. Rising above and behind it is job number 534, the MASSEE APARTMENTS, built in 1924.

(33.2)

(34.1)

(34.2)

ALTERATIONS FOR *T. D. TINSLEY, job number 145, 1911.*

HOUSE FOR *DR. H. W. WALKER, job number 111, 1911.*

HOUSE FOR *E. W. STETSON, job number 120, c. 1911.*

(34.3)

(35.1)

(35.2)

ALTERATIONS TO HOUSE FOR MRS. J. W. SHINHOLSER,
job number 146, 1911. Above left: Entrance facing College Street. Above right: Loggia.
Below: Living room. The red lacquer secretary-desk purchased by Reid for another
Macon house is at home here.

(35.3)

(36.1)

HOUSE FOR EUGENE STETSON, *job number 141, 1911.*

(36.2)

HOUSE FOR GEORGE DERRY, *job number 174, 1912.*

(36.3)

House in the Vista Circle neighborhood, attributed to Neel Reid, similar to the T. H. Hall house (30.1).

(36.4)

HOUSE FOR T. C. PARKER, *job number 175, 1912*

(37.1)

HOUSE FOR ARTHUR CODDINGTON, job number 210, 1913.

(37.2)

ALTERATIONS TO HOUSE FOR WILL MILLER, job number 253, 1914.

(38.1)

HOUSE FOR ALBERT BACH,
job number 266, 1915.
Below: Entrance elevation.
Opposite page, top: Second floor plan.
Opposite page, bottom: First floor plan.

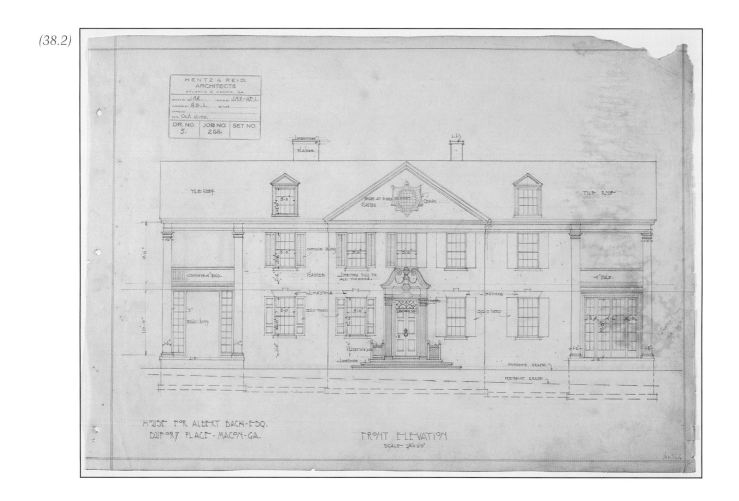

(38.2)

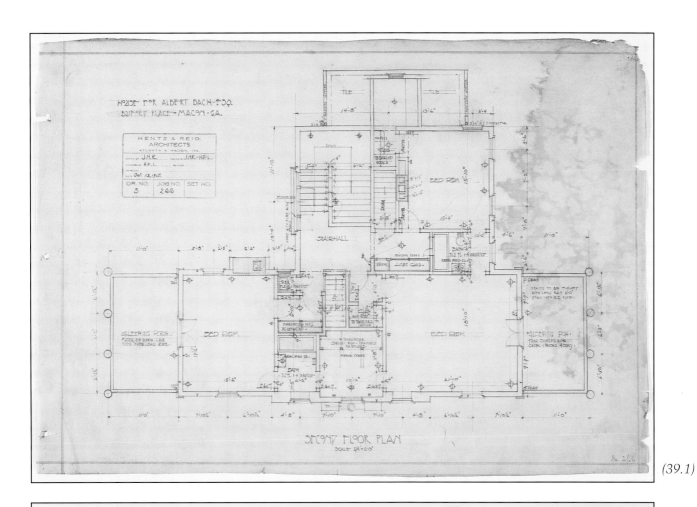

(39.1)

(39.2)

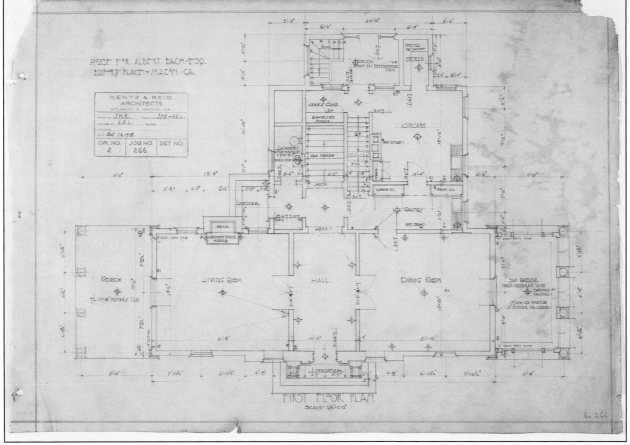

(40.1)

HOUSE FOR MAX MORRIS,
job number 267, 1915.

(40.2)

EXTERIOR ALTERATIONS, PORCH AND PORTE
COCHERE, FOR MRS. T. C. BURKE,
job number 335, 1917.

(40.3)

APARTMENT HOTEL FOR W. J. AND O. J. MASSEE, job number 534, 1924.

(41.1)

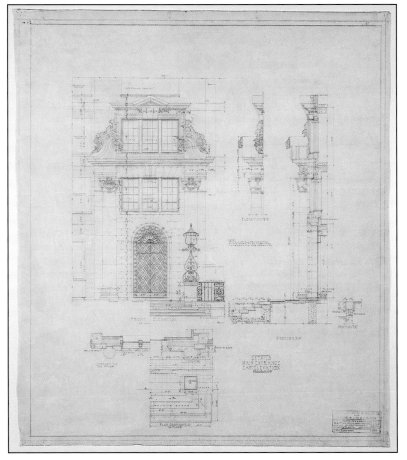

(41.2)

Massee Apartment Hotel.
Above: Elevation of front pediment.
Left: Details of main entrance.
Drafted by Mack Tucker. The design of
the building reflects the sophisticated
and expansive spirit of the New South.

HILLS AND DALES / FERRELL GARDENS

(42.1)

Hills and Dales south elevation c. 1916.

With this grand project, five years into their partnership, Neel Reid, age twenty-nine, and Hal Hentz, thirty-one, came into their own. It was the first of fifteen projects in Troup County, Georgia, where Reid's great-grandfather, Samuel Reid, laid out the county seat of LaGrange in 1828.

Hentz & Reid and the Callaways created an elegant modern classical "home place," which the Callaways called Hills and Dales. It suggests the classic plantation traditions of the region and rises from a setting unequaled in the state—the five-acre, terraced boxwood parterre gardens begun by Mrs. Sarah Coleman Ferrell (1817–1903) in 1841. Mrs. Ferrell called her creation The Terraces, but it was known throughout the area as Ferrell Gardens. In 1912 Fuller Callaway acquired the fifteen-hundred-acre estate from Judge Blount Ferrell as the late Mrs. Ferrell had hoped, because she knew the industrialist greatly admired her gardens.

The culmination of the first half of Reid's career is the suburban villa that he designed to complement Mrs. Ferrell's formal, Italian Renaissance revival landscape, to which he added touches of renaissance-style garden ornaments. This project came at the end of his period of training and first works and set the stage for other large, villa-like commissions, especially in Atlanta, such as the Andrew Calhoun estate of 1922–23.

When he began the Callaway project in 1914, the firm was still Hentz & Reid of Atlanta and Macon; when he completed the project in 1916, it was Hentz, Reid & Adler; the firm was growing to include a number of talented young assistants; the Macon office had been closed; and the work was concentrated in Atlanta where the commissions increased, both in number and scale, as the New South flourished.

The house on its landscaped antebellum site, where the Ferrells' cottage had stood, suggests but does not replicate the classical plantation traditions of the Old South. Reinvigorating the historic architectural background of a locale was a major interest of these American beaux arts architects of the early twentieth-century classic revival, usually called the American Renaissance. They sought to extend tradition and graft onto the roots of Colonial and Federal architectural culture, a revived classicism thought appropriate for modern life.

The Callaway project, which was a pivotal point in Reid's career and life, began ten years of accomplishments that ended with his early death in 1926. A landmark of the American Renaissance, it is an emblem of the culture of that era as expressed in the South by a group of architects born and bred there. In

(43.1)

(43.2)

Above: Postcards from Neel Reid's collection depict Ferrell Gardens.
Below: Hal Hentz and Neel Reid at Hills and Dales 1916.

Georgia, instead of a proto-modernist figure such as Frank Lloyd Wright, we have Neel Reid and his colleagues, who sought to explore and invigorate the native classicism in which they were raised by creating an eclectic dialogue with past styles—using the traditional designs of their region as sources of inspiration for graceful and livable new structures to serve the twentieth century.

The formative years of the American Renaissance period for Reid and his contemporaries was in the first decade of the century, during the administration of President Theodore Roosevelt, whose mother was from Roswell, Georgia. In 1902 the Roosevelts invited Charles Follen McKim, with whom Reid would be acquainted at Columbia University, to direct a comprehensive renovation of the White House. McKim removed the Victorian alterations from the classical design to emphasize its place in

(43.3)

the nation's early heritage. This was an apotheosis for the Colonial Revival movement, a general term that embraced early American architecture from the seventeenth century through the Roman and Greek revivals. Another was the well-known fact that the president's mother's family home in Roswell, Bulloch Hall, was a temple-form Greek Revival house in that much-admired style from the architectural heritage of the antebellum South. In 1907 Teddy Roosevelt opened the Jamestown Exposition, and *The Old and New South, 1607–1907*, was published with a photograph of "The Georgia Building" at the exposition. "A Reproduction Bulloch Hall, Roswell, Georgia, the Home of President Roosevelt's mother," the caption read (p. 628).

Such classical images, often called Southern Colonial, were icons of the first decades of this cen-

(44.1)

Images from Reid's scrapbook (probably photographed by Reid) show Hills and Dales as construction was being completed. Above: A view of the north entrance. Below: Living room and stair hall c. 1916. Opposite page, top: The south, or garden, elevation framed by a trellis arch. Opposite page, bottom: The two-story portico on the east end of the house. Right: An early floor plan shows a rectangular rather than semi-circular portico, and a long hall separated the living room from the stair hall.

(44.2)

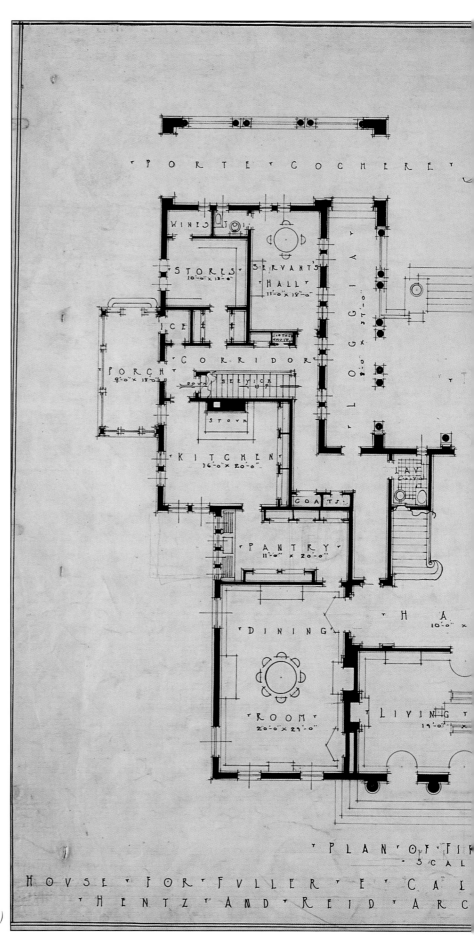

(44.3)

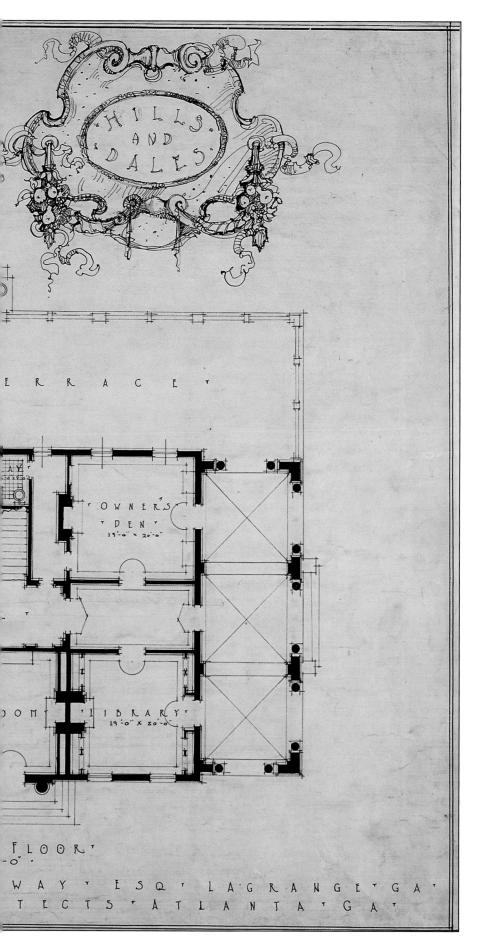

(45.1)

(45.2)

tury. The Callaway country-house villa fits into that pattern exactly, especially with its antebellum garden setting. Although Bulloch Hall was built about 1840, and therefore was not Colonial (just as the White House actually dated from the post-Colonial, Federal period) the white-columned type became the model for many a modern Mount Vernon and White House. (For proud Southerners, yet another high point in the movement had been McKim, Mead & White's renovation of Thomas Jefferson's library/rotunda at the University of Virginia in 1895 after it was wrecked by fire; this prompted a revival of red brick, white columned neoclassicism, which Reid would include in his eclectic repertory.

That was the Colonial Revival environment in which Neel Reid began his career and which led to the design solution he devised for Hills and Dales. He celebrated and extended the tradition of that place and site without copying local landmarks. Representing an eclectic classicism that looked to the ultimate Italian Renaissance prototypes that had inspired Mrs. Ferrell's Italianate boxwood garden, it suggests the Palladianism of the eighteenth and early nineteenth century behind American neoclassicism. Reid described the finished product to the Callaways as "Georgian Italian," according to Alice Hand (Mrs. Fuller E. Jr.) Callaway, the current resident.

In 1916, as Hills and Dales was being completed, Neel Reid purchased to renovate as his primary residence Mimosa Hall, c. 1840, which is similar in date and style to Bulloch Hall and literally its next-door neighbor in Roswell. This acquisition identified Reid's background and values, and by then his career could afford him such a luxury.

The Callaway commission was the largest he had received to that time. This success allowed, and probably necessitated, Hentz and Reid taking on their friend and colleague, Rudolph Sartorius Adler, also influenced by McKim at Columbia University, as a busy partner in their beaux arts enterprise. RSA, as he signed working drawings, some for Hills and Dales, was, like Hal Hentz, both artist and practical architect with a fine business sense.

Hills and Dales is a LaGrange landmark on a popular, established site, as well as a landmark in Reid's career and that of his partnership. This grand project made his reputation as an architect, garden designer and restorer, and interior decorator and

assures it to this day. This villa–country house stated his approach to McKim's American Renaissance. It extended and enlarged the Troup County plantation tradition with sophisticated allusions to Charles Adams Platt's villa houses in the New York, Philadelphia, and Chicago areas, such houses as Sylvania (1904), Timberline (1907), and Villa Turicum (1908). Platt, one of Reid's favorite designers, was a generation older than Reid, but the *Platt Monograph* of 1913 made his work widely known. Many of Platt's designs were Colonial Revival adaptations of Italian villas set in formal landscape gardens. They were illustrated in the magazine *House and Garden*, for example, after three Philadelphia architects began its publication in 1901 to promote, as they wrote in volume one, number one: "The point of view of the architect to whom the house and its garden seem so intimately related that the attempt to design the one without the other can never reach the highest level of success" (p. 16). Pratt, like Reid, also designed interior decorating schemes, as Reid did for Hills and Dales.

The McKim renaissance was spread by several generations of American designers such as Platt and Reid. Reid's work was being illustrated nationally as he designed Hills and Dales and was included in Fiske Kimball's special country house issue of *Architectural Record* in 1919. These designers throughout the country influenced each other, especially through the medium of books and magazines. The Italian Renaissance and the American were both bookish, but copying was considered bad form, in all senses; learning and emulation, however, were not—learning could produce good form, the Renaissance ideal of reviving the most classic "antique."

Reid's description of Hills and Dales as "Georgian Italian" for our purposes should be interpreted broadly, emphasizing Georgia, the place, as well as the Georgian period and style, and LaGrange, Georgia, the location, in Reid's own ancestral county. The Italian was clearly suggested by Mrs. Ferrell's renaissance parterre gardens on what had been cotton-growing terraces, in the Italian terraced-garden tradition.

The seat of Troup County, LaGrange, is located seventy miles southwest of Atlanta near the Chattahoochee River border between Georgia and Alabama. This is the forested, rolling topography of the pied-

(47.1)

Reid, far right, posed with his cousin, Mrs. John M. (Sally Grant) Slaton, Fuller E. Callaway, Mrs. Fuller Callaway, and Miss Martha Slaton in 1916 as Hills and Dales was being completed.

mont plateau. Early settlement was begun in 1825–26 when an Indian treaty allowed for expansion westward of plantation cotton culture along the Oakfuskee Trail. The county was organized in December 1826, and LaGrange became county seat in 1828, after Neel Reid's great-grandfather, Samuel Reid, arrived. By 1830 there were nearly six thousand settlers, and by 1840 more than twice that. The county became one of the state's wealthier areas, with larger plantations and better designed plantation houses than the average in the region. Railroad development, as in much of the state, followed the settlers. The first railroad through the county, the Atlanta and West Point, came in 1854. A small-scale textile industry associated with the quantities of cotton grown in the Chattahoochee Valley had it origins before the Civil War, but did not get underway until the 1970s and '80s. By 1895 Fuller E. Callaway (1870–1928), a native of the county, had begun his leadership of the textile industry in the valley. In 1907 his Calumet Company took the lead, at the same time that the Atlanta, Birmingham, and Coastline Railroad came to town. In 1915, at the time Callaway was building Hills and Dales, he created Hillside Cotton Mills, a leading new facility. (In 1932 his sons Fuller E. Callaway Jr. and Cason Callaway, who commissioned a Reid house near Hills and Dales in 1921, would organize Callaway Mills, Inc.)

All of the LaGrange and Troup County Hentz, Reid & Adler commissions after Hills and Dales were related in some way to the Callaway textile interest and family. The Callaways were exceptional clients to acquire at age twenty-nine. What a sublime scenic creation for Georgia the Callaways and their architects fashioned from Sarah Coleman Ferrell's dwarf boxwood parterres she designed in the spirit of Pliny the Younger's classic precedent of spelled-out mottoes in geometric patterns! Just as he would with later projects, Reid allowed the gardens and landscape to dominate; he created a garden façade with French doors on the south elevation, which was the elevation toward the gardens and the road, with a porte cochere entrance on the north and a semicircular portico in the Ionic order at the main pedestrian entrance on the east—a Palladian portico in the spirit of the antebellum South. As with Charles Platt, Reid synthesized the Italian villa tradition of house and garden with the native classicism of America.

Hills and Dales is an original creation but conservative, with past styles and forms as a starting point, seeming at home in its Deep South setting, at the same time adding fresh aspects to a continuing classical tradition. With Hills and Dales, the American Renaissance came to Georgia in the finest way. It set a standard for Reid's later work. The house that client and architect built for the terraced Ferrell parterre gardens beautifully merged the Old South and New, an expression of J. Neel Reid's Georgia school of classicism, when the economic prosperity of the New South 1920s had begun to come into view. It is a legacy to preserve.

HILLS AND DALES
PORTFOLIO

*House for Fuller Callaway, Hills and Dales,
job number 233, 1914.*

(48.1)

*Right: The south elevation at Hills and Dales looks out on
Mrs. Ferrell's gardens. Above: This fountain, which serves
as a focal point for the landscape of the south elevation,
was designed by Hentz & Reid as part of the overall house
and garden composition.*

(48.2)

(50.1)

The landscape plan (opposite) for Hills and Dales was a collaboration of Neel Reid and the Callaways based on the legacy of Mrs. Ferrell. Above: A view from the greenhouse. Below: The greenhouse. Opposite, below: Garden elevation from a lower terrace.

(50.2)

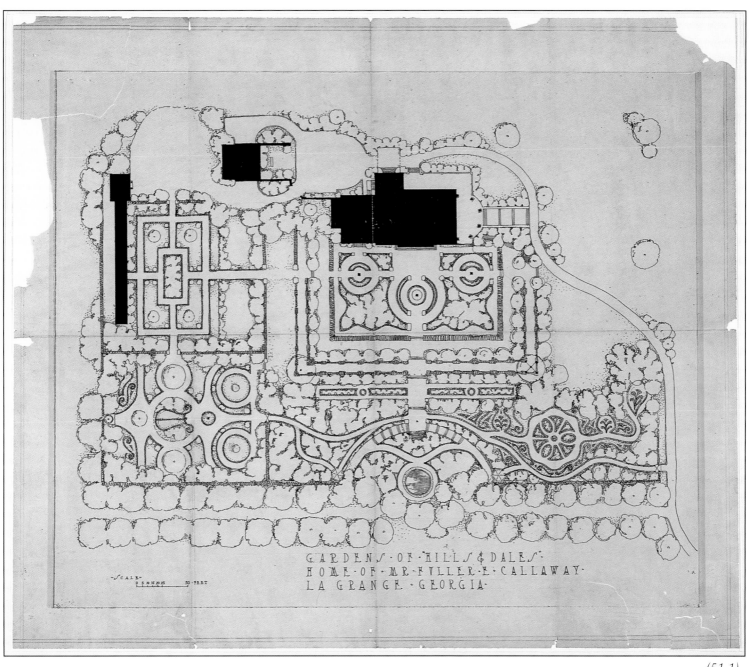

GARDENS·OF·HILLS&DALES·
HOME·OF·MR·FULLER·E·CALLAWAY·
LA·GRANGE·GEORGIA·

SCALE
0 5 10 15 20 25   50 FEET

(51.1)

(51.2)

(52.1)

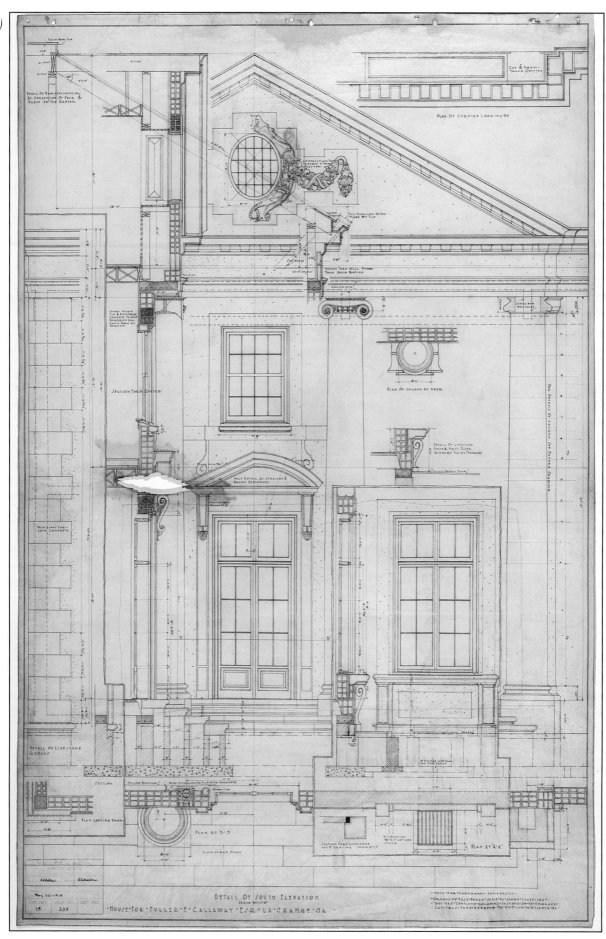

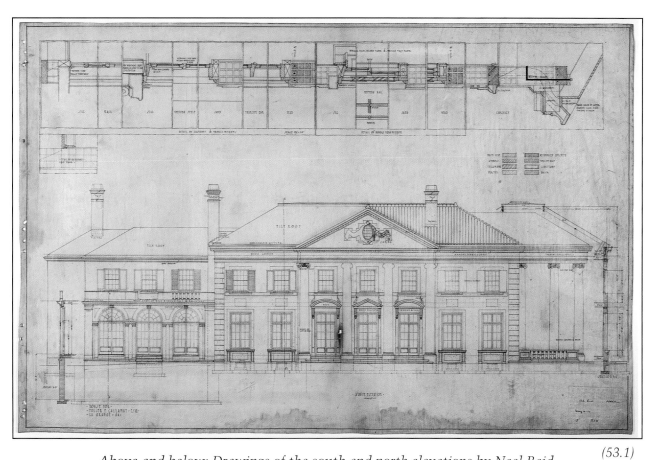

(53.1)

Above and below: Drawings of the south and north elevations by Neel Reid.
Opposite page: Details of south elevation; drawings by Rudolph Adler.

(53.2)

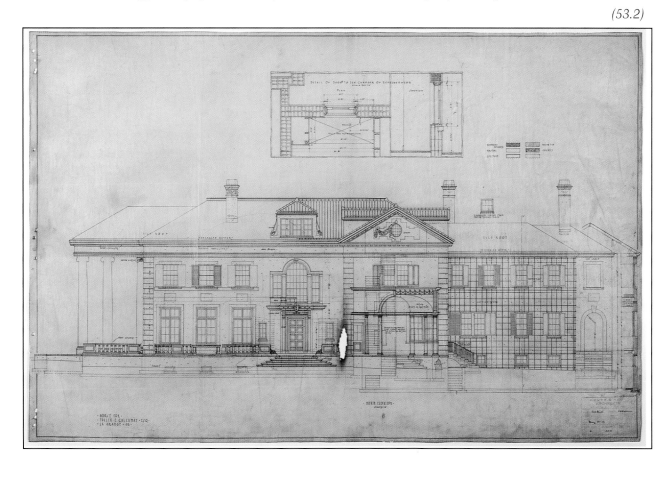

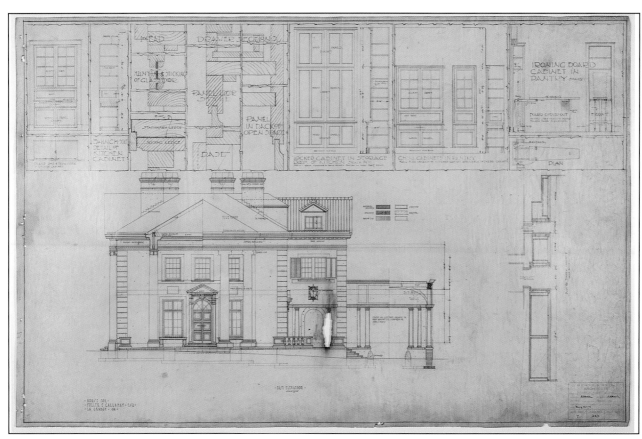

(54.1)

Drawings of the east and west elevations and
cabinet details by Rudolph Adler.

(54.2)

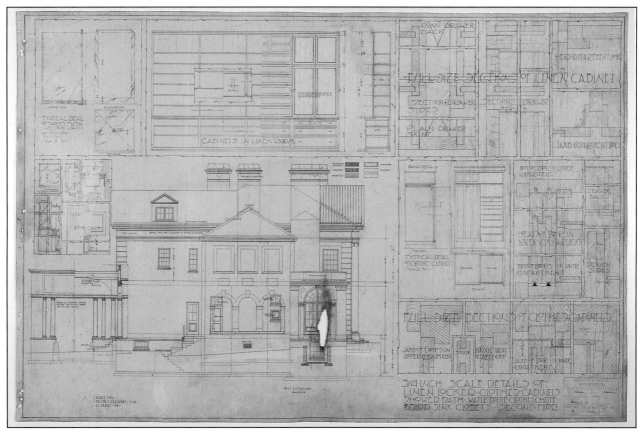

(55.1)

(55.2)

(55.3)

Top: View from the northeast. Left: East elevation.
Above: Porte cochere on north elevation.

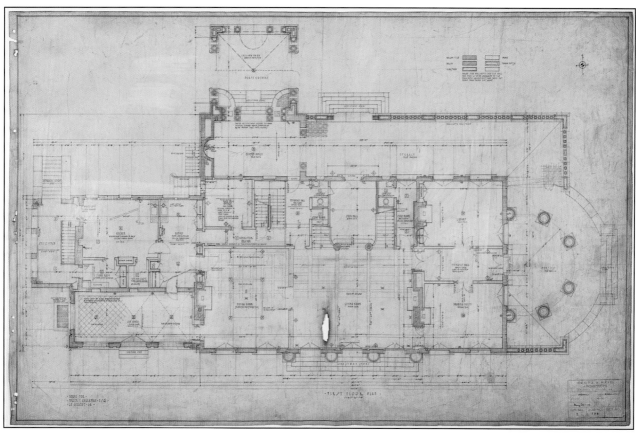

(56.1)

Floor plans drawn by Rudolph Adler.
Above: First floor. Below: Second floor.

(56.2)

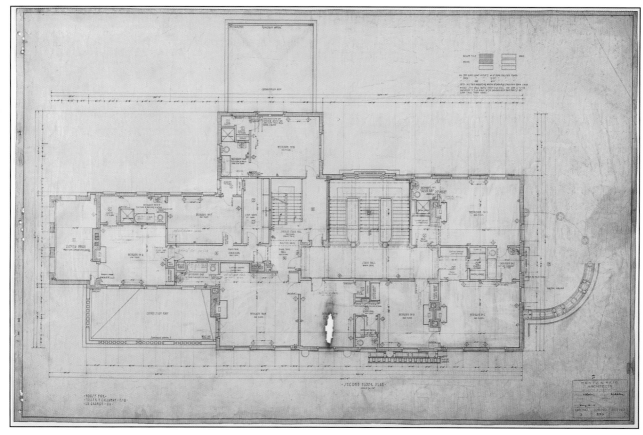

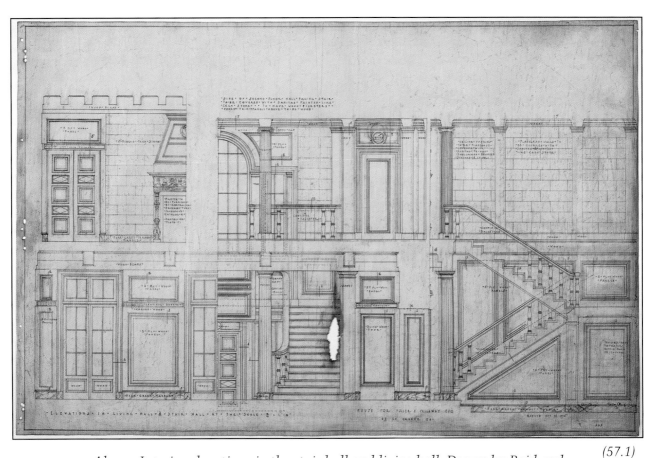

(57.1)

Above: Interior elevations in the stair hall and living hall. Drawn by Reid and Philip Shutze. Below: Interior elevations in dining room drafted by Shutze.

(57.2)

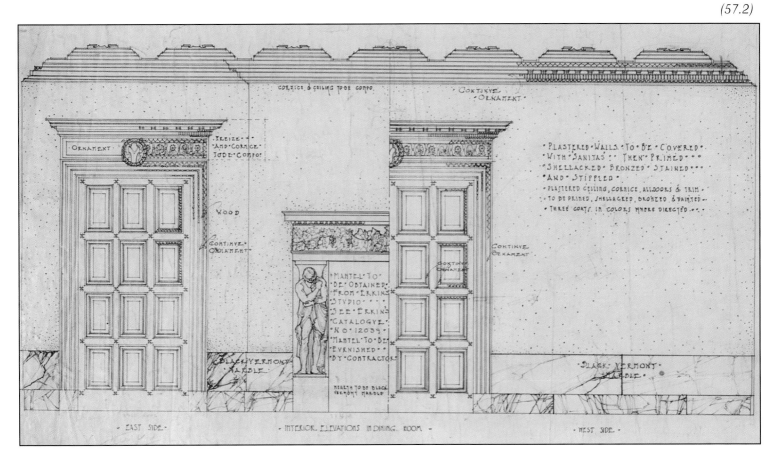

(58.1)

Above: Dining room, still furnished and decorated essentially as by Neel Reid. Right: Living hall and stair hall. The original mantel shown in the drawing on the preceding page (illustration 57.1) has been replaced.

(58.2)

(60.1)

(60.2)

Above: Library. Left: Music room (originally called the drawing room) with view of Reid's fountain in front of the south elevation. Opposite page, top: Elevation in library drawn by Neel Reid. Opposite page, bottom: Library details.

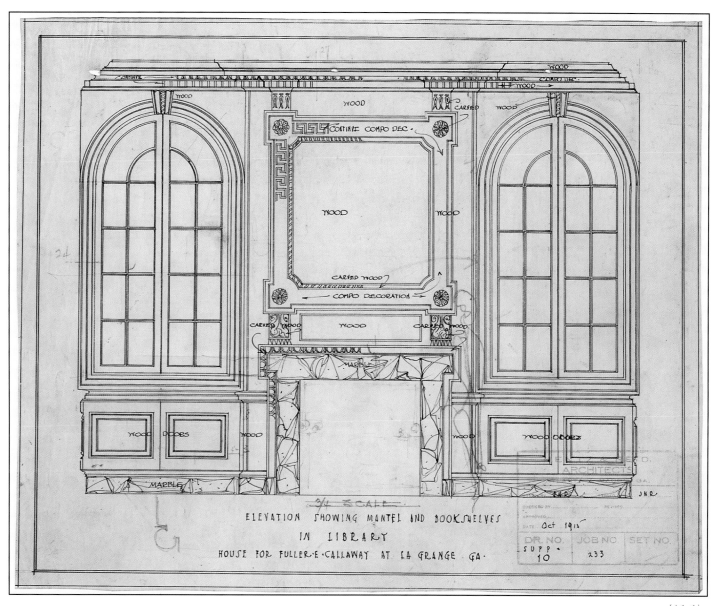

(61.1)

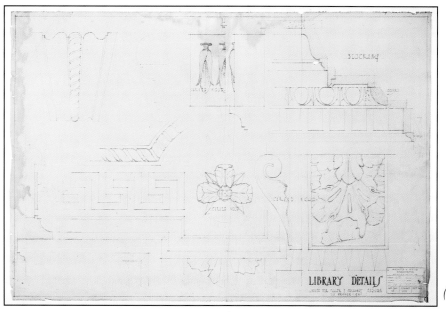

(61.2)

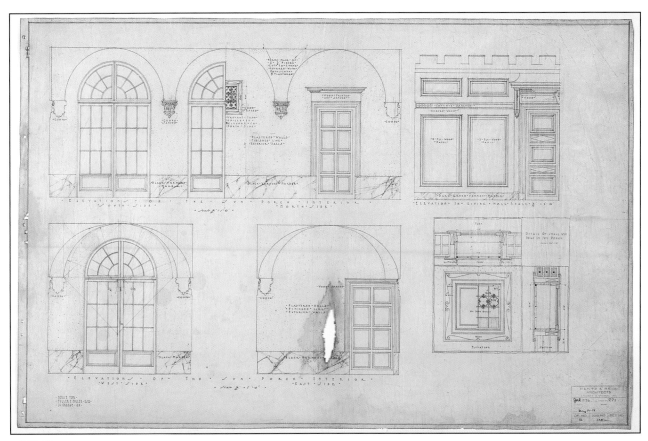

(62.1)

(62.2)

Above: Interior elevations of sun porch, drawn by Neel Reid. Left: Sun porch.

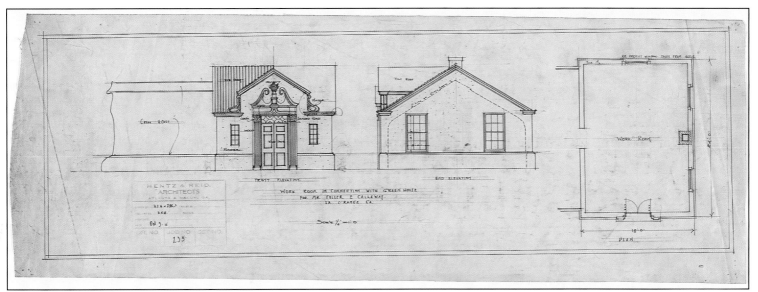

Above: Workroom for greenhouse, drawn by Neel Reid and Hal Hentz.
Below: Details of wrought iron on well, drawn by Reid.

(63.1)

(63.2)

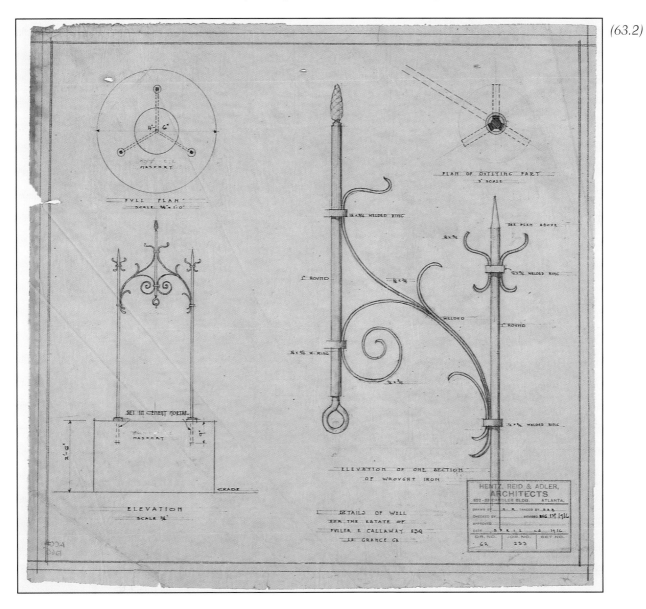

ATLANTA

Above: Atlanta skyline, in 1907. Below: Neel Reid in his Candler Building office, c. 1916.

The name Neel Reid had become a standard brand, like Coca-Cola and Bobby Jones, in Atlanta folklore in the architect's lifetime, and when death cut short his career in February 1926, front-page news and editorial eulogies praised him and his work and mourned his loss. Some seventy-five years later, this book documents his aesthetic contributions to the cultural history of Atlanta and the region.

Brought to Atlanta as a babe in arms, Joseph Neel Reid lived there for his first five years before his parents moved to Macon to be near their friend and business associate Joseph Neel, for whom they named their first-born son. We have seen Neel Reid's Macon, the middle Georgia city that played such an important part in his early life and that his architectural career and aesthetic genius affected significantly with the buildings he and his partners carefully designed and sited to grace the landscape. At first

(64.2)

the firm was of Atlanta and Macon, and both cities reflect his influence, even today—perhaps Atlanta, the larger and younger of the two, even more than Macon, the smaller and older.

Reid's architectural apprenticeship began in Macon with Curran Ellis and continued in Atlanta with Willis Denny, Ellis's associate there; after Denny's death in 1905, Reid went on as a special student to architecture school at Columbia University, along with his friend Hal Hentz, with whom he would form his partnership in Atlanta in 1909. They would bring back to Georgia the American Renaissance eclecticism and revivalism of Columbia's Charles McKim, the great beaux arts classicist.

Atlanta in 1909 had 1,300 "horse-less carriages" and numerous streetcar lines; the population was around 150,000. Since 1868, following the Civil War, Atlanta had been the capital of the state; it was a railroad crossroads that was beginning to become a

Hal Fitzgerald Hentz, c. 1916.

Rudolph Sartorius Adler, c. 1916.

small metropolis in the image of much larger north-ern cities. In 1908 a school of architecture was begun at Georgia Tech, because architects were needed to direct the great volume of construction in the grow-ing New South city. In *The Old South and the New* (1907), Charles Morris wrote, "In Atlanta . . . the old everywhere has made way for the new." By 1920 the population had grown by 50,000 and the place, both urban and suburban, had begun to resemble the city of today.

Neel Reid and his associates were, indeed, an important part of the story. They found a small, pic-turesque, Victorian city and helped make it new according to the fashion of historical revivalism as practiced in the architectural schools, both in the United States and abroad. Atlanta wanted to resemble Chicago and New York with perhaps a touch of Lon-don. As Charles Morris wrote in 1907: "It resembles a Northern business city in the number of 'skyscrapers' which have gone up within recent years, each of them a great hive of industry. It is different in this respect from any other city in the South. It might, so far as appearances go, be a Northern city lifted up bodily and dropped down here" (p. 507).

Of the firm's list of commissions housed at the Atlanta History Center, there are 325 Atlanta jobs

from the Reid years, 1909 to 1926, when his fine aes-thetic hand directed design. A great percentage of those listed have been identified (see Appendix 3), and survive much as they were built. During those years, Reid and his office associates and clients, such as the Adairs of the Adair Realty Company, transformed Atlanta according to the manner and style of McKim, Mead & White's New York, which the Atlanta part-ners knew in the first decade of the century.

Hal Fitzgerald Hentz, who signed his drawings HFH, was a native of Florida, who became a Georgian in 1904 upon his graduation from Emory College at Oxford, Georgia. Hentz settled in Atlanta then before going to Columbia for architecture and worked for Asa G. Candler, owner of the Coca-Cola Company. It was an important connection. An industrialist, Mr. Candler included real-estate development among his investments. In May 1908 he headed a syndicate to buy the fledgling Druid Hills suburb and to complete and enlarge it. Candler was assisted in this work by the Adair Realty Company as exclusive sales agents. Through its friendship with Candler and the Adairs, Hentz & Reid, later Hentz, Reid & Adler, would be closely associated with the architectural quality of the Druid Hills neighborhood in the design of numer-ous houses along Ponce de Leon Avenue and Oakdale, Springdale, and Fairview Roads. Fairview would have ten of the firm's designs, including two houses where Neel Reid would live for a short time himself before moving to Roswell to renovate Mimosa Hall.

Rudolph Sartorius Adler, who studied with Reid and Hentz at Columbia, was a native of Atlanta. His father was president of the Atlanta Paper Company, and his family was part of the old Jewish mercantile community. His first cousin was Walter Rich, president of M. Rich & Son, historically Atlanta's leading department store—its slogan was "Atlanta Owned, Atlanta Operated." The firm designed a house for

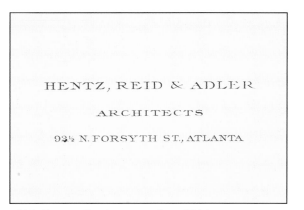

(66.1)   *Business card, c. 1916.*

Walter Rich in 1916 and received the design commission for the department store, Rich's, job number 403, in 1921. Adler signed his working drawings RSA. He was obviously a talented architect who contributed to all phases of the practice. He is buried among his family at Oakland Cemetery, Atlanta's oldest burial ground.

A combination scrapbook and sketchbook, signed "Joseph Neel Reid" on the inside front, which was evidently assembled in New York City when Reid was an architectural student, survived almost miraculously in the basement of Atlanta's Candler Building on Peachtree Street, where the

(66.2)   *Pages from Neel Reid's scrapbook show an early appreciation of garden design.*

partners practiced throughout their career. From a private collection, this and two others were made available to the author during research. Reid had filled it with magazine photographs of favorite McKim, Mead & White buildings in New York, and works by Charles Platt and others, both urban and suburban, commercial and residential. All three dusty books are splendid glimpses into Reid's taste in architecture, interiors, and gardens; these are apparently only a small portion of such idea books Reid and his partners assembled in their extensive library in the Candler Building.

Writing in the late 1940s in an American Guide Series edition about Atlanta, Paul W. Miller expressed an understanding of the Atlanta aspect of Reid's reputation, which was by then the accepted version. Miller, a journalist, emphasized Reid's residential contribution in the context of a short but

brilliant career: "One architect who included a strong influence on the quality of Atlanta's best residential areas was Neel Reid. His execution was not limited to any particular style, but his talent was shown most frequently in houses of renaissance or Georgian design. Reid was young and just beginning to attract national fame at the time of his death in 1926" (p. 133). Another statement of the Reid reputation as a figure based in Atlanta appeared about the same time in Francis Butler Simkins's scholarly *The South, Old and New* (1947): "At Atlanta . . . Neel Reid, an architect who became active around 1907, persuaded the suburbanites to abandon their varied extravagances in favor of the simple reds and whites of the Georgian style set against the forest and hills. Thus Atlanta—and Southern cities that followed its example—came to possess some of the most beautiful suburbs in all America" (p. 357). *Life* magazine,

Reid's postcard album is filled with images of classical designs from across the United States. (67.1)

(68.1)

(68.2)

Top: Station for Southern Railway at Peachtree Crossing, *job number 282, 1916, Brookwood. Bobby Jones was
greeted at the Brookwood station when he returned home
to Atlanta after winning the U. S. Open in 1923 (above,
Jones in center). Right:* Bank and office building for the
Hillyer Trust, *job number 102, 1911. Below: Identified
as* "Coca-Cola Factory" *on the firm's list of jobs, this
was job number 77, 1909.*

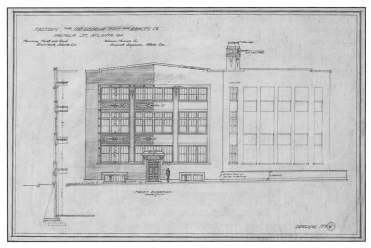

(68.3)

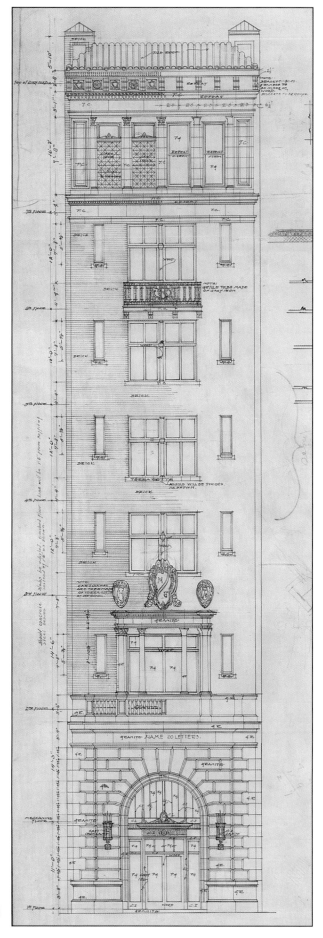

(68.4)

Rich's, job number 403, for M. RICH & *(69.1)*
BROTHERS, 1921–22.

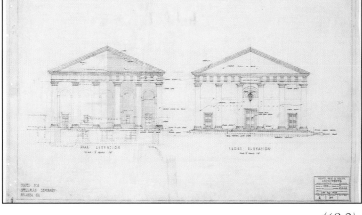

SPELMAN SEMINARY CHAPEL, job number 519, *(69.2)*
1923–24.

June 7, 1948, might have been using a press release distributed by the Atlanta Chamber of Commerce or the Garden Club of Georgia in an article on Atlanta homes: "Atlantans give much credit for the beauty of their estates to an architect, Neel Reid, who died 22 years ago. He designed many of the hundreds of handsome Northside homes which now spread over 12 square miles of park-like woods. By never building a house without also planning a lavish garden for it, Reid did much to father Atlanta's passion for gardening. Reid set a style which has been conscientiously and admiringly followed by most of the architects who came after him" (p. 80).

Although there is much truth in this suburban, residential factor, the impact of Neel Reid of Hentz, Reid & Adler on urban Atlanta should not be overlooked. Of the 325 jobs Norrman, Hentz & Reid, Hentz & Reid, and Hentz, Reid & Adler received from 1909 until Reid's death were a number of important commissions for nonresidential, urban structures. There were also semi-urban/semi-suburban Hentz, Reid & Adler buildings along Peachtree Street from North Avenue, in what is today called Midtown, passing by Ansley Park on through the area at Twenty-fifth and Twenty-sixth Streets called Brookwood, where Peachtree Street becomes Road, on to Buckhead, centered at the West Paces Ferry/Roswell Road crossroads. This corridor has had semi-urban/semi-suburban Reid-designed apartment buildings and residences; there were seven Reid residences at Brookwood, all now either moved or demolished. Only Reid's Southern Railway (Brookwood) Station of 1917 and one Reid house, the Logan Clarke, job number 490, 1922, in the Brookwood Hills garden suburb just off of Peachtree at 14 Palisades Road remain of that settlement.

The second Atlanta commission (job number 77) on the jobs list is a "Coca-Cola Factory" built in 1909 at 56 Magnolia Street just southwest of downtown and now demolished. The thirteenth is the Hillyer Trust Company Office Building, from 1911, at 140 Peachtree Street, just north of the old Five Points financial district and across from the Candler Building. Originally an eight-story concrete and steel high-rise structure, it was reduced to three stories in 1977, destroying much of Reid's renaissance details. Following along from 1911 was a variety of jobs, including work over a period of years for the Piedmont Driving Club on Piedmont Avenue, where both Reid and Hentz were members. There were small stores of many kinds, an automobile showroom, movie theaters, a candy factory, a Masonic lodge, an athletic club, a YMCA, a hospital clinic, a railroad station, a bakery, a children's hospital, a number of apartment buildings, a large clothing store, a small downtown skyscraper, a hotel, a sanitorium, and a small real-estate office, among other constructions.

The Howard Theater (later the Paramount) was built for George Troup Howard in 1919–20 on Peachtree Street downtown. It was demolished in 1960, but part of the entrance elevation survives as the façade of a house in Moultrie, Georgia. This was job number 369.

(70.3)

Especially in the early years of the practice, JNR and NR, Reid's initials, appeared on practically every working drawing, as did those of this partners and those of young architect apprentices. Usually Reid's initials appeared on drafts for important elevations and ornamental details. Although drafting is not proof of design conception, it is certainly proof of participation in the creative process. The office followed the beaux arts design procedure, beginning with an initial esquisse, or idea sketch, proceeding through the final working drawings from which blueprints result for distribution to clients, builders, contractors, and others. That these are usually called "plans" indicates the importance of that element of design. From plans, in theory, an entire structure can be envisioned. In fact, the client was often presented a rendu or color rendering, sometimes in perspective, of the front elevation.

The design of suburban (and semi-suburban) residences, sometimes called "country houses" or "estates," was certainly Reid's greatest love, combining architecture, interior decoration, and gardens,

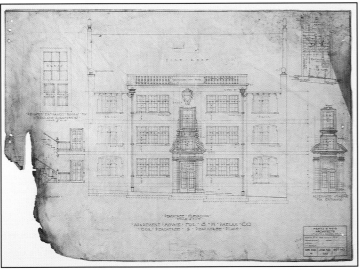

(71.1)

Apartment house for Sid H. Phelan Company,
job number 257, 1915, drafted by Neel Reid and
Philip Shutze. This building is now known as the
Palmer House.

(71.2)

(71.3)

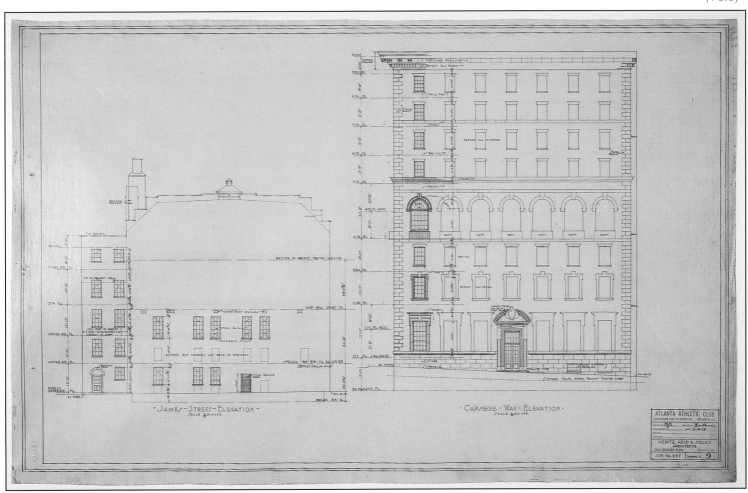

The Atlanta Athletic Club, job number 557, was built on Carnegie Way in 1925–26. It was demolished in 1973.

(72.1)

The clubhouse drawings for the ATLANTA ATHLETIC CLUB at East Lake (job number 241, 1914) illustrate the talents of all of the principals in this remarkable Atlanta firm. The exterior elevation below was drawn by Hal Hentz and Rudolph Adler. The interior elevations (opposite, top) were drafted by Neel Reid and Philip Shutze. Shutze drew the dining room wall detail (opposite, below).

(72.2)

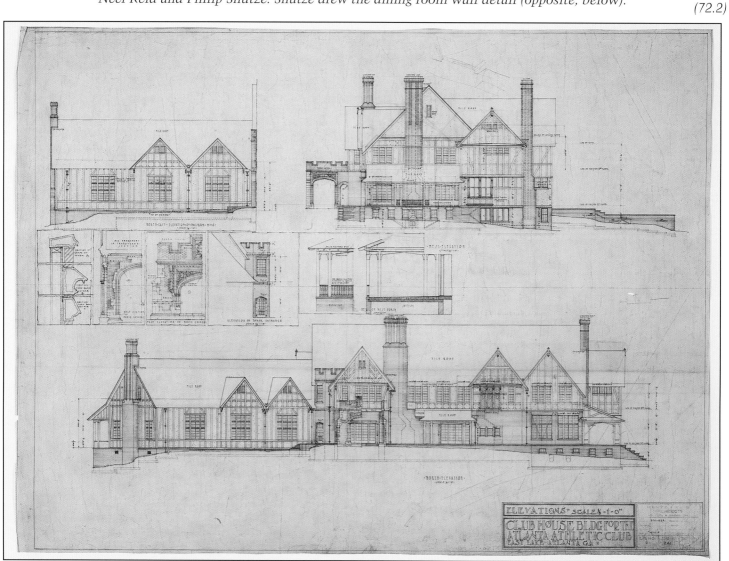

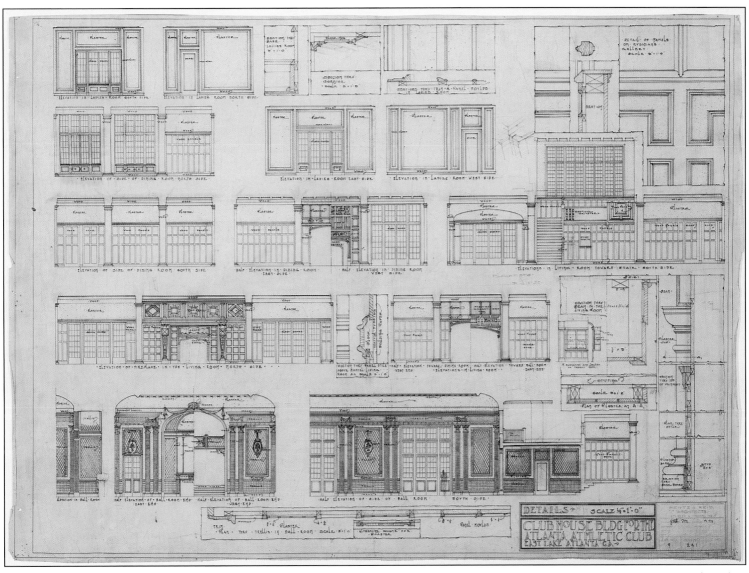

(73.1)

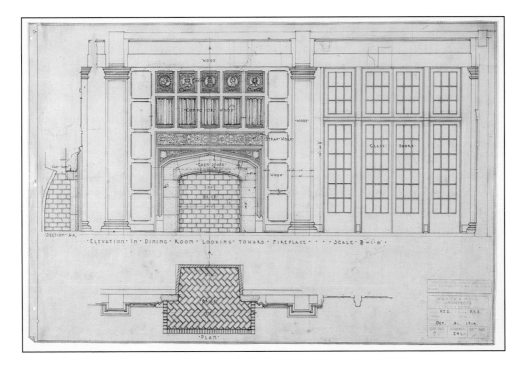

(73.2)

Druid Hills is the location of many Reid designs, with notable concentrations on Fairview (right) and Oakdale Roads. Neel Reid lived for a time on Fairview in two different houses he designed.

FRANK ADAIR house, job number 136, 1911.

(74.1)

(74.2)

harmonious compositions with details that contribute to a unity of effect. Often segments of neighborhoods would be designed, house by house, as in Druid Hills and Ansley Park in northeast Atlanta and Peachtree Heights Park in the northwest, in the Buckhead area. Characteristic of Reid's work was the concentration of a few boldly scaled ornamental elements at focal points on otherwise comparatively plain façades. There is often a hipped roof, villa-like rectangular horizontality, a central block with side porches, sometimes in wings, placed in landscape garden settings reached through French doors, very much in the manner of the "casual classicism" of Charles Platt. Many could be described as Colonial, Federal, or Georgian Revival, but nearly always with the Italian Renaissance villa set in a garden in the back of his mind. Reid's impact on the northside Atlanta suburbs was and remains significant and valuable. It is no exaggeration to assert that concentrations of designs from the Hentz, Reid & Adler "atelier," led by Neel Reid, found in these well laid out, tree-shaded green enclaves on the rolling piedmont terrain of North Atlanta, do constitute what Dr. Frances Simkins called "some of the most beautiful suburbs in all America."

The first of these was Druid Hills, begun by Joel Hurt, a civil engineer developer, in the city's northeastern quadrant centered on Ponce de Leon Avenue

from Briarcliff Road east toward Decatur, the seat of DeKalb County. Hurt developed the garden suburb of Inman Park just prior to this, but Reid did only two houses there. The pastoral residential neighborhood of Druid Hills, with its original landscape plan by Frederick Law Olmsted Sr. and later revision by his sons became the location of numerous Reid designs. This occurred largely because of his and Hentz's friendship with Frank Adair and Hunter Perry (who married sisters) and Forrest and George Adair, all of the Adair Realty Company, which was in charge of sales and development after Asa Candler and several associates purchased Hurt's Olmsted-planned suburb. The first Neel Reid designs for Druid Hills began to appear soon after 1909. Frank and Margaret Adair's own house at 1341 Ponce de Leon Avenue,

SIGMUND MONTAG house, job number 259, 1915. (75.1)

WALTER RICH house, job number 288, 1916.
Below: Garden of Rich house. (75.2)

(75.3)

job number 136, overlooking Olmsted's Virgilee Park, was completed in 1911 and still stands very much as designed. One can sit in the long living room and gaze out one of the four French doors on the front of the house facing toward the other side of busy Ponce de Leon Avenue and across Virgilee Park, without actually seeing pavement—only the tops of passing cars, giving the illusion that one is in a country house in the city ("semi-urban/semi-suburban"?).

A pamphlet, "Marvelous Story of Atlanta Real Estate," published in 1921 by the Atlanta Title and Trust Company, extolled the business virtues of a number of valuable real-estate transactions and developments in the city, including Druid Hills and Ansley Park. The president of the Atlanta Real

Estate Board, Henry B. Scott, wrote about Ansley Park: "Perhaps the most phenomenal growth of any residential section within a decade [1904–14] is contained in the story of the evolution of Land Lot No. 105. On June 14, 1847, George W. Collier purchased this land lot containing 202 ½ acres, for $150.00. On May 5, 1904 . . . the Collier estate sold the same to Hugh T. Inman for $300,000.00." Scott said Edwin P. Ansley developed the property and sold some of the lots for as high as $31,250 an acre, and he reported, "There is one block that is worth approximately what Mr. Inman paid for the whole land lot."

(76.1)
        Ansley Park, c. 1910.

Below: THE DELLA MANTA APARTMENTS, *designed for Dunbar and Sewell, job number 307, 1917. This building is on the*
(76.2)   *National Register of Historic Places, because Margaret Mitchell lived here in the 1930s and '40s.*

The enthusiastic real-estate man did not mention how well-planned E. P. Ansley's garden suburb was or how Neel Reid and his associates, early in the firm's and the development's history, set high standards of residential design for the neighborhood, but in the years since that pamphlet was published, both of these aspects have often been mentioned. In 1979, when an Ansley Park Historic District was added to the National Register of Historic Places, several residences designed by Neel Reid, who was described as "one of Atlanta's most important early-twentieth century architects," were cited.

From job number 87, 1909, when the firm was still known as Norrman, Hentz & Reid, through job number 606, 1923–26, there were at least sixteen important commissions within Ansley Park: from Fourteenth Street on the south, to Peachtree Circle at Peachtree Street on the north, West Peachtree Street/Spring Street on the west, and Golf Circle, Piedmont Avenue/Piedmont Park on the east. (Piedmont Park and Ansley Park were known as "Twin Parks" in the early days of the neighborhood development.) Among these commissions were two large apartment buildings, the Della Manta, 1917, job number 307, for a firm called Dunbar and Sewell, at One South Prado and Piedmont Avenue, and the larger of the two, the Garrison Apartments (now Reid House condominiums), 1923–24, job number 533, on the east side of Peachtree Street, between Sixteenth and Seventeenth Streets.

During research for this book, three residences, job numbers 112, 114, and 134, which were built in the earliest part of the development, were identified. They had long ago been lost as Reid houses: job number 112 for Mrs. R. T. Dorsey, 1910–11, on the

A landmark of the Ansley Park area is the GARRISON APARTMENTS *(now the Reid House), job number 533, 1923–24, shown here in construction photographs.*

(78.1)

(78.2)

Ansley Park. Above: Two views of job number 112, built for MRS. R. T. DORSEY, 1910–11. Below: Elevations of a house built for W. M. HAYNES in 1911–12, job number 114.

(78.3)

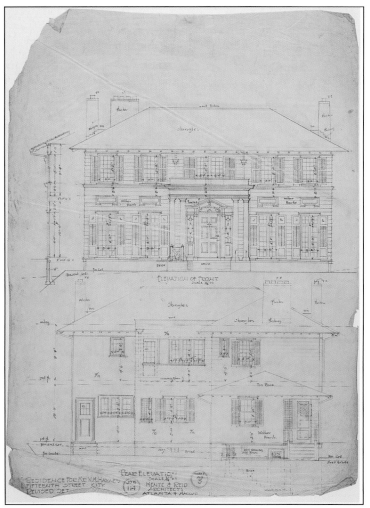

(78.4)

Prado; number 114, 1911–12, for W. M. Haynes; and number 134 for the Misses Nagle, 1911–12. These still look much as they were designed and were easily identified from the original working drawings housed at the Atlanta History Center.

Job number 87, which stood on East Fourteenth Street, was demolished many years ago, as was job number 133, on Peachtree Street just north of the Garrison Apartments (Reid House). Job number 156 no longer survives on West Sixteenth Street, the sec-

(79.1)

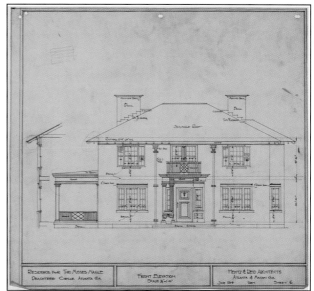

(79.2)

Above: Elevations of job number 134,
for the MISSES NAGLE, in 1911–12.

(79.3)

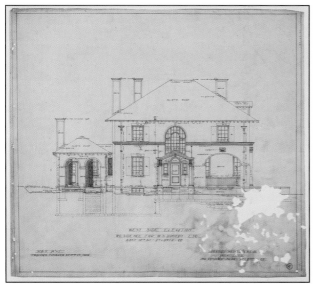

(79.4)

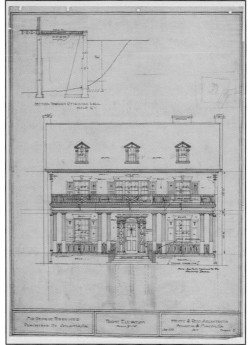

Three Reid designs in
Ansley Park, job num-
bers 87, 133, and 156,
have been demolished
over time. Far left: The
W. S. DUNCAN house,
number 87, 1909.
Left: The house for
GEORGE FORRESTER, job
number 133, 1911, stood
on Peachtree Street.
Below: Job number 156,
1912, was the second
house for MRS. R. T.
DORSEY, designed in 1912
and built on West Six-
teenth Street.

ond Mrs. R. T. Dorsey house in Ansley Park, but all of the other Reid contributions to the neighborhood remain, including various interior designs at the Piedmont Driving Club on Piedmont Avenue.

In addition to documenting those "lost" houses, the history of the splendid Villa Apartments at 200 Montgomery Ferry Drive has been partly resolved. Converted to condominiums in 1979, this regal two-story apartment building, located next to the Ansley Golf Club on about an acre of land at the northeast

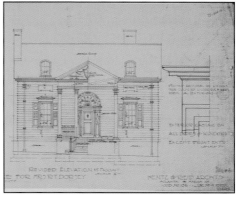

(79.5)

Designs for the Piedmont Driving Club were made by Reid and his associates at several times over the first three decades of the century because of expansion and fire damage. The first job was number 106 in 1910. The ballroom (below) was redesigned in 1921 after a fire.

(80.1)

(80.2)

(80.3)

Ballroom, job number 415, 1921.

Entrance hall, 1921.

edge of the neighborhood, has long been somewhat of a mystery. Speculation and gossip have given its date as about 1920 and its reason for being as "golf suites" for the Ansley Park Golf Club, as it was originally called. After the club was organized in 1912 as part of Ansley's original neighborhood concept, a small golf house was begun in 1915, but the Ansley Park club struggled along for a number of years before it became solvent or capable of the sort of endeavor the Villa represents. Research, in fact, can document that the Italian Villa Apartments, as the building was originally called, were being constructed in the summer of 1926 by a firm called Co-operative Plan, Inc., headed by Asa Griggs Candler Jr. and Martin B. Dunbar, as officers in a group of investors who began assembling parcels of land at Golf Circle

in 1921. There is a building permit from 1923 for a sign directing people to the proposed site. This hard evidence comes from corporate loan and deed records, which produced Candler's and Dunbar's names. Dunbar's name is an important clue, for job number 606 on the Hentz, Reid & Adler list is for the "Martin Dunbar Apartments." (Dunbar had also been involved in the Della Manta project at One South Prado.) Number 606 is the last one on the jobs list before Neel Reid's death. Unfortunately drawings for that project have not survived, or have not been located.

Oral history has also asserted that the designer was Philip Trammell Shutze when he was still a draftsman-architect in the firm. Clearly the project was begun several years before Reid died and Shutze

VILLA ("Martin Dunbar") APARTMENTS, job number 606, 1923–26.

took over as head designer. Loan records definitely point to a completion date of December 1926, with 1921 as the beginning of corporate aspects of the project. Other than its location next to the Ansley Golf Club at Golf Circle, there is no evidence that its intended purpose was "golf suites." As the Villa Apartments (now condominiums), it retains part of its original name and almost all of the 1920s Neo-Palladian stylishness worthy of Neel Reid and his associates in the Georgia school of classicists. Its somewhat exotic stucco style next to the frame Colonial Revival golf house is yet another reminder of the affluent mid-1920s in the South when the Florida boom spawned a Mediterranean Revival, in which Hentz, Reid & Adler participated, as with the Tampa Terrace Hotel, job number 535, 1923–24, when the firm maintained a Tampa office prior to the 1926 Florida "bust." Certainly in December 1926, when the Italian Villa was completed, Philip Shutze was a Hentz, Reid & Adler employee and would have contributed to the project, but when it was begun Neel Reid was the acknowledged chief designer, which he remained until early 1926.

The Villa is one more chapter in the "Marvelous Story of Atlanta Real Estate," in which the architecture of Neel Reid and his associates took center stage. Ansley Park is the location of an important part of Reid's legacy, but it did not end there, as it extended into nearby Brookwood and thence northward toward the Buckhead section of Atlanta. Here, too, Hentz, Reid & Adler was in the forefront, perhaps even more than in Ansley Park, but no less so than in Druid Hills. Today, Druid Hills, Ansley Park, and Buckhead are even more semi-urban, semi-suburban than they were in the 1940s when *Life* magazine featured Atlanta homes. Emblematic of how times have changed as Atlanta has grown is the way early twentieth-century north Atlanta areas are being recognized as historic districts, representing earlier patterns of life—and always the name Neel Reid is featured as a major contributor, a cultural hero, as he was considered in his own day.

Neel Reid's influence was evident as one left Ansley Park and proceeded north on Peachtree Street and Road and into the adjacent neighborhoods along the way toward the historic Buckhead intersection of Peachtree, West Paces Ferry, and Roswell Roads. Along this path there were at least thirty-five com-

missions, including the Peachtree/Brookwood Station at 1688 Peachtree, job number 282, 1916–17, at the old Brookwood settlement. Reid's serenely Palladian design has become a Peachtree landmark.

Referring to the Brookwood area, which began to be known by that name in the late nineteenth century, William Bailey Williford asserted in *Peachtree Street, Atlanta* (1962): "The stretch of Peachtree from its northern intersection with West Peachtree [at Ansley Park] to the wooded area near Huntington Road was at one time the most beautiful residential area in Atlanta" (p. 123). Much of the beauty was due to seven Neel Reid houses built from 1911 through 1922–23:

Job number 78, Willis Timmons, 1911
Job number 162, Mrs. H. P. Cooper, 1912
Job number 163, Winship Nunnally, 1912
Job number 450, Hunter Perry, 1921
Job number 457, Willis Jones, 1922
Job number 472, J. Carrol Payne, 1922
Job number 490, Logan Clarke, 1922

All but the last of these, which was built on Palisades Road just east of Peachtree in the Brookwood Hills neighborhood, have been removed. (The current owner of number 490 led a civic group that has had that elegant c. 1920 subdivision listed in the National Register of Historic Places.)

"Brookwood" shows on old maps as the northern edge of the extended city limits of August 1908, which also covered Ansley Park and Druid Hills. These new limits stopped where Palisades Road would be built into Brookwood Hills and where Peachtree Street now changes to Road. About the time of this limits extension, Peachtree was widened and paved north to Buckhead, opening that large territory to development. In 1907, even before the paving, a streetcar line was opened to Buckhead. There were already some summer estates, and the Walter Andrews family moved full time to Peachtree Road at the future Andrews Drive by 1910, assembling thirty-five acres, which would later become part of the E. Rivers land developments. The increased use of automobiles also helped with the development of suburban Buckhead.

Indeed, suburban Brookwood Station was built because of the growth of north Atlanta. Neel Reid designed it as a domestic-scaled, red-brick and limestone commercial villa to compliment the residen-

(83.1)

Mrs. Hunter Cooper house, number 162, 1912.

(83.7)

Logan Clarke house, number 490, 1922.

J. Carrol Payne house, (83.2)
number 472, 1922.

(83.3)

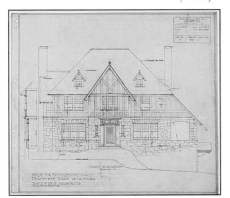

*Above: Winship Nunnally
house, number 163, 1912.
Below: Willis Jones house,* (83.8)
number 457, 1922.

 *This map locating Reid projects
at Brookwood is based on a 1926
map, when the city limits came
just south of Palisades Road, and
shows the neighborhood before
much of it was erased by the
interstate highways at Brookwood interchange. (Foust Street
is now Deering Road.) Only the
train station, the Adair stores,
and the Clarke house remain.*

(83.6)

*Above: Hunter Perry house,
number 450, 1921.
Below: Willis Timmons house,
number 78, 1911.*

(83.4)

(83.5)

tial neighborhood. Reid's influence was evident throughout the former farm land of this area that, in only a matter of years, would go from countryside to suburban to semi-suburban to semi-urban, which it remains. From Brookwood, his influence extended north into the planned residential neighborhood of Peachtree Heights Park, West and East (including an area sometimes called the West Andrews district, a 1922 extension of Peachtree Heights along Habersham Road and Andrews Drive north to West Paces Ferry), and ended at Buckhead with the West Paces Ferry/Tuxedo Park district. All were residential except for two of the thirty-five Reid commissions in north Atlanta, the railroad station and the Blackman Terrace sanitarium, 1925, job number 558. (Now destroyed, it stood on the west side of Peachtree where Brookwood Square stands.)

In 1908 Eretus (E.) Rivers and Frank C. Owens began subdividing the area east of Peachtree between present-day Lindbergh Drive and East Wesley Road in what had been Wesley G. Collier farm land. Laid out by Atlanta civil engineer O. F. Kauffman, Peachtree Heights East had the first Neel Reid house built north of Brookwood. When the firm was still Hentz & Reid, it built the first of numerous houses it would design for clients in the Buckhead area before Reid's death. Job number 169, 1912, was for Mrs. Samuel C. Porter on a short street paralleling Peachtree Road, Parkside Drive, overlooking the duck pond in Peachtree Heights East. For the head of

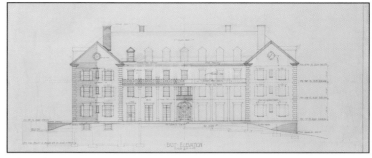

(84.1)

BLACKMAN TERRACE SANITARIUM, *job number 558, 1925, which became the Colonial Terrace Hotel, was destroyed.*

the noted Porter & Porter interior decorating firm and a close friend of his, Reid designed one of his, to coin a phrase, "casual country classicals," which still stands, but has not been known as a "Neel Reid." The drawings show the still-surviving, large-scaled, Italian Renaissance focal point doorway that the designer often favored, on a frame, horizontal, two-story block, with a hipped roof.

The farthest residence from Peachtree and the Buckhead crossroads was the second Winship Nunnally house, on West Paces Ferry near Northside Parkway, job number 517, 1923, now destroyed. The very last of these in which Reid participated was job number 591, the Edward H. Inman house, 1925–26. Known as Swan House, it was completed in 1928 after Reid's death and after, in 1927, Hal Hentz and Rudolph Adler had formed a new partnership, Hentz, Adler & Shutze. Swan House is now a house muse-

The house for S. C. PORTER on Parkside Drive is job number 169, 1912.

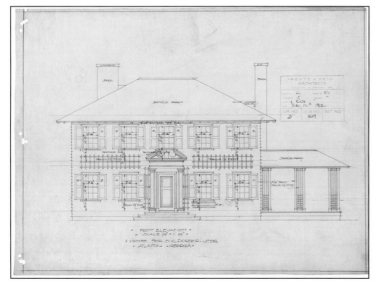

(85.1)

Above: House for WINSHIP NUNNALLY, *job number 517, 1923–24.*
Below: EDWARD H. INMAN *house (Swan House), job number 591, 1925–26.*

um at the Atlanta History Center.

The character of the residential architecture in north Atlanta during these years when Reid was the most influential designer was described in an *Atlanta Journal* article from July 18, 1915. Although Reid was not mentioned by name, the comments were based on Hentz, Reid & Adler houses in Ansley Park, Druid Hills, and the Buckhead area. Among those cited were job number 222, Alsop; number 235, Whitman-Dannals; number 251, Dickey; number 259, Montag; and number 268, Crumley. The *Journal* account said: "Among the types of homes in Atlanta are the Southern and the New England colonial; the early English; Georgian; Italian, Spanish, and French Renaissance. A great effort is also being made to harmonize architecture and interior decorations. Always, though the rooms be colonial, Adam, renaissance, or other period or feeling, they show the same harmony of design and furnishing."

Singling out "the residence of Charles Dannals,"

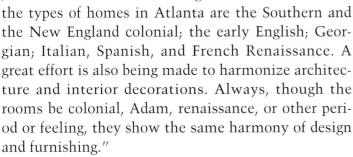

(85.2)

the newspaper account said that it is "of particular interest from an artistic standpoint, and is of pure colonial design" (p. 662). This Reid house that stood at 2662 Peachtree Road and that was demolished in 1978 was originally furnished, according to Charles Dannals Jr. "with chairs, sofas, chandeliers, porcelains, vases, and other pieces, which Neel Reid had gotten for us."

The Whitman-Dannals house was part of a development called Peachtree Heights Park, or West, put together by the E. Rivers Company beginning in 1910–11. A revised plat for the area, dated February 18, 1915, shows Carrère & Hastings as consulting architects for the planned "subdivision," as the plat indicates. Carrère & Hastings was a New York beaux arts firm which had been closely associated with the Columbia University school of architecture where Thomas Hastings, like Charles McKim, had headed a student atelier when Hentz, Reid, and Adler studied there. Peachtree Heights West and East by the E. Rivers Company are the core of what today is resi-

(86.1)

The house designed for J. B. WHITMAN in 1914 (and first occupied by his son-in-law, Charles Dannals) was job number 235 and stood at 2662 Peachtree Road (view below, 1919) until it was demolished in 1978.

(86.2)

dential Buckhead. The West segment is the more affluent and stately of the two areas flanking Peachtree Road, and it is listed on the National Register of Historic Places.

The Reid houses in Peachtree Heights West are almost too numerous to list; there are groups of them on Habersham, Cherokee, and West Wesley Roads and on Andrews Drive. One of the earliest of Reid's designs in the neighborhood, the Charles C. Case house, job number 372, 1919–21, at 2624 Habersham Road, signaled a change in taste of the public toward a somewhat more archaeological eclecticism. It is undoubtedly by Neel Reid himself, and still stands in cherished condition, owned by members of a family that has had it since the Cases sold it, a family with close ties to Hal Hentz. It is a preeminent example of the beautiful suburban Atlanta homes *Life* magazine featured in 1948, perhaps today more beautiful than ever.

When Reid designed the Case residence, based on a small English country house, for a beautiful site at the top of a hill on winding Habersham Road, this was the suburban country. A park-like neighborhood landscape plan was enhancing the natural beauty of the forested piedmont topography, in the manner of the naturalistic school of Frederick Law Olmsted. Reid's house designs were setting the standard of taste in the north Atlanta suburbs from Olmsted's Druid Hills, through Ansley Park, to here. As the neighborhood was built, period revival was the mode, with style precedents from the Tudor, Georgian, Federal, and Italian Renaissance periods. Archaeologically authentic, even erudite, forms and details were prized, based on measured drawings and sketches of historical models. The learning was subtle, and so were the results.

Neel Reid had traveled in England during his two years of special studies at Columbia University and abroad, and he kept a diary in which he described the purchase of architectural books in London; writing in September 1907, he said: "Indulged in two books, *Works of Inigo Jones* and a later work, English houses, line drawings." The second of these was evidently the 1905 edition of *English Domestic Architecture of the XVII and XVIII Centuries* by Horace Field and Michael Binney (revised in 1928). Its subtitle reads "A Selection of Examples of Smaller Buildings, Measured, Drawn

and Photographed." A featured example from this book's English Renaissance vernacular architecture is "The Manor House, Tintinhull, Somerset, c. 1720." There are a photograph and a measured drawing of what, in fact, is the garden or west elevation. No floor plan is given. Field and Binney describe it as "dignified yet homelike." From this garden elevation in Tintinhull, Reid made his own dignified design with a nearly identical walled forecourt and sculptured eagles on piers near Habersham Road. Sometimes called the Eagle House, it is a sort of "suburban town house," a near twin on the front elevation to its English country cousin.

In the village of Tintinhull, the house was usually called the Mansion. The older eastern section was a farmhouse from about a hundred years earlier. The west elevation was intended as a new, symmetrical entrance front facing a formal garden. Reid was an expert in this matter of houses integral with gardens, with more than one formal elevation and with more than one processional approach for resident and visitor alike. He began exploring this subject for the Fuller Callaways in 1914–16 in his design of Hills and Dales with its several elevations in a garden setting.

Both Reid's Atlanta adaptation, called Somerset House, and the original in Somerset, England, are well-known houses and have long been featured together in magazines and books. Tintinhull House, Somerset, has belonged to the English National Trust since 1954. In the booklet distributed by the English conservation organization, the American "twin" is mentioned in this way: "In 1918 the West Front was accurately reproduced at a house in Atlanta, Georgia, USA, named Somerset House in compliment to its original" (pp. 6–7).

Mrs. Charles C. (Kareen G.) Case (1884–1970) acquired the lot in Peachtree Heights Park on May 8, 1919, according to the deed. Soon afterwards, Neel Reid drew plans, first for the garage with garage apartment, which was built on the property first; those drawings are dated August 14, 1919. A founding member of the Peachtree Garden Club (Reid's club), Mrs. Case sold the house to Sally Connally (Mrs. H. Warner) Martin, on May 29, 1935. Mrs. Martin was the aunt of Hal Hentz's wife, Frances Connally Hentz. (The Hentzes would build their own home on nearby West Muscogee in 1937–38.) The

(88.1)

The CHARLES C. CASE *house (above and right), job number 372, 1919–21, was featured in the August 1926 issue of* Southern Architect and Building News.

(88.3)

Above and right: "The Manor House, Tintinhull, Somerset, c. 1720." Because Reid used the garden elevation of this notable English house as a model for the façade of the Case house on Habersham Road, it is called Somerset House.

SECOND FLOOR PLAN
HOUSE OF C. C. CASE, ESQ., ATLANTA, GA.
HENTZ, REID & ADLER, ARCHITECTS

(88.2)

(88.4)

house then passed from Mrs. Martin to Frances Spalding (Mrs. Robert F.) Bryan, her niece, in March 1959. The present owner, Mrs. Jarrett L. (Mary Virginia Bryan) Davis III, is the Bryans' daughter and great-niece of Mrs. Warner Martin. Mrs. Davis's file on the house contains Reid's original working drawings on architect's linen, job number 372. Uncle Hal Hentz told her family that it was "Reid's idea" to do an Atlanta version of the English Renaissance house in Somerset. Neel Reid became thirty-four years old October 23, 1919, as this house was underway.

In Mrs. Davis's house archive is a copy of the August 1936 *House Beautiful*, which sensibly reported: "The manor house of Tintinhull was the model for this new house designed by the late Neel Reid of the firm of Hentz, Reid & Adler. They made changes, of course. But in its main outlines, Somerset House follows its original. Even the eagles were copied. For modern convenience they put a circular motor drive at the front, sacrificing the lawn and garden. But they kept the classic pediments, the pilasters, the stone quoins, the entrance itself." In August 1926, *Southern Architect and Building News* featured the house. Expressing the spirit of the time that produced this landmark of Peachtree Heights Park, the writer observed: "In the past, we have seen many attempts by those who would be original, to start a new style in architecture, leaving behind examples that stand as a warning to those who would come after, and rendering the dependence upon historical form and precedent more secure than ever before." Praising the Charles Case house, he said: "Few houses in Atlanta possess greater charm and dignity than this house of Mr. Case designed by that talented artist Neel Reid." Opinion has not changed.

It is a rare passerby who does not notice the handsome stone wall and eagles near the roadway and glimpse the limestone façade and circular court paved with cobblestones and who is not permanently charmed by this quintessential Buckhead "Neel Reid." Arguably, the Case house was the model home for the garden suburb of Peachtree Heights Park, and it set the stage for other evocative designs which followed along on Habersham, West Wesley, and Cherokee Roads and Andrews Drive—it could rightfully be called "Neel Reid country." (The Whitman-Dannals House, job number 235, of 1914, which

stood on Peachtree frontage of Peachtree Heights, chronologically preceded the Case house.)

Counting the Whitman-Dannals and the Case house, there were seventeen Hentz, Reid & Adler domestic designs in Peachtree Heights Park from 1914 through 1925–26, ending with number 591, the Edward H. Inman house at 3099 Andrews Drive. Of these, only one has been demolished, number 455, the John Bulow Campbell house, 1922, which crowned a hill on Andrews Drive at Habersham Way. Except for the Charles Shelton house, number 572, 1925–26, on Habersham Road, a large Tudor revival evocation, all of the houses are subtly eclectic classical variations, including American Georgian Colonial, English Georgian and Adamesque, American neoclassical revival, and Anglo-Italian. All are set in the lush stretches of shade and dogwood trees and sweeping lawns of Peachtree Heights Park. Lawns remind one of golf greens and fairways, as though Atlanta's golf hero, Bobby Jones, were in charge of the landscape—and as Atlanta's architecture hero, Neel Reid, was for the houses and gardens. There were six "Neel Reids" on Habersham, five on Andrews, three on Cherokee, and two on West Wesley.

Habersham Road:
> Job number 372, Case
> Job number 460, Manry
> Job number 510, Wright
> Job number 527, Dorsey
> Job number 562, Thornton
> Job number 572, Shelton

Andrews Drive:
> Job number 455, Campbell
> Job number 503, Alston
> Job number 509, Witham
> Job number 555, Nixon
> Job number 591, Inman

Cherokee Road:
> Job number 467, McDuffie
> Job number 468, Draper
> Job number 469, Newman

West Wesley Road:
> Job number 496, Street
> Job number 504, Tompkins

The Robert C. Alston house, 2866 Andrews Drive, number 503, 1922–23, at Cherokee Road, is a red-brick synthesis of American Georgian and Greek Revival details and forms. Let us single it out

(90.1)

Designs by Hentz, Reid & Adler were often featured in print during the 1920s and '30s.
Among those from Peachtree Heights Park were
the CAM DORSEY house, job number 527,
1923–24 (above and left), the JESSE DRAPER
house, job number 468, 1922, on Cherokee
Road (below), and the HENRY TOMPKINS house,
job number 504, 1922–24, on West Wesley
Road (opposite page).

(90.2)

(90.3)

(91.1)

Peachtree Heights Park.
Above: Habersham Road, the MANRY (left, job number 460) and WRIGHT (right, job number 510) houses.

(91.3)

Below and right: The HENRY TOMPKINS house
(job number 504), façade and entrance hall.

(91.2)

(92.1)　*Peachtree Heights Park, Andrews Drive.*
Above and below: House for LAURA B.
(MRS. JOHN BULOW) CAMPBELL, job num-
ber 455, 1922. Right: VAUGHN NIXON
(92.2)　*house, job number 555, 1925.*

(92.3)

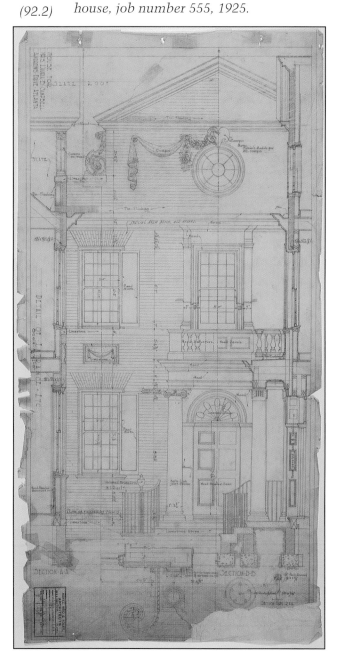

because of an eye-witness account of the architect's morning visit there when it was new. He came for a conference with the owner, Caro du Bignon (Mrs. Robert C.) Alston. The exact date is unknown, but probably 1924. A niece of Mrs. Alston, who was visiting her aunt from out of town, recalled that she was asked to greet Reid at the porte-cochere door; he either had been driven there on his way to the Candler Building or had possibly walked from the William Manry house just west of there on Habersham, where he often spent the night with his friends, instead of returning to Mimosa Hall in Roswell. The young lady had heard about this handsome young man-about-town architect, who was considered an aesthetic genius, and she wanted to meet him. They had been seated for only a few moments when, remaining in his chair, Mr. Reid excused himself as he suffered an attack of epilepsy brought on by his worsening malignant brain tumor. The story goes, "He took from his suit coat a large linen pocket handkerchief to cover his face and head as he had a momentary seizure." This troubling but fascinating moment passed quickly before her aunt came downstairs to confer about some practical design matter she wanted to bring to her architect's attention. It is a moment that the young lady has not forgotten even as she has seen the age of her aunt, then, come and go.

There are those who still remember such extraordinary things which shed light into the shadows of that era. For a new book, *Buckhead, A Place for All Time* by Susan K. Barnard, a daughter of Phillip C. McDuffie reminisced about her family home at 7 Cherokee Road, job number 467, designed in 1922 and, since 1987, the residence of Mrs. Henry Florance, who also loves it: "Mother and Daddy drew the plans, and Neel Reid was the architect. They had a beautiful formal garden in the back and they brought Neel Reid out on a stretcher to approve the beautiful gazebo that was in the garden" (p. 112).

The classical gazebo, a domed temple, was given a separate job number, 605, because it was built slightly later, when Reid was making those final inspections in late 1925 and early 1926. He even went by train to Columbus, Georgia, to check on the R. E. Dismukes house, job number 513, completed in 1925 when he was not well.

The Vaughn Nixon house, 3083 Andrews Drive,

job number 555, 1925–26, is one of Reid's last designs and last final inspections. Like its next-door neighbor, the Edward Inman house, job number 591, it is located in the extension of Andrews Drive made to West Paces Ferry Road in 1922. Mrs. Frank A. Player, a daughter of the Vaughn Nixons, who grew up in the house, recalled her family's memory of a "thin Neel Reid, dragging a bit from the paralysis in his left side, but with the help of cane, coming to the house as it was being completed." She said, "Father knew both Hal Hentz and Neel Reid well, but of course Neel was the *artiste*." Named Vaughn for her father, Mrs. Player has some of the furnishings and art objects that Reid selected for the house; some are at the Piedmont Driving Club; and some are still in the house, which has belonged to the Wayne Watsons since 1964. Neel Reid selected and placed a pair of large landscape-seascape paintings in the spacious entrance-stair hall, where they still hang.

Hentz, Reid & Adler was at its prime in the mid-1920s during the expansive economy of that decade following World War I. The firm had a great deal of work under contract, on the drawing boards, and under construction as Reid passed away. The Nixon-Watson house was one of the last that Reid himself saw from conception to completion. In a period of fewer than twenty years, Reid and his partners helped to create a Southern American Renaissance. Atlanta was born too late to share in the colonial eighteenth century or very much of the antebellum Greek Revival, yet had tried to rectify this just before and just after the Great War. It was an effort from which we continue to benefit.

Just as the Case house was Reid's interpretation of a specific small English Renaissance house at Tintinhull, Somerset, here is his cream stucco version of the red brick Hammond-Harwood house (1773–74) at Annapolis, Maryland, one of the primary landmarks of colonial American Georgian domestic architecture. Reid's Vaughn Nixon house is not a copy of the Maryland precedent, but an eclectic design based on the Hammond-Harwood façade, especially its beautiful fanlighted doorway. Few enter the house on this formal front facing the great lawn and Andrews Drive; instead they arrive by automobile at the one-story classical loggia of the garden elevation and enter the wide Tidewater hallway with its romantic-classical maritime vistas that

(95.1)   (95.2)

*The façade of the VAUGHN NIXON house, job number 555 (above, right), was Neel Reid's
interpretation of the Hammond-Harwood house (above, left), 1773–74, Annapolis, Maryland.*

Reid selected for his interior architectural scheme.

Neel Reid's classic precedent for the design of the front of the house is one of the most admired of early America. His suburban version beautifully replicates the spirit of the original Annapolis town house. A coincidence which adds another facet to the Reid legend is that the Hammond-Harwood house was built according to the design of another gifted architect, William Buckland (1734–74), who also died at the top of his career in his last house, the masterpiece Reid and his clients found worthy of emulating in Peachtree Heights.

Then why is it said that this early twentieth-century contribution to the American classical tradition is Neel Reid's last house? It is only job number 555, and there are job number 561, the Alex Smith house in Tuxedo Park, just off of West Paces Ferry Road;

number 562, the Lawson Thornton house on Habersham Road; number 572, the Charles Shelton house on Habersham; number 591, the Edward Inman (Swan) house, on Andrews Drive, a house listed in the National Register of Historic Places; and 598, the Bolton house near Social Circle, Georgia. (See Other Locations.) These were all under way before Reid's death.

The office records of the firm of Hentz, Reid & Adler and the records of his estate for February-May 1926 in the possession of his heirs give actual and prospective jobs with estimated costs of projects and commissions being owed "in office February 14, 1926," including the Cooperative Apartments (the Villa), job number 606, in Ansley Park.

Included on these valuable records are, in descending order: job number 591, E. H. Inman; number 572, Charles Shelton; number 555, Vaughn Nixon decorating; number 542, Joseph D. Rhodes decorating; and number 513, R. E. Dismukes residence decorating (Columbus, Georgia; see Other Locations). In these records, an account for the firm's year ending December 31, 1925, documents that each partner earned $18,000.00 for that year and each partner's account was credited with almost $9,000.00 additional profits. There was an item, "Loss on Florida Office" in the amount of $10,946.12, as the Florida real estate boom came to an end.

The Vaughn Nixon house, number 555, is clearly among Reid's last works; the firm had not yet sent the last interior decorating invoice for it when he died. It was probably the last residence he was able to see to its conclusion, although he had participated in all works of the firm through December 1925 and was so remunerated or, in some cases, his estate was. After he died and his will had been probated, March 1, 1926, with Roy Dorsey as executor, the surviving partners paid Reid's estate $18,000, in six $3,000 installments, as the purchase price of the Neel Reid interest in actual and prospective jobs. This settlement also covered the purchase of Reid's personal architectural library, as listed February 28, 1926. (See bibliography for some of these books, including *Brick Architecture of the Colonial Period in Maryland and Virginia* [1919], which shows the Hammond-Harwood entrance doorway Reid used at the Vaughn Nixon house.)

On the day after his death, the Georgia Chapter of the American Institute of Architects issued a memorial deploring their member's passing, which was published in the *Atlanta Journal* funeral report, February 15, 1926. Words from that memorial help explain why the Nixon house could be called a last house, in the truest sense of Reid's approach to his work: "In all his work he did not consider his job complete until the last shrub was planted in relation and the last bit of interior decorating was handled in his own peculiarly happy style."

A design by Reid was not a drawing-board dream, a paper product, but an executed work down to the "last shrub." Even though Reid was involved in all the work until his death and remained the principal designer until the last, he was not able to complete, through the execution stage, job numbers 591 through number 606, in his own "peculiarly happy style."

That is not to say that these jobs do not remain Hentz, Reid & Adler works, however. Hentz, Adler & Shutze was not incorporated until 1927, as Reid's former partners, Hal Hentz and Rudolph Adler, added Philip Shutze, a thirty-seven-year-old protege of their former firm, who became the new partnership's chief designer and thus the inheritor of a great tradition. In that way, Shutze, a graduate of Georgia Tech's and Columbia University's schools of architecture and a fellow of Charles McKim's American Academy in Rome, was Reid's successor among the Georgia classicists in the Southern school of McKim, Mead & White's American Renaissance.

Peachtree Heights Park, an expression of that same renaissance, came toward the end of Reid's life and career, but there are other areas in Buckhead in which Reid's influence was felt, such as on West Paces Ferry Road and in Tuxedo Park. These houses, in scale and style, reflect Atlanta's New South affluence and the exotic Florida mentality before the Florida real estate debacle of 1925–26.

It started with "Arden," the residence of James L. Dickey Jr., designed in 1914–15 and completed in early 1917, job number 251, 456 West Paces Ferry Road, NW, only blocks west of the main Buckhead intersection. (At about the same time as Arden, on land purchased from the Dickeys, is job number 222, "alterations and additions" for Edward Alsop; the present address is 490 West Paces Ferry Road. For Alsop, Reid improved a summer cottage, adding a porte cochere, porches, urns, and large flower boxes outside and paneled walls inside. JNR himself drafted some of the Alsop's working drawings.) Soon after Arden's completion *Architectural Record* featured it in the Portfolio of Current Architecture section of the October and December 1917 issues. Many of its working drawings were by Rudolph Adler and Philip Shutze; both were superb and prolific draftsmen; Adler was especially adept at staircases. That, of course, does not mean they were the designers of this, the largest frame house by Hentz, Reid & Adler, but they played a significant part.

From an autobiographical sketch (which is housed in his extensive archive at the Atlanta History Center) that Philip Shutze wrote in 1976, a few years before his death, we get an important insight about the design of such houses: "At the outset, let me repeat again and again, that in my opinion, no one member of an architectural firm, over a period of years can be designated as the author delineator absolute of any particular structure" (box 1, folder II).

Shutze listed in capitals the "usual constituents" of a "closely knit" organization: "The Job Getter; the Designer; Engineer; Experienced Draftsmen; Specifications Writer, and Superintendent." Shutze says all of these together usually make "for a smoothly and effectively performing partnership, contributing to the whole effort. If any of these spheres of activity malfunction, failure will surely result." Neel Reid has usually been considered the "author delineator absolute" of the Dickey house, which may be an overstatement because of the contributions of the entire team to the successful results.

The façade of Arden is considered a derivation of the Potomac River piazza at Mount Vernon, a popular colonial revival model for the front of houses. Outside, it is basically Federal, with a two-story entrance portico made up of eight attenuated white columns in the Tuscan order—George Washington's columns were square piers. Inside, the moldings are American Georgian, and there is an impressive entrance hall and double staircase. Just as with Hills and Dales, this is an Old South/New South monument for a "lord of the manor" of his neighborhood, which the Dickeys have been in Buckhead for many years. (Poet Jim Dickey, who wrote "Buckhead Boys," was a nephew of James L. Dickey Jr.)

In the fall of 1903 Dickey's father purchased four hundred acres at fifteen dollars per acre, which included the West Paces Ferry Road frontage where Dickey Jr. built in 1915–17. In the spring of the next year, Robert Foster Maddox, the best friend of James Dickey Jr., bought seventy-three acres of this land across the road from the Dickey family's original spread, and in 1911 Maddox built the first Buckhead country estate, Woodhaven, where the Governor's Mansion stands today. After Dickey Sr.'s death in 1910, the Tuxedo Park Company, headed by Charles Black, bought a large portion of the Dickeys' land for development, selling large lots for spacious estates.

Arden, Dickey Jr.'s Neel Reid house, remains as one of the earliest landmarks of the West Paces Ferry corridor of mansions. Much of the surrounding land of the estate, however, has been subdivided, continuing the process that began with James L. Dickey Sr.

Arden, the JAMES L. DICKEY JR. house, job number 251, 1914–15. (97.1)

Arden stair hall. (97.2)

Arden parterre garden. (97.3)

(98.1)

The ANDREW CALHOUN estate, Tryggveson, viewed from West Paces Ferry Road, before it was reduced by subdividing the grounds. The designs for the house and gardens, job number 396, 1921–22, evolved over several years utilizing the varied talents within the firm. Below: The sunken garden, from a c. 1930 photograph.

(98.2)

(98.4)

Interiors of the Calhoun house, c. 1930. Below: Stair hall. Right: Dining room.

(98.3)

but not all of it as enlightened as his and his son's generations.

The Andrew Calhoun estate, which was developed west of the Dickey place on the same side of Paces Ferry beginning in 1921, was job number 396. Today the address of the house is Pinestream Drive because the property has been subdivided. Andrew Calhoun originally had one hundred acres, developing some eighteen of them formally. Calhoun was in real estate, a gentleman farmer, and part of the prominent Atlanta and Georgia branch of the South Carolina Calhouns. Here Mrs. Calhoun, Mary Guy Trigg of Chattanooga, Tennessee, founded the Peachtree Garden Club, Atlanta's first, in 1923. Neel Reid was closely associated with this club from its inception; his mother, Mrs. John Reid, was a member, and its roll was made up of ladies who lived in his houses, among them Mrs. Frank Adair, Mrs. Robert C. Alston, Mrs. Andrew Calhoun, Mrs. J. Bulow Campbell, Mrs. Charles C. Case, Mrs. James L. Dickey, Mrs. Cam D. Dorsey, Mrs. Jessie Draper, Mrs. Philip C. McDuffie, Mrs. Winship Nunnally, Mrs. Henry Newman, Mrs. Hunter Perry, and Mrs. Trammell Scott. Mrs. Cason Callaway and Mrs. Fuller E. Callaway, like Mrs. Reid, were out-of-town members. In 1948, when Mrs. Charles Case was president of this influential club during its twenty-fifth anniversary year, Constance Knowles (Mrs. Jesse) Draper, wrote about Neel Reid in a club publication that Atlantans owe much of their "appreciation of all the arts" to him. (The Peachtree Garden Club founded the Neel Reid Scholarship at the University of Georgia in 1946.)

The Calhoun estate, which was called Tryggveson, included an orchard, a garden, a lake, tennis courts, and formal gardens. It was entered through baroque piers on West Paces Ferry modeled after some in Verona, Italy. Although these fanciful piers still stand, they have been moved apart to form an entrance to Pinestream Road, built in the valley between West Paces and the house when the terraced gardens and the surrounding acreage were subdivided and developed in the 1960s.

Neel Reid's first trip to Italy came in 1907. With his signature and bookplate, his guidebook, *The Old Gardens of Italy, How to Visit Them* (London, 1907), survives in his family's Neel Reid collection. Among the gardens Reid visited then as checked in his guidebook are Albani and Corsini in Rome, Gori in Siena, and Cuzzano in Verona. Reid returned to Italy in the spring and early summer of 1922 with a protege, Lewis Edmund Crook Jr., when Reid was already slowed a bit by his brain cancer, after the Calhoun house was under contract. Reid bought furnishings and art objects for the house. The working drawings, mostly dated November 1922, were prepared by Philip Shutze, Lewis Crook, James Means,

and Ernest Ivey. The house was under construction in mid-1923, after Mr. Crook and Mr. Ivey had formed their new partnership, Ivey & Crook, on May 1, 1923; for them it was job number 105, "supervision." The Villa Gori, Siena, and the Villa Cuzzano, Verona, were two of the villas that Reid and his associates used as inspiration for the eclectic design the Calhouns contracted them to create. In this project, as with others during this period of Hentz, Reid & Adler's history, there was a studio-like collaboration of artistic and practical talents and temperaments of varying degrees of training and experience, working together with Reid and his partners to satisfy the client and the firm's architectural and aesthetic standards.

One of the earliest houses built in Tuxedo Park, a development on the north side of West Paces Ferry Road, was the Joseph D. Rhodes residence, Hentz, Reid & Adler job number 542, designed in 1924 and completed in 1926. The address, as presently reckoned on West Paces Ferry, is 541; Tuxedo Road runs along its east side. The tile-roofed, stucco villa was designed when the firm maintained a Tampa office in the midst of the Florida boom, when exotic, even baroque, Mediterranean styles were fashionable. The Tampa Terrace Hotel, job number 535, also dated 1924, has details quite similar, for example, to the Italianate Calhoun house on the south side of West Paces Ferry. The working drawings for the Tampa Terrace were mostly drafted by McKendree A. (Mack) Tucker (1896–1972), who also signed the Rhodes house drawings MAT in the identification block. Mack Tucker was a talented Georgia Tech–trained architect who drafted many a "set of plans" for buildings during this period of the firm, and sometimes he signed his work McK. In 1929 he formed his own firm of Tucker & Howell, with Atlanta native Albert Howell, another Georgia classicist. Rudolph Adler's initials, RSA, also appeared on the Rhodes house and Tampa Terrace drawings.

In 1923 Neel Reid ceased to draft but not to oversee design, and the Rhodes house is another of the firm's 1920s projects in which his name should not be minimized. This would include interior decorating; a charge for that service was on the firm's books when Reid died. Some have seen the hand of Philip Shutze in the Rhodes project, but during the years 1923 through 1925, Shutze seems to have been

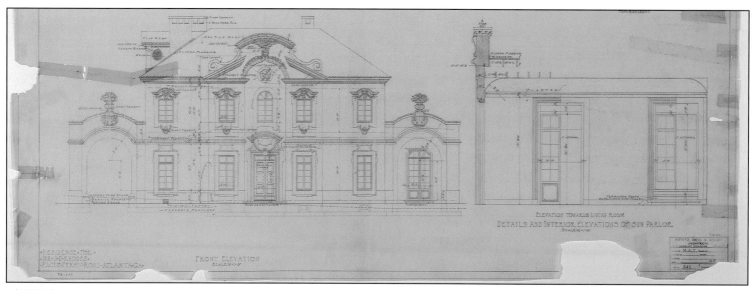

(100.1)

Above: Joseph D. Rhodes *house, job number 542, 1924, drafted by Mack Tucker.*

Below: Details of entrance and terrace, Tampa Terrace Hotel, *job number 535, 1924–25.*

(100.2)

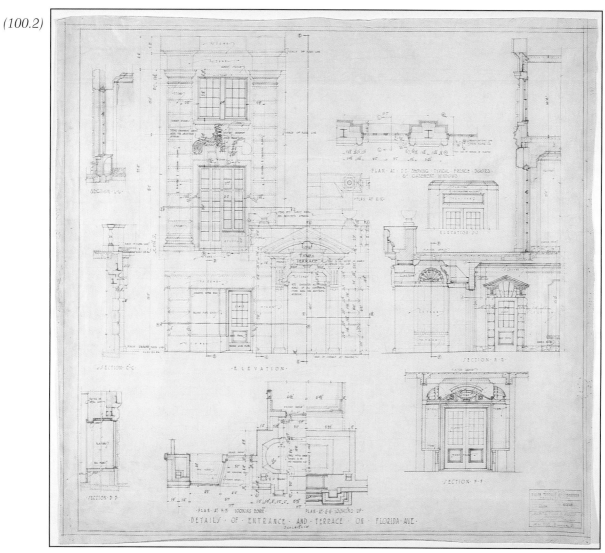

(101.1)

House for ALEXANDER W. SMITH,
job number 561, 1925, Tuxedo Park.

(101.2)

JOHN W. GRANT garden,
job number 584, c. 1925, at Craigellachie.

somewhat of a gypsy, working as an associate with various firms in New York City. In an interview with James Means in 1971 regarding who designed the Dan Horgan house, an Italian baroque pavilion, c. 1926, on the outskirts of Macon, Jimmy Means told this historian-writer that a major contribution Philip Shutze made to the firm of Hentz, Reid & Adler was a collection of Italian photographs Shutze brought with him when he returned from his years studying abroad. Means said that they all benefitted from these new additions to the firm's books and photographs used in the creative-eclectic process of fashioning new designs based on historical precedents. Means, who came to work for Hentz, Reid & Adler in 1917 and became a fine domestic architect in the eclectic traditionalist manner, had done the working drawings (JM) for the Horgan house, but he did not consider it his design.

Presently standing at 520 West Paces Ferry Road, on the south side of the street, is the Willis B. Jones house, job number 457, 1921–23, which was moved to that site in the late 1960s from 1753 Peachtree Street, at Brookwood. Although it is not exactly as it was originally, especially inside, enough of Reid's design work, inspired by English Renaissance models, survives as a credit to his name and to its new Buckhead location. Nothing, however, survives of job number 584, "John W. Grant garden," c. 1925, which was made behind the Grant house, Craigellachie, c.

1917, at 155 West Paces Ferry Road, now the Cherokee Town Club. For Barnard's *Buckhead* (1996), John W. Grant III remembered: "John Grant's cousin, eminent architect Neel Reid, redid these gardens and built a summer house where they used to put the orchestra when they had lawn parties" (p. 97).

On that elegiac note, we take leave of Neel Reid's Buckhead and Atlanta. But it brings to mind another leaving, another elegy, published December 25, 1925, in the *Atlanta Journal*, O. B. Keeler's column entitled "Neel Reid and Bobby Jones": "On and about this particular Christmas two champions set out from Atlanta, one north, one south. One who departed Wednesday is Neel Reid. One, who departs either Saturday evening or Sunday morning, is Bobby Jones." Jones was leaving Atlanta for another golf tournament; Reid was going to Boston, yet again, to see the great brain surgeon Dr. Harvey Cushing. Within weeks Dr. Cushing wrote Reid's mother, Mrs. John W. Reid, Mimosa Hall, Roswell, Georgia: "I have just heard from round-about sources that Neel has had his end. I hope it was peaceful and without pain. He was a splendid fellow and . . . I came not only to be much attached to him but to have the greatest respect for his character, manliness and courage" (February 25, 1926).

Reid had worked to the end, and we have many accounts of his dedication during 1925 and early 1926, as he made his last rounds like a champion.

House for Frank Adair,
job number 136, 1911, Druid Hills.

(102.1)

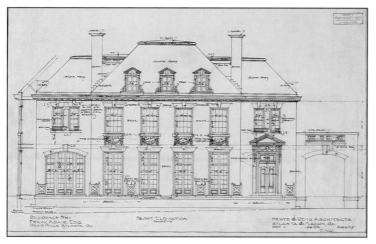

Above and right: Entrance elevation.
Below: Bay window with ornamental lattice,
a decorative device Reid used frequently.

(102.2)

(102.3)

(104.1)

Above: French doors in the living room of
the Frank Adair house offer views of Virgilee
Park and across Ponce de Leon Avenue.
Right: Elevation and section of fountain on
the tea porch, drafted by Philip Shutze.
Trellis was a Reid favorite, indoors and out.

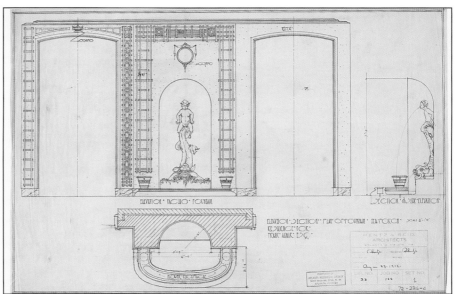

(104.2)

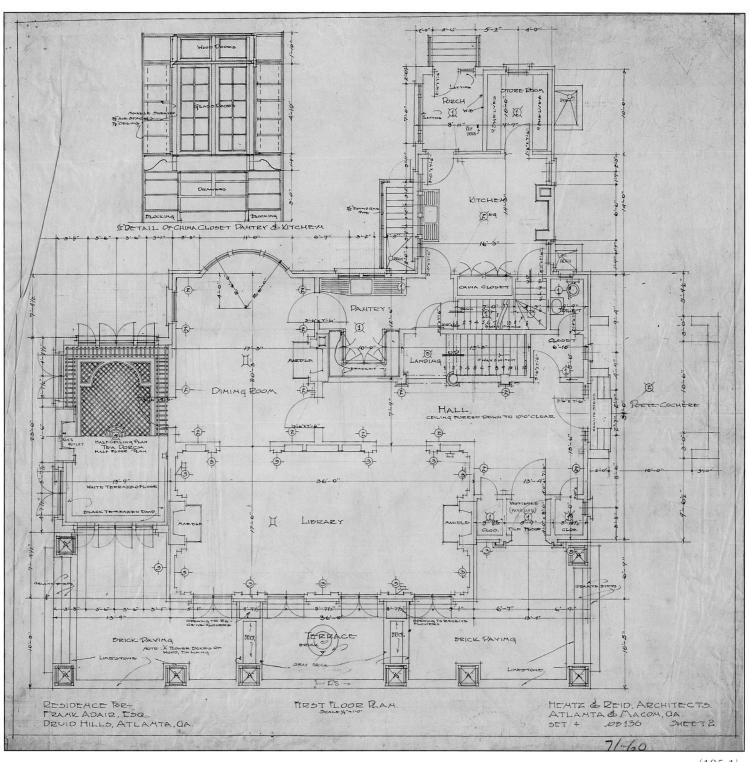

(105.1)

Plan for the first floor of the Frank Adair house.

(106.1)

HOUSE FOR NEEL REID, *job number 249, 1914, Druid Hills. Reid lived here less than a year, selling the house in 1915. He then moved into nearby job number 271, which he built for sale before moving to Roswell. Reid based this design on a house (1904) by Charles Platt in Hadlyme, Connecticut.*

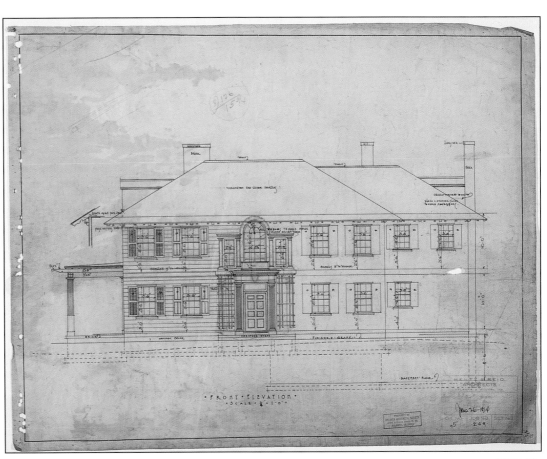

(107.1)

Above: Entrance elevation, drafted by Reid. Left: Detail of column on pergola porch, drafted by Philip Shutze.

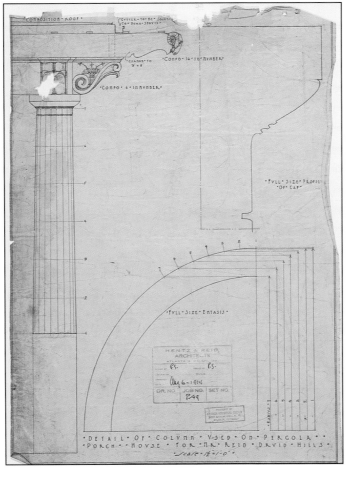

(107.2)

(108.1)

Neel Reid house, number 249. Right and below: Except for screen on the kitchen porch and sleeping porch, the rear elevation appears much as it did when Reid lived there briefly in 1914–15.

(108.2)

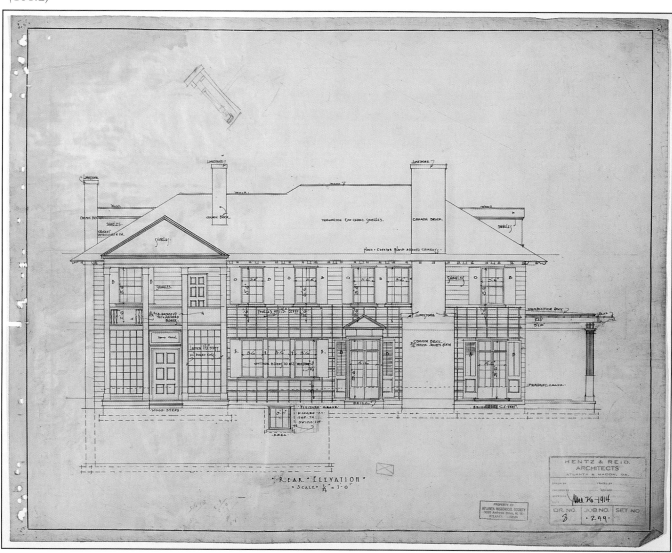

(109.1)

(109.2)

Several houses designed for resale were built along a two-block stretch of Fairview Road in Druid Hills near the house Reid lived at that time. Among them were job number 219, 1913, above left, job number 238, 1914, below, and job number 255, 1915, above right.

(109.3)

(110.1)

(110.2)

HOUSE FOR A. C. NEWELL, *job number 258, 1914–15. The firm's list of jobs gives Jesse Draper, but the working drawings show A. C. Newell, who acquired this house in 1915 from Draper and commissioned Reid alterations.*

(111.1)

(111.2)

Newell house.
Above: Garden elevation.
Left: Porch detail.

(112.1)

Newell house, job number 258.
Above: Living room.
Right: Dining room.

(112.2)

(113.1)

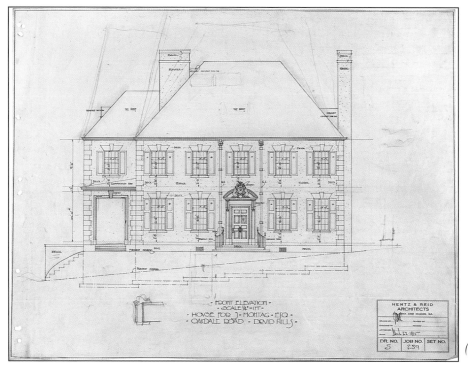

(113.2)

HOUSE FOR SIGMUND MONTAG,
job number 259, 1915, Druid Hills.
Entrance elevation drafted by Neel Reid.

(114.1)

House for Walter Rich, *job number 288, 1916, Druid Hills.*

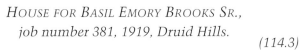

This selection of homes on Fairview, Clifton, and Springdale Roads illustrates the broad eclecticism of Reid's work.

House for William R. Prescott, *job number 275, 1915, Druid Hills.*

House for Basil Emory Brooks Sr., *job number 381, 1919, Druid Hills.*

(114.2)

(114.3)

(115.1)

HOUSE FOR O. R. STRAUSS, *job number 292, 1917, Druid Hills.*
Below: The layout of grounds, drafted by Neel Reid, was typical of the integrated design
service the partnership provided.

(115.2)

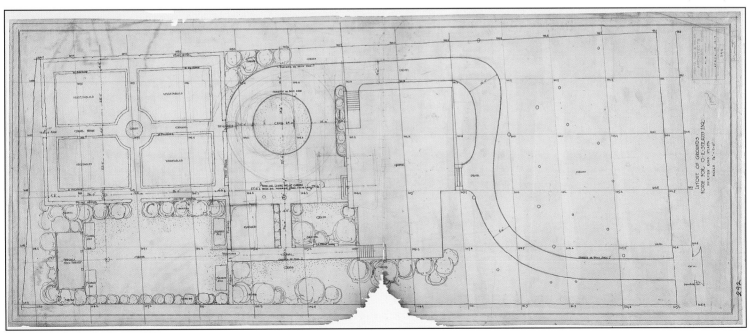

HOUSE FOR ROBERT M. CRUMLEY, *job number 268, 1915, Ansley Park.*
Opposite: Plan of first floor, drafted by Neel Reid and Rudolph Adler.

(117.1)

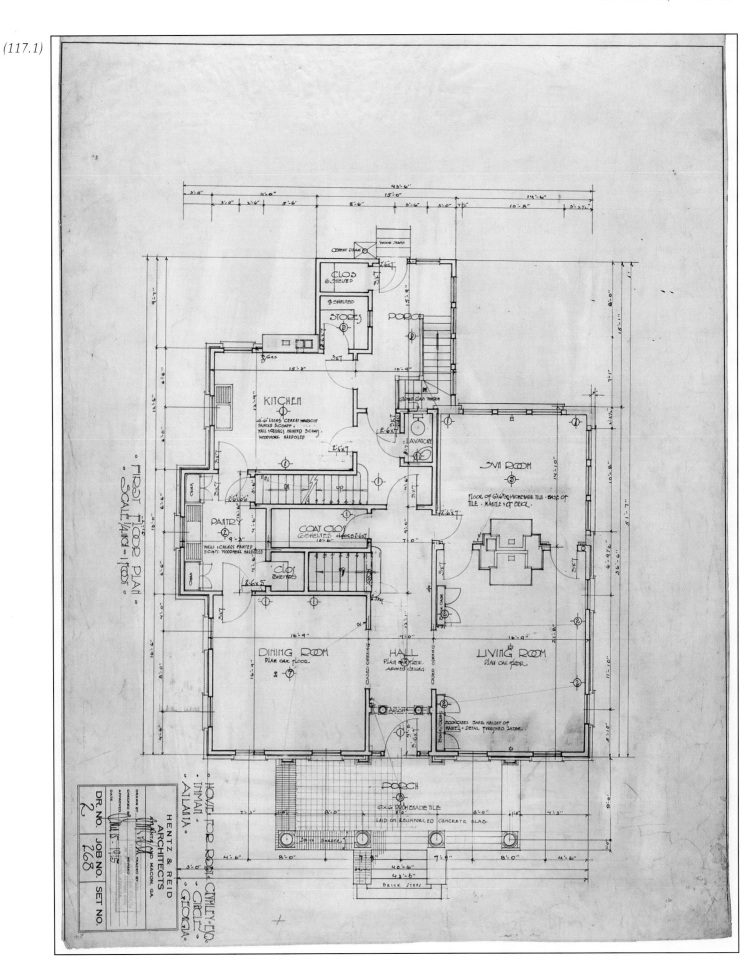

Robert Crumley house, entrance hall.

Robert Crumley house, stair hall.   *(119.1)*

HOUSE FOR STEPHAN A. LYNCH, job number 387, 1920–21, Ansley Park.
Entrance elevation.

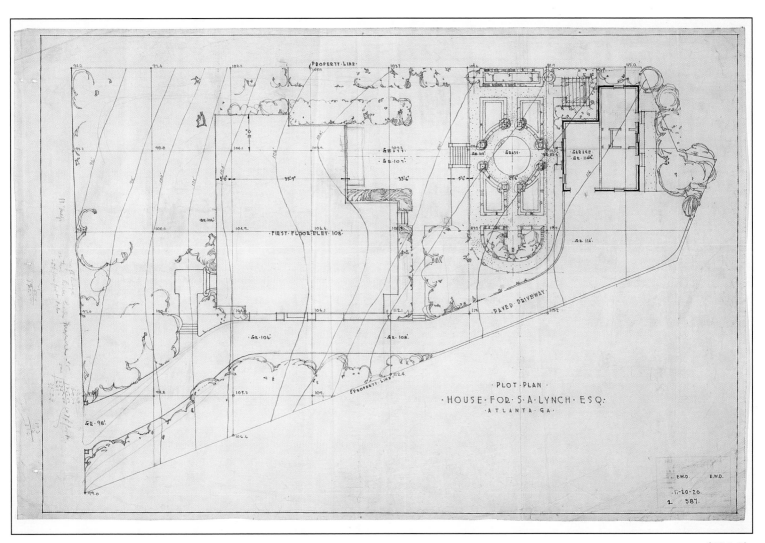

(121.1)

Stephan A. Lynch house. Plot plan.

House for David C. Black, job number 456, 1921–22, Ansley Park.

(122.1)

Above: Entrance elevation.
Left: Den.

(122.2)

David Black house, entrance/stair hall.

(123.1)

(124.1)

APARTMENT HOUSE FOR THE GARRISON COMPANY,
job number 533, 1923–24, Ansley Park; now called Reid House Condominiums.

(125.1)

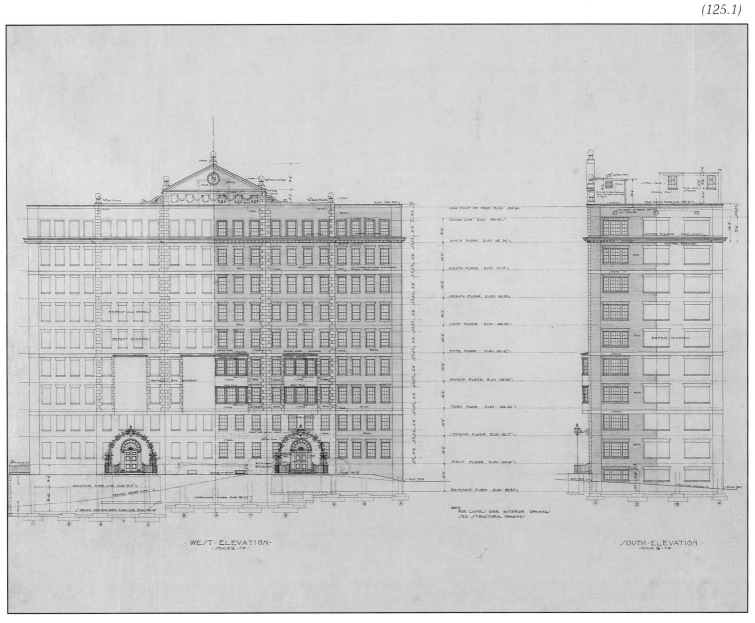

Entrance (west) and south side elevations, drafted by Philip Shutze and CJT.

(126.1)

Southern Railway Passenger Station, job number 282, 1916–17, Brookwood.
Roof originally had green Ludowici tiles. Below: East elevation and entrance details, drafted by Neel Reid.

(126.2)

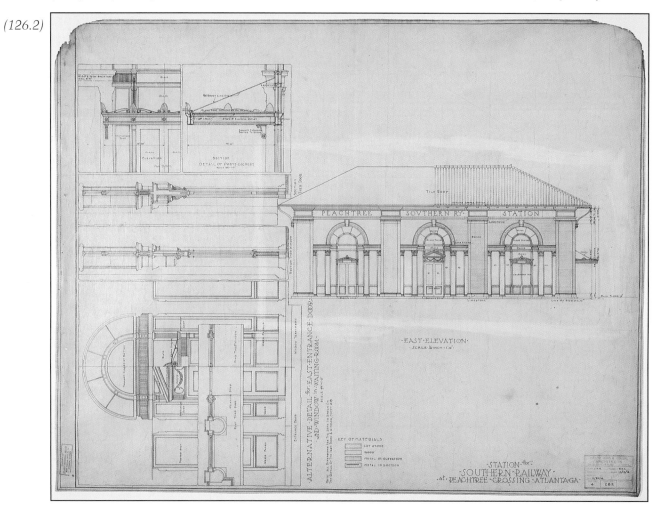

Southern Railway Passenger Station interior.

(127.1)

(128.1)

House for Willis Jones,
job number 457, 1921–22, Brookwood.
This house was moved to 520 West Paces Ferry Road from Brookwood.
The original design was altered somewhat during renovation.

(129.1)

HOUSE FOR LOGAN CLARKE, job number 490, 1922, Brookwood Hills.
Above: Entrance elevation. Below: Living room.

(129.2)

(131.1)

HOUSE FOR JAMES L. DICKEY JR., ARDEN,
job number 251, 1914–15, West Paces Ferry Road.
The entrance elevation of Arden is Reid's
version of the piazza at Mount Vernon.

(132.1)

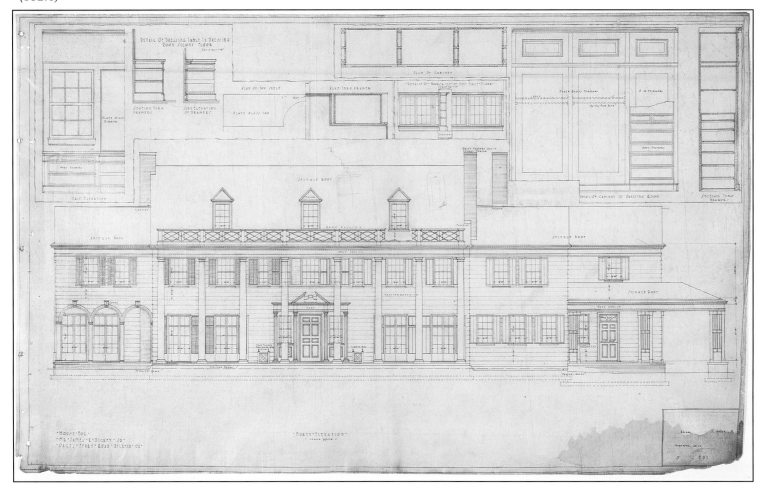

James L. Dickey Jr. house, entrance elevation, drafted by Rudolph Adler.

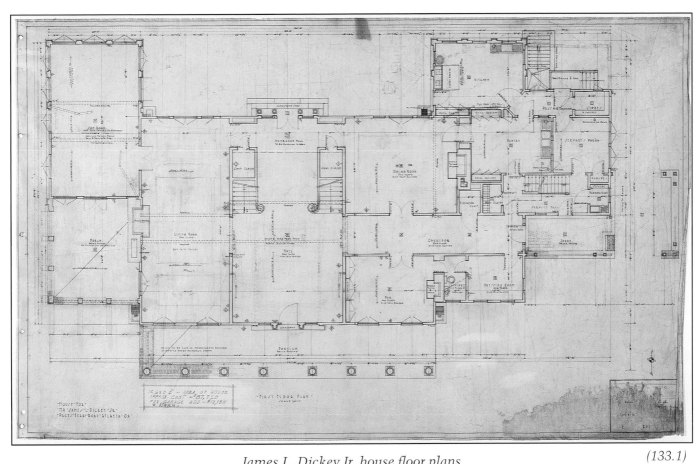

(133.1)

James L. Dickey Jr. house floor plans.
Above: First floor. Below: Second floor. Drafted by Rudolph Adler.

(133.2)

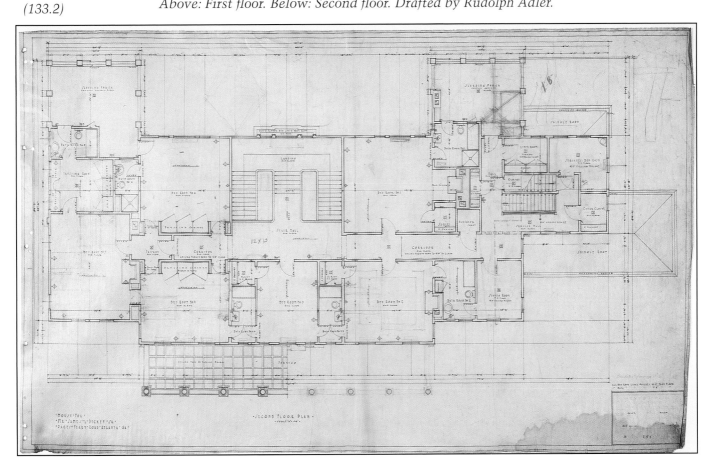

James L. Dickey house, view from living room into stair hall.

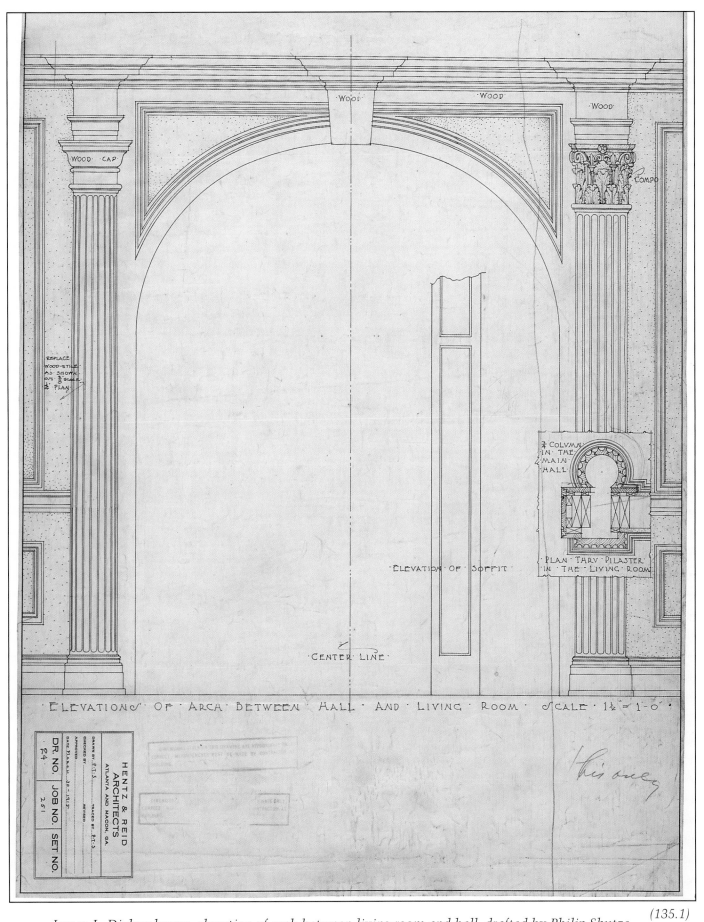

James L. Dickey house, elevation of arch between living room and hall, drafted by Philip Shutze.

(135.1)

James L. Dickey house, view from stair hall into living room.

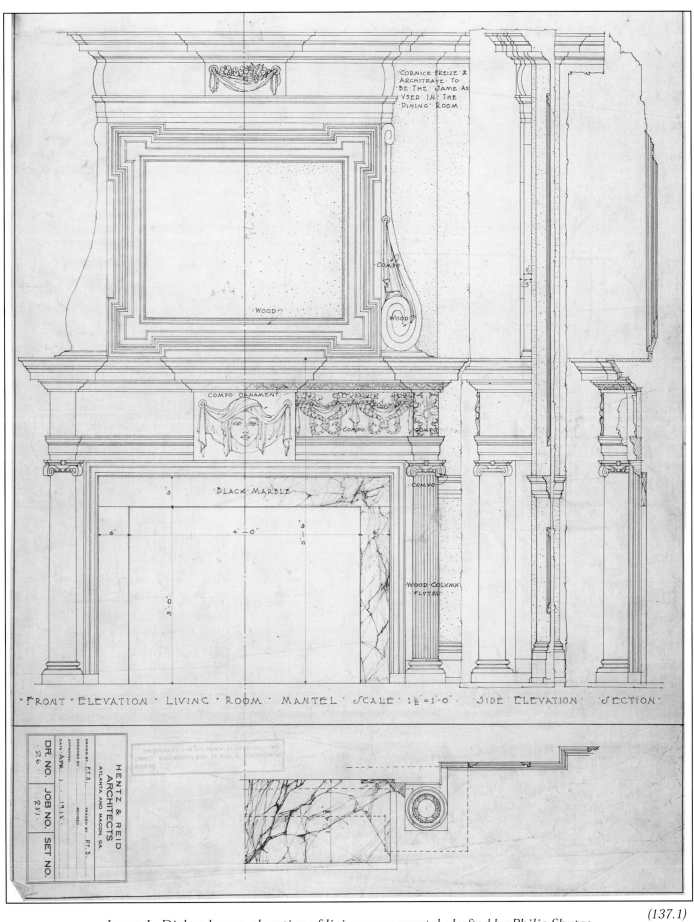

James L. Dickey house, elevation of living room mantel, drafted by Philip Shutze.

(137.1)

(138.1)

HOUSE FOR ANDREW CALHOUN, TRYGGVESON, job number 396, 1921–22, West Paces Ferry Road.
Above: Front (garden) elevation. Below: Rear (entrance) elevation.

(138.2)

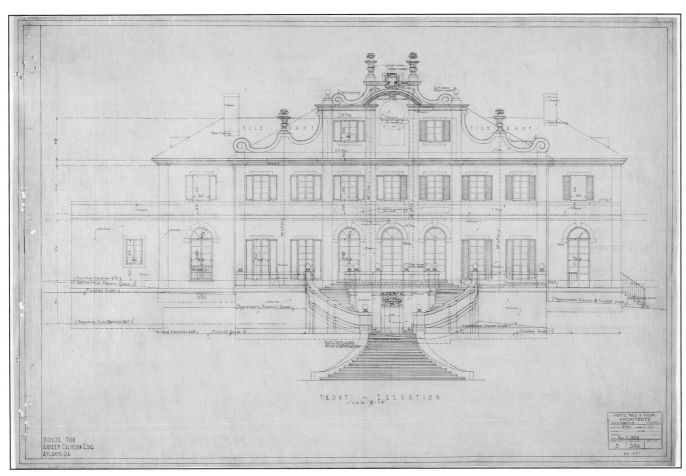

(139.1)

Andrew Calhoun house.
Most of the key figures at Hentz, Reid
& Adler worked on the design for the
Calhoun estate. Above: Front (garden)
elevation, drafted by Philip Shutze in
1922 and checked by Lewis Crook.
Right: The first design for the front
elevation was drafted in 1920 by Neel
Reid and Mack Tucker and checked
by Rudolph Adler and Ed Ivey.

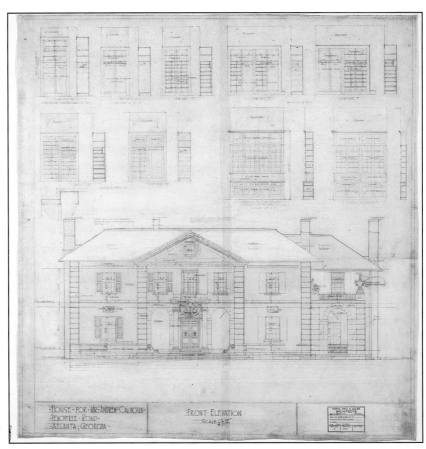

(139.2)

(140.1)

(140.2)

(140.3)

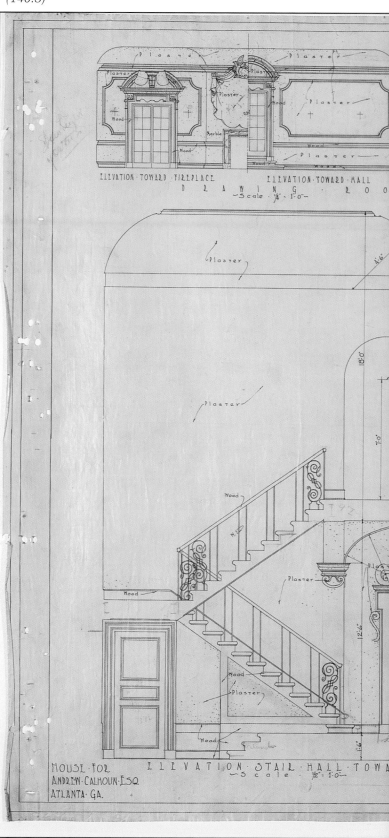

Andrew Calhoun house. Above: Interior elevations, drafted by Philip Shutze and Lewis Crook. Top left: View from drawing room through stair hall. Left: Stair hall.

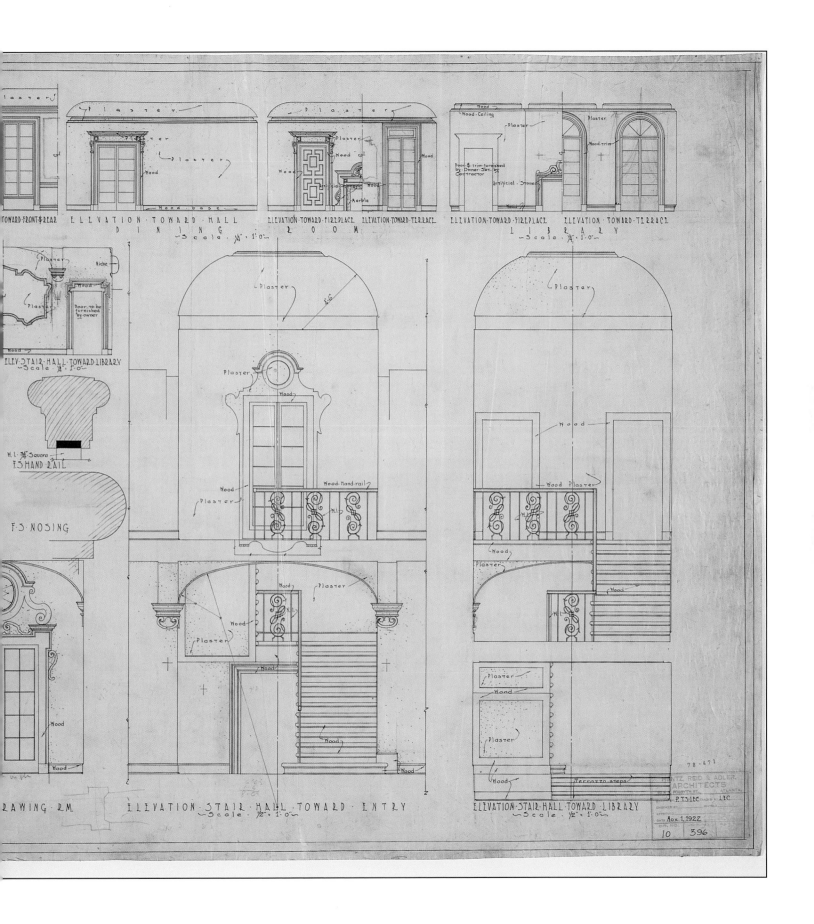

ELEVATION·TOWARD·FRONT·&·REAR ELEVATION·TOWARD·HALL ELEVATION·TOWARD·FIREPLACE ELEVATION·TOWARD·TERRACE ELEVATION·TOWARD·FIREPLACE ELEVATION·TOWARD·TERRACE

DINING·ROOM LIBRARY
~Scale·¼"·1'-0"~ ~Scale·¼"·1'-0"~

ELEV·STAIR·HALL·TOWARD·LIBRARY
~Scale·¼"·1'-0"~

F.S·HAND·RAIL

F.S·NOSING

DRAWING·RM. ELEVATION·STAIR·HALL·TOWARD·ENTRY ELEVATION·STAIR·HALL·TOWARD·LIBRARY
~Scale·½"·1'-0"~ ~Scale·½"·1'-0"~

HOUSE FOR CHARLES C. CASE,
job number 372, 1919, Peachtree Heights Park.

(143.1)

*Left: The garden elevation at Tintinhull in Somerset,
England, was the model for the entrance elevation.
Above: Entrance driveway.*

(143.2)

(144.1)

(144.2)

Charles C. Case house.
Above: Living room. Left: The rear
elevation and garden have alterations
in keeping with the spirit of Reid's
original design.

(145.1)

Charles C. Case house, dining room.

(147.1)

HOUSE FOR WILLIAM F. MANRY JR.,
job number 460, 1921, Peachtree Heights Park.
Above: Side view showing unusual double-flue chimney design.
Below: Rear elevation.

(147.2)

(147.3)

(148.1)

William F. Manry Jr. house. Above: Stair hall. Right: Living room.

(148.2)

HOUSE FOR P. C. McDUFFIE,
job number 467, 1922, Peachtree Heights Park.

(150.1)

Above: Entrance elevation.
Right: Dining room.

(150.2)

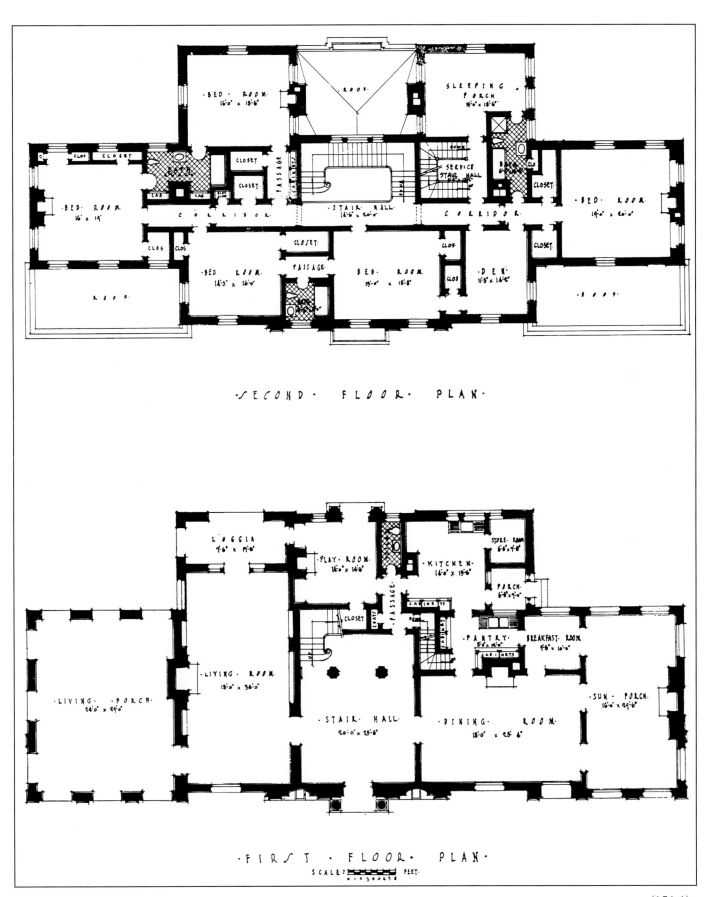

·SECOND· FLOOR· PLAN·

·FIRST · FLOOR· PLAN·

SCALE: FEET

(151.1)

Floor plans of the McDuffie house drawn for publication in the 1920s.

(152.1)

P. C. McDuffie house.
Above: Rear elevation. Below: Garden plan.

(152.2)

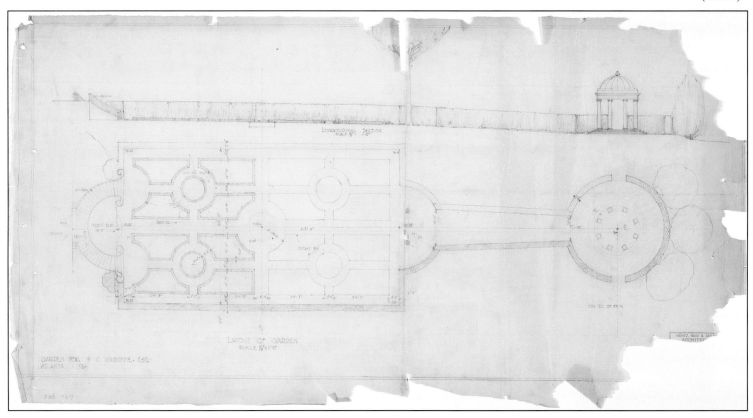

(153.1)

(153.2)

P. C. McDuffie house. Above: Garden gazebo
Left: Detail of drawing for entrance pilasters,
drafted by Rudolph Adler.

(154.1)

*The sweeping lawns and towering trees of Peachtree
Heights Park are handsome settings for many Hentz,
Reid & Adler compositions. The houses designed for Jesse
Draper and Henry Newman have been a visual ensemble
on Cherokee Road for more than half a century.*

(154.2)

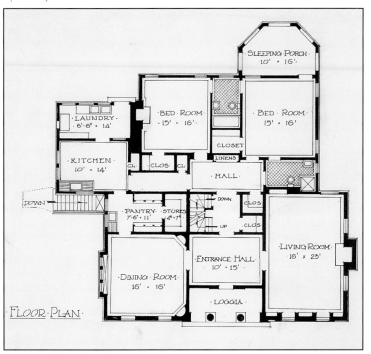

*HOUSE FOR JESSE DRAPER,
job number 468, 1922 (left).
This floor plan for the Draper
house (above left) was drawn for
an article in* House and Gardens
Book of Houses *(1925).*

(154.3)

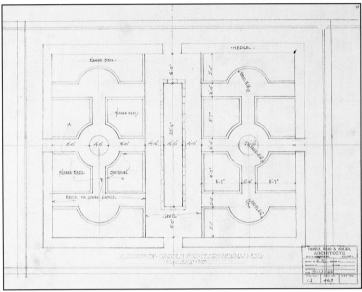

(155.1)

House for Henry Newman,
job number 469, 1921–22.
The elevation for the Newman house (below) was drafted
by AEC. The garden layout was drawn by Neel Reid.

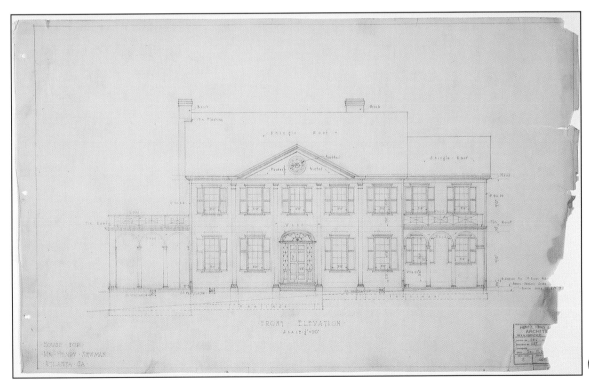

(155.2)

(156.1)

House for Robert C. Alston,
job number 503, 1922–23, Peachtree Heights Park.
Opposite page, top: Elevation drafted by Lewis Crook.
Opposite page bottom: Grounds plan drafted by James Means.

(157.1)

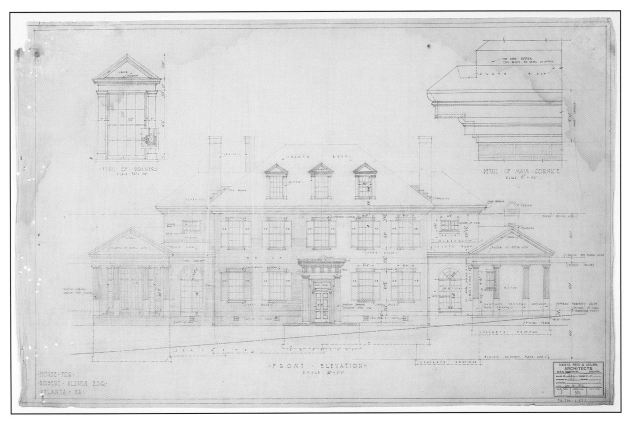

(157.2)

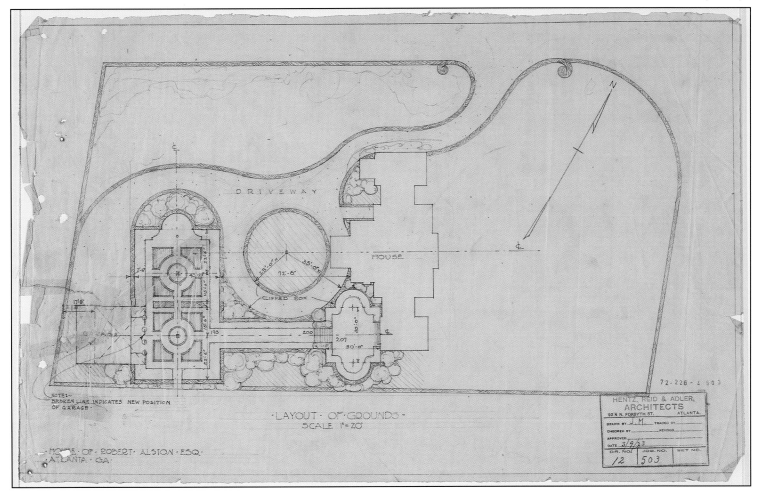

HOUSE FOR HENRY TOMPKINS,
job number 504, 1922–24, Peachtree Heights Park.

(158.1)

Above: Entrance elevation.

*Right: Plan of first floor,
drawn for publication in the
April 1928 issue of* Southern
Architect and Building News.

(158.2)

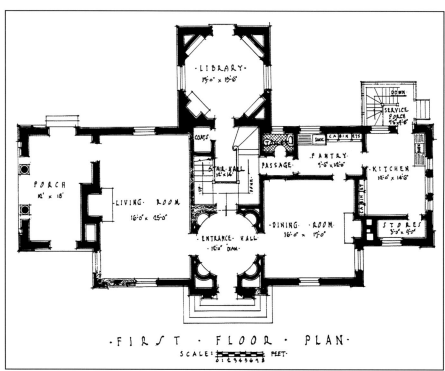

(159.1)

Henry Tompkins house. Elevation and details of entrance.

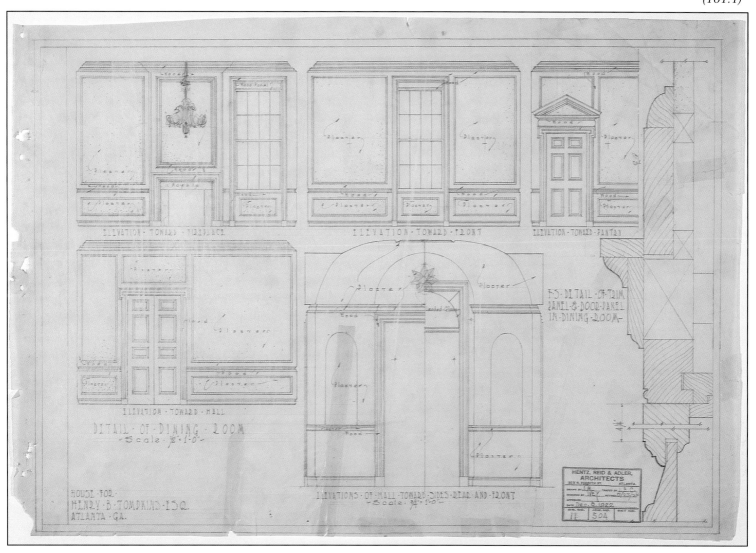

Henry Tompkins house. Opposite page: Entrance hall. Above: Interior elevations and details, drafted by James Means.

(162.1)

The garden of the Henry Tompkins house is an outstanding example of the complete design capabilities
of Hentz, Reid & Adler. Above: Walled garden and
rear elevation. Left: View of garden toward garage.
Opposite page: The design for the garden was
drafted by James Means in 1925. In 1997 the garden
remains much as designed.

(162.2)

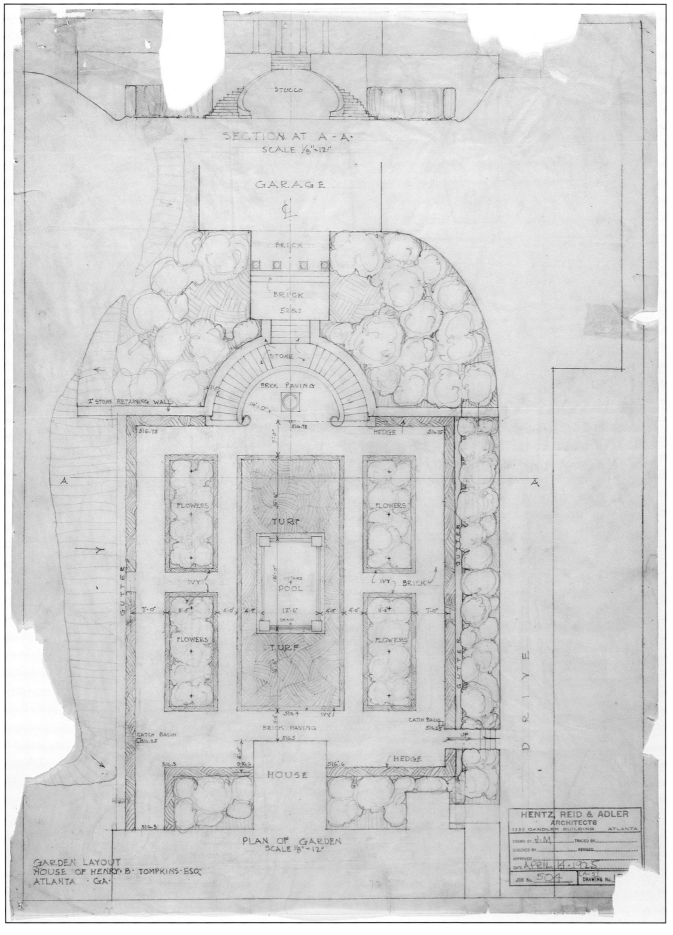

STUCCO

SECTION AT A · A ·
SCALE ⅛" = 12"

GARAGE

BRICK

BRICK
52 BS

STONE

BRICK PAVING

7" STONE RETAINING WALL

516-T5   516-T5   HEDGE   516-T5

A   A

FLOWERS   FLOWERS

TURF

IVY   POOL   IVY   BRICK

FLOWERS   FLOWERS

TURF

516-4   IVY

BRICK PAVING
516-5

CATCH BASIN
516-25   CATCH BASIN
516-25

516-3   516-6   HEDGE

HOUSE

516-5

PLAN OF GARDEN
SCALE ⅛" = 12"

GARDEN LAYOUT
HOUSE OF HENRY · B · TOMPKINS · ESQ·
ATLANTA · GA·

DRIVE

HENTZ, REID & ADLER
ARCHITECTS
1330 CANDLER BUILDING   ATLANTA
DRAWN BY L.M.   TRACED BY
CHECKED BY   REVISED
APPROVED
DATE APRIL 14 · 1925
JOB No. 504   DRAWING No.

(165.1)

HOUSE FOR STUART WITHAM,
job number 509, 1923, Peachtree Heights Park.

(165.2)

The Witham house was featured in House and Garden in
January 1928 as "A Georgian House in Atlanta." Left: Entrance
elevation. Above: Rear elevation. Below: Garden.

(165.3)

(166.1)

Stuart Witham house. Above: Living room. Below: Dining room.

(166.2)

(167.1)

Stuart Witham house. Left: Stair hall. Below: Neel Reid drew these interior elevations in 1923 when his drafting days were about over.

(167.2)

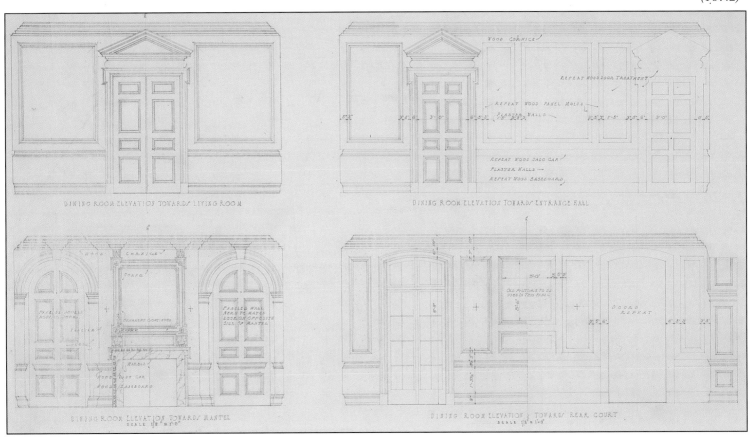

(168.1)

HOUSE FOR JAMES LIVINGSTON WRIGHT,
job number 510, 1923, Peachtree Heights Park.
Above: Entrance elevation. Below left: Rear and south side. Below right: Living room.

(168.2)

(168.3)

James Livingston Wright house. Stair hall with view into dining room.

HOUSE FOR VAUGHN NIXON,
job number 555, 1925, Peachtree Heights Park.

(170.1)

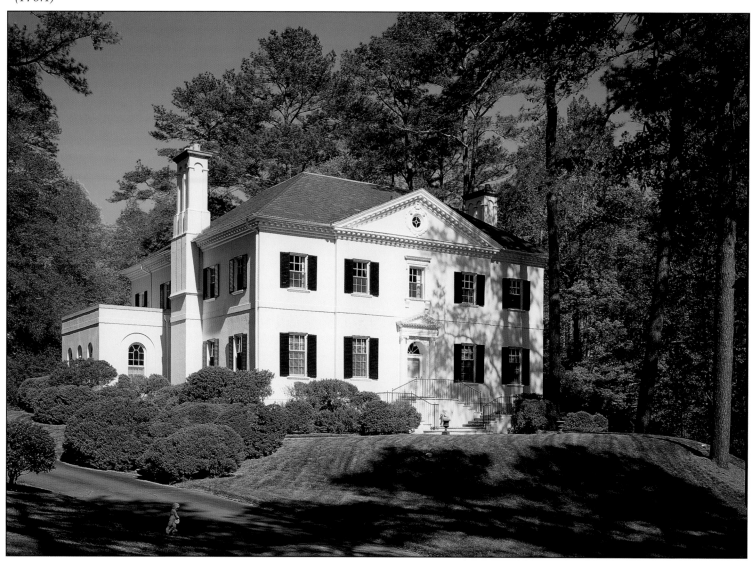

(170.2)

Above: Front elevation.
Left: Library.

Vaughn Nixon house. Above: View of the rear elevation from the garden.

(172.3)

(172.1)

Vaughn Nixon house. Above: Living room fireplace wall.
Right: Entrance/stair hall with view into dining room. Reid purchased
a pair of large European maritime scenes for this hall. They are still
where he placed them for the Nixons. Below: Dining room.

(172.2)

HOUSE FOR DR. LAWSON THORNTON,
job number 562, 1925, Peachtree Heights Park.

(174.1)

(175.1)

(175.2)

Dr. Lawson Thornton house.
Above and left: Rear elevation and view of
the rolling Peachtree Heights landscape.
Reid also designed the guest house.

House for Edward H. Inman, Swan House,
job numbers 547 and 591, 1925–26.

(176.1)

The first plans for the Inmans show a house somewhat larger than the one actually built.
Above: Original design for garden elevation. Below: Original plan for first floor.

(176.2)

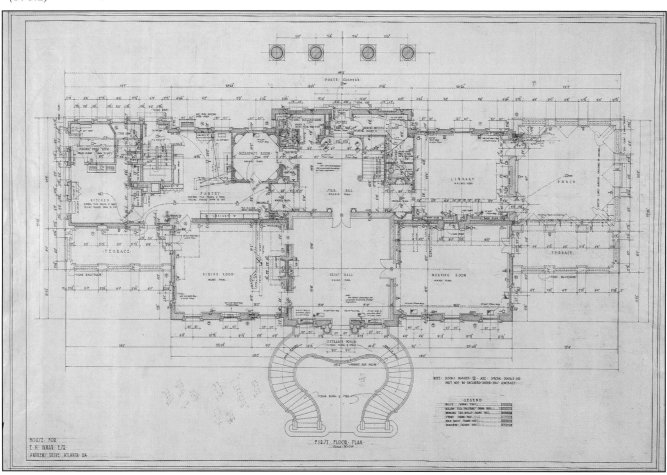

(177.1)

Edward H. Inman house.
The final drawings for the garden elevation reflect the Italianate influences
that shaped many other Hentz, Reid & Adler designs of the period. The plan
below has been inverted for comparison to the first floor plan opposite.

(177.2)

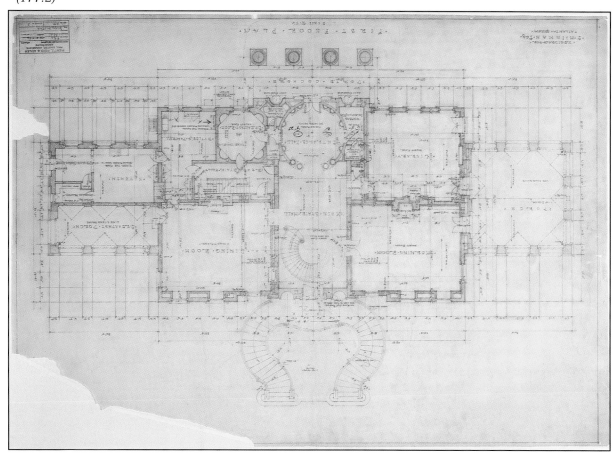

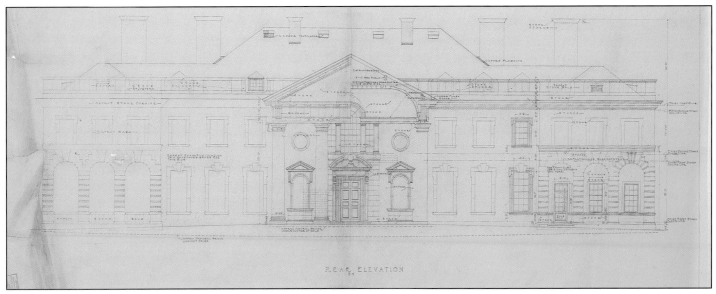

Edward H. Inman house, rear (east) elevations.
Differences between the original (above) and final (below) designs for the rear
elevation are not so striking as those for the garden façade.

(178.2)

(179.1)

Edward H. Inman house.
Above: Garden façade. Below left: Rear (east) elevation. Below right: Library

(179.2)

(179.3)

(180.1)

TAMPA TERRACE HOTEL,
job number 535, 1924–25, Tampa.

FLORIDA

Young architects beginning practice usually depend on friends and acquaintances as first clients. The new firm of Hentz & Reid was of Atlanta and Macon because both men had connections in those cities, Reid especially in Macon. But Florida from the first was also the location of work because Hal Hentz was a native. He was born at City Point on the east coast and grew up at well-to-do little Quincy. Quincy is just northwest of the state capital of Tallahassee in the Panhandle near the Georgia line, where his father had settled to practice medicine. It is the governmental seat of Gadsden County, and Hentz & Reid job number 99 is the county courthouse. Designed in 1909–10 and built in 1912–13, it still stands on the public square in the nationally registered Quincy Historic District. (At the time of registration, its style was aptly characterized as "classical eclecticism.")

This county courthouse was the first of twenty-five Florida jobs between 1909, the first year of the partnership, and 1926, which was both the year of Reid's death and the end of the state's real estate boom. The northern half of Florida, including Quincy, Monticello, and Jacksonville, was the site of their work until 1923, when the locus moved to Tampa, Saint Petersburg, and Lakeland, after the partners established an office at Tampa to take advantage of the state's sudden prosperity and growth, especially that of south Florida.

At Monticello, just northeast of Tallahassee, in 1912 there was a high school, job number 178; with later additions, number 250; and there, a residence, job number 188. The first Jacksonville work came in 1913, job number 242. Then, after the firm was Hentz, Reid & Adler, came a Methodist church, number 309, 1917, again at Quincy. A residence for Judge William B. Lamar was number 354, 1918, at Monticello, and in 1922 another residence at Quincy, number 480.

The first job of the Florida boom era came in 1923, one of several Adair Realty and Trust Company commissions in Florida, job number 505, at Jacksonville, the 310 West Church Street Apartments. The character and scale of this downtown landmark reflect its time and place with the firm's stylish red brick and limestone synthesis of Georgian Revival–Italian Baroque. Still standing in downtown Jacksonville, although not in pristine condition—the elaborate main doorway has been compromised—it is on the National Register of Historic Places and is now a hotel. That same year there was a beach cottage for Frank Adair out at the ocean.

The Atlanta Adairs were friends and clients with a number of Florida investment and development projects that Hentz, Reid & Adler designed. Probably, the most outstanding of these was the Tampa Terrace Hotel, job number 535, 1924, which stood until the late 1960s at the southwest corner of Lafayette and Florida Avenues in downtown Tampa. This tall and elegant Italian Renaissance derivation, drafted by Mack Tucker, was financed by Adair Realty bonds. The hotel opened in 1926. After the crash, the bond holders sold it to a New York financier. Popular for many years, it went out of business in 1965 and was subsequently demolished. Stylistically, it was similar inside and outside to Atlanta commissions, among them the Andrew Calhoun house, number 396, the Joseph D. Rhodes house, number 542, and the Edward H. Inman house, number 591.

The second of the boom commissions was job number 514, 1923, the Lakeland Terrace Hotel, Lakeland, Florida, in the center of the state—near where Hal Hentz retired in 1943 to Redwings, his house at Winter Haven. Still in fairly good condition and about to be restored as a hotel, the Lakeland Terrace, too, is reminiscent of work in the firm's Italian Renaissance Baroque manner also used in Georgia. A nine-story, tile-roofed stucco design, it has a Baroque entrance similar to that used in 1924 at the red-brick Massee Apartments, job number 534, in Macon. Some of the Lakeland Terrace's elevations and decorative elements were drafted by Lewis Edmund

(181.1)

LAKELAND TERRACE HOTEL, *job number 514, 1923–24, Lakeland.*

Crook (LEC), who had just returned in 1922 from his European tour as Reid's companion. The treatment of the roofline pediment is a simplified Baroque motif similar to that used at the Tampa Terrace the next year. These late Renaissance elements capture the extravagant spirit of that expansive and vibrant, but short-lived, era of the New South.

Not only was the real estate market booming but, of course, so was the population. For example, Sarasota, Florida, jumped in population from 3,000 in 1920 to 15,000 in 1926. Miami's population doubled in 1925–26; but all of this expansion slowed down considerably with the hurricane of '26, the coming of the boll weevil, the bank failures and all of the other evils of that year, which brought on a depression in the South several years before it hit the rest of the country.

Hentz, Reid & Adler closed the Tampa office at the end of 1925 with a loss of nearly $11,000. But the interaction between the Atlanta firm and the boom mentality of the neighboring state had created a mid-1920s scale and style, a sort of Florida-Mediterranean Madness that was felt in Buckhead, especially along West Paces Ferry Road and in Tuxedo Park. Adair Realty and Trust failed in late 1926, was reorganized, withdrew from Florida, and was never quite so expansive again.

And Neel Reid died. What an odd coincidence that he did so as the era which he had helped give artistic form drew to a close. What if he had lived, even as long as Adler, who died in 1945, or Hentz, who retired in 1942–43 and died in 1972 at age eighty-eight at Winter Haven? Hentz was still praising his late partner and the days of their youthful practice when he told Neel W. Reid, Reid's nephew, in 1943: "As an architect I was good, but your uncle was great." This Florida work is more evidence that Neel Reid, of Hentz, Reid & Adler, was achieving greatness as his life and that era came to an end.

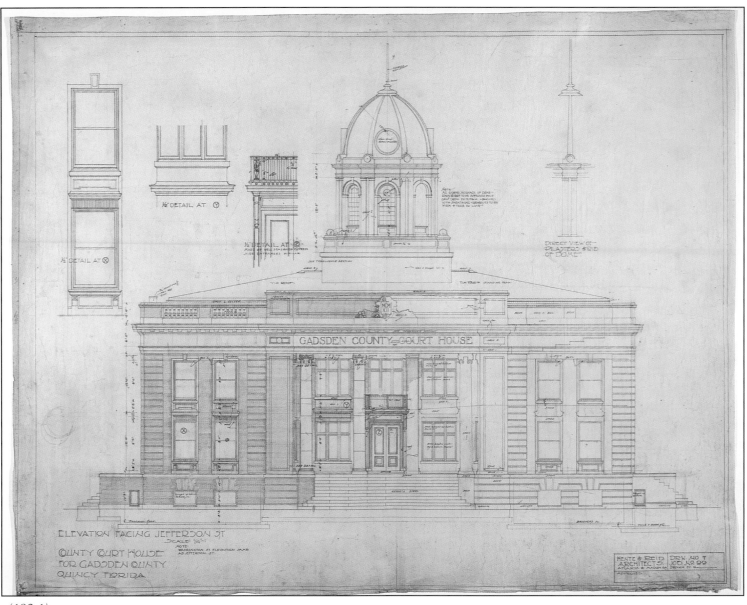

(182.1)

GADSDEN COUNTY COURTHOUSE,
job number 99, 1912, Quincy, Florida. Below: Construction photograph, 1913.

(182.2)

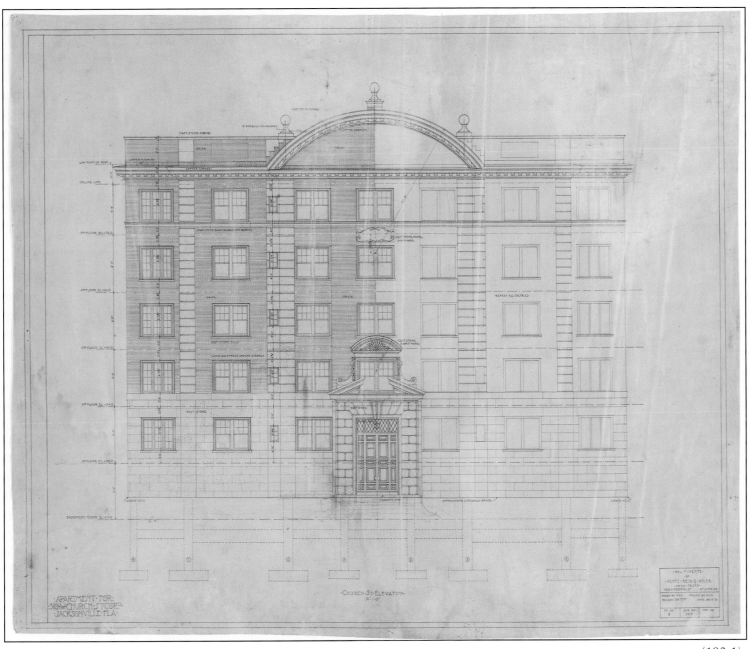

(183.1)

*APARTMENT FOR ADAIR REALTY'S 310 WEST CHURCH STREET CORPORATION,
job number 505, 1923, Jacksonville.*

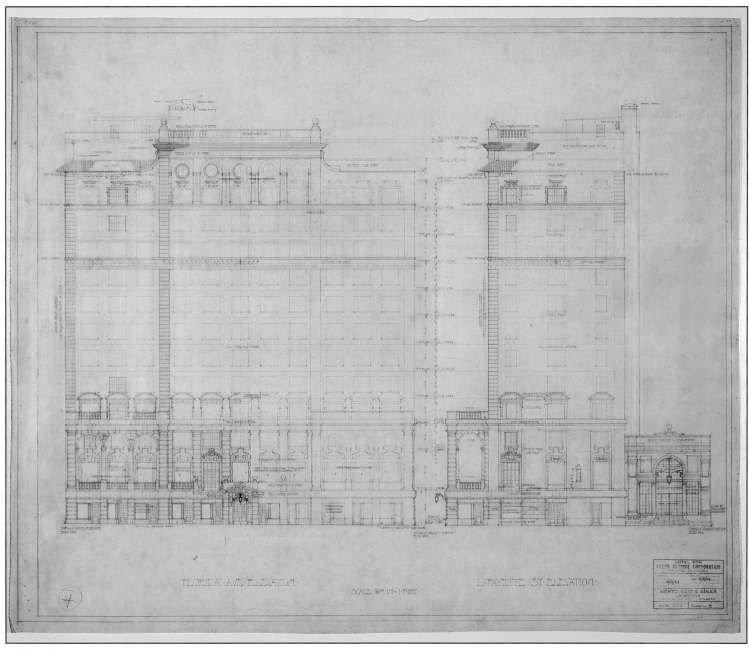

(184.1)

Tampa Terrace Hotel,
job number 535, 1924–25, Tampa.

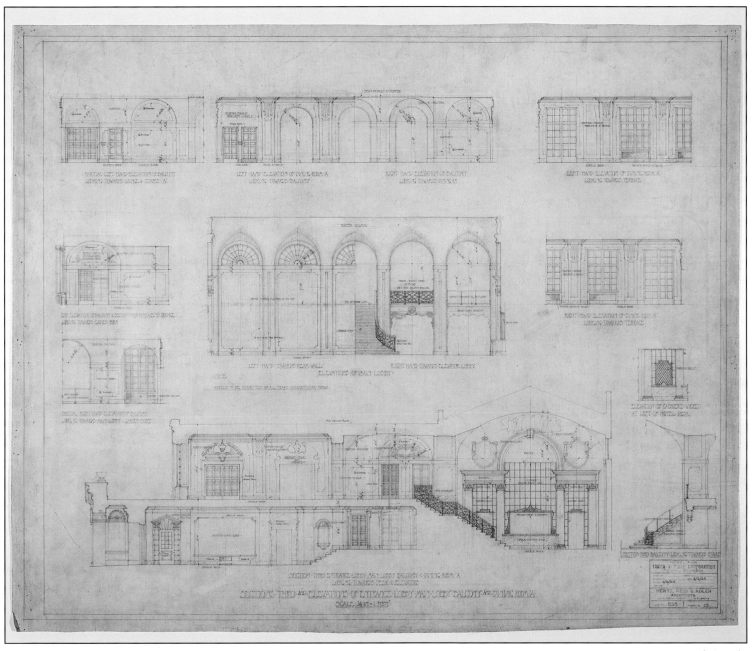

(185.1)

Tampa Terrace Hotel,
interior elevations and sections.

Mimosa Hall, c. 1920.

Roswell, Georgia

When Neel Reid purchased Mimosa Hall to renovate as his home in 1916, Roswell's antebellum classical houses, especially Mimosa and its next-door neighbor, Bulloch Hall, were beginning to be known for their history, beauty, and style. The great art historian Fiske Kimball, in *Thomas Jefferson, Architect*, published that year, referred to Mimosa Hall by the name of one of its longtime owners, the Hansells, and cited it with Bulloch as a nationally important derivation of Jefferson's neoclassicism. Kimball said, "The Bulloch and Hansell houses at Roswell, Georgia, are almost purely Jeffersonian. The full temple-form—as it had been employed in Jefferson's pavilions at the University of Virginia—was imitated widely."

That year of 1916, Reid and his partners completed one of their most important neoclassical commissions, Hills and Dales, the Fuller Callaway house at LaGrange, Georgia, which was Reid's New South version of an antebellum classical house.

Bulloch Hall, the other temple-form house at Roswell, was perhaps even better known than Mimosa. President Roosevelt visited Bulloch in 1905 because it had been the home of his mother, Martha (Mittie) Bulloch, where she married the president's father in 1853. And in 1907 it was the

Neel Reid and his mother, Elizabeth (front left), and sister, Louise (directly behind Elizabeth), at Mimosa Hall with friends.

(187.1)

(187.2)

(187.3)

Interior views of Mimosa Hall from the Reid family album.
Below: View of Neel Reid's garden design at Mimosa Hall.

(187.4)

model for the Georgia building at the Jamestown (Virginia) Exposition, for which Roosevelt cut the ribbon on opening day.

When Reid bought Mimosa, the style of antebellum Southern plantation houses was becoming fashionable again as the North and South reunified, and it was the period of the Colonial Revival movement. People considered white-columned Southern houses to be "Southern Colonial" and prized them highly. Charles McKim's renovation-restoration of the White House in Washington, D.C., in 1902 set a national neoclassical standard that Reid, his colleagues, and their clients made into a vogue.

In 1902 also, these Roswell neoclassical houses received national attention. They were published in *The American Architect and Building News* in an article, "Savannah and Parts of the Far South," written by an astute Atlanta lady, the amateur architectural historian Corinne Ruth Stocker (Mrs. Thaddeus) Horton, who signed herself C. R. S. Horton and made her own photographs. Mrs. Horton's insightful, illustrated article was probably where Fiske Kimball and Neel Reid first became acquainted with the architecture of Roswell's temple-form houses.

But for an architect actually to renovate an ante-

bellum example as his residence was rather ahead of its time. And for Reid it was somewhat of an adventure, because he did not drive, and Roswell is nineteen miles north of Atlanta. Mimosa Hall was indeed a "country house," even though located in the village of Roswell near the town square. In those days, the Chattahoochee River bridge was a noisy wooden contraption. Neel Reid crossed this covered bridge almost daily, riding in the Roswell jitney driven by Mr. D. H. Brantley, the "jitney driver," who asked the architect to design and build him a "Neel Reid house that he could afford." Job number 361, 1918–19, was the result. Built on Mimosa Boulevard, this modest one-story frame house still stands. Sarah Newton, who has owned it since 1952, cannot say enough nice things about Reid's version of a Dutch Colonial cottage. (The entire neighborhood is on the National Register of Historic Places as a historic district.)

Mimosa Hall was completed in 1847 for Major John Dunwody and his wife, Jane Bulloch, sister of Major James Stephens Bulloch of Bulloch Hall. The builder-architect was Willis Ball of Windsor, Connecticut, which was the birthplace of Roswell King, for whom Roswell was named. Ball also designed and

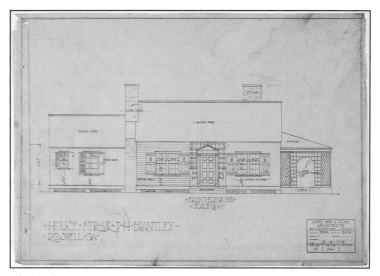

HOUSE FOR D. H. BRANTLEY,
job number 361, 1918–19, Roswell.

built the other great houses of the village as well as its Presbyterian Church.

Mimosa as it appears now is much as Reid renovated the place in 1916–17, when he found it in dilapidated condition. Today it is in the hands of the Hansell family, which has owned it twice, giving it the name Mimosa Hall after General A. J. Hansell purchased the property in 1869. He sold it in 1899, and his great-grandson Granger Hansell repurchased it in 1947. Granger's son, C. Edward Hansell, and his wife, Sylvia, cherish the place now and keep it much as Reid had it in 1926. Reid designed the fieldstone drive and courtyard, but his extensive gardens (possibly five acres), for practical reasons of maintenance, have almost disappeared except for a reflecting pool and a few indications of formal parterre beds.

Neel Reid's nephew, Neel W. Reid of Baltimore, Maryland (who provided the quotation from Hal Hentz at the end of the Florida section), was born at Mimosa Hall on December 20, 1922. The son of Neel Reid's brother, John W. Reid Jr., he lived there on and off for seven years, a period which extended beyond his uncle's death when the place had become his grandmother's and aunt's house. Those Neel Reid ladies moved with Reid in 1916–17 when he left Atlanta's Druid Hills to live in Roswell. They inherited the ten-acre property from Neel, remaining there until they sold it in July 1937. They moved to Whitlock Avenue in Marietta, into a smaller house, still standing, that Hal Hentz designed for them.

Neel W. Reed, whom his grandmother sometimes called Neel II, spent a great deal of time there and inherited much of the contents. Mrs. Reid died in the spring of 1938 and Louise Reid in 1953. Many of the furnishings, art objects, and personal belongings from that house had been in Mimosa Hall and are now in the possession of Neel II and his sister. Neel and Meredith and their mother (d. 1939), who was originally from Maryland, moved to Baltimore in the early 1930s after John W. Reid Jr. died in 1930. Color photographs were made for this book in Neel W. Reid's Baltimore apartment in the summer of 1996 to illustrate items from Mimosa Hall, some of them designed by the architect himself.

Some of these objects show in a November 1926 article on Mimosa Hall in *Southern Architect and Building News* (pp. 49–54). The illustrations from that magazine document how Mimosa Hall looked inside and outside in Neel Reid's era, and the text by his mother is helpful for that period. Neel Reid's niece and nephew, to whom we have dedicated this book because of their essential and loyal support of this project, have fond memories of Mimosa Hall during their childhood when their relatives lived there in the style that their uncle had made possible.

Neel Reid died here February 14, 1926, in the double parlor he had made into one large room, where he had placed a bed and was convalescing from the effects of brain cancer.

(189.1)

Furnishings and Reid family heirlooms from Mimosa Hall are now preserved by Neel Reid's neice and nephew in Baltimore.

(189.2)

(189.3)

COLUMBUS, GEORGIA

Columbus is located on the east bank of the Chattahoochee River at the Fall Line, about 110 miles west of Macon and 120 miles southwest of Atlanta. Historically, it has been a center of textile manufacturing. Hentz & Reid received two commissions from there and Hentz, Reid & Adler, one. All were residential.

The first job came in 1914, number 227, for Harry L. Williams, and the other two were for the Dismukes family, E. P., number 260, 1915; and R. E., number 513, 1923. They were father and son and were cousins of Hal Hentz from Quincy, Florida, where Hentz grew up. Elisha Paul Dismukes came to Columbus in 1894. His son, Robert Ernest Dismukes, was born at Quincy in 1877. E. P. Dismukes was president of the Georgia Manufacturing Company, a large textile business, and was a civic leader. R. E. graduated from Princeton University and then Harvard Law School and, like his father, became prominent in many phases of Columbus life. R. E. was married to Lenora Swift, the daughter of George P. Swift Jr., another textile family.

Harry L. Williams and his wife, Maude Lowndes Williams, also were prominent citizens. Their home, now destroyed, stood on Wynnton Road at Eighteenth Street in the Overlook area; it was a two-story white frame house with a hipped roof in Neel Reid's Colonial Revival mode, with a pergola-like front and side porch and four French doors placed symmetrically across the façade. A black-and-white photograph dated 1915 shows the house when it was completed, with typical features of Reid's "casual classicism" in place: a house-long front terrace is built of brick and has trellis work and flower boxes; the full-length blinds for the French doors are painted the color of the clapboards; and those at the second floor windows are dark green. The Doric columns of the bracketed pergola-like porches are unfluted one-third of the way up in the Roman-Pompeiian manner that Reid adopted from Charles Platt. Overall, the house has the character of the Colonial Revival–Italian villa eclectic style from Platt's Cornish, New Hampshire, art colony.

The E. P. Dismukes house, also gone, stood in the downtown Columbus residential area, now a historic district, on the west side of the 1500 block of Third Avenue. This later became the home of the John C. Martins, and members of that family have a photograph. This, too, was Colonial Revival, but in Reid's red-brick with white-trim Jeffersonian manner, featuring a one-story classical front porch, in the Tuscan order, and three dormers, similar in style to Edgehill and Redlands in Albemarle County, Virginia. Reid used that approach in Atlanta several times, especially for the Robert Crumley house, job number 268, 1915–17, in Ansley Park.

The Robert Ernest Dismukes house, which Reid designed in 1923, was completed the next year at 1617 Summit Drive on a knoll in the beautiful little garden suburb of Peacock Woods. Somewhat similar in style to the Robert Alston house in Peachtree Heights Park of the same year, the R. E. Dismukes house is red-brick Georgian with Federal and Greek Revival details. The two-story main block is flanked by one-story wings containing porches. Like many of Reid's designs, there are two main elevations, front and rear, and, as with the Alston house, there is a garden-side porte-cochere entrance. On that side are a columned servants' quarters and tea-house gazebo, a small Tuscan temple with treillage. The working drawings also show formal parterre beds linking the symmetrically placed dependencies, where there is now a grass lawn.

When this house was added to the National Register of Historic Places, this writer-historian researched the property. An interview with the late Edward Shorter of Macon and Columbus, who knew Neel Reid and Hal Hentz, produced the fact that Shorter was there the day Reid came to the house for a final inspection, sometime in 1925. Reid had designed furniture for the house, including a desk for the library that is still in place. Reid was coming to inspect the entire ensemble, interiors, exterior, and garden, to see that everything was as he intended. (Shorter, an artist, connoisseur, and museum director, was aware that the Dismukes and Hal Hentz were related and that Neel Reid had been the designer.)

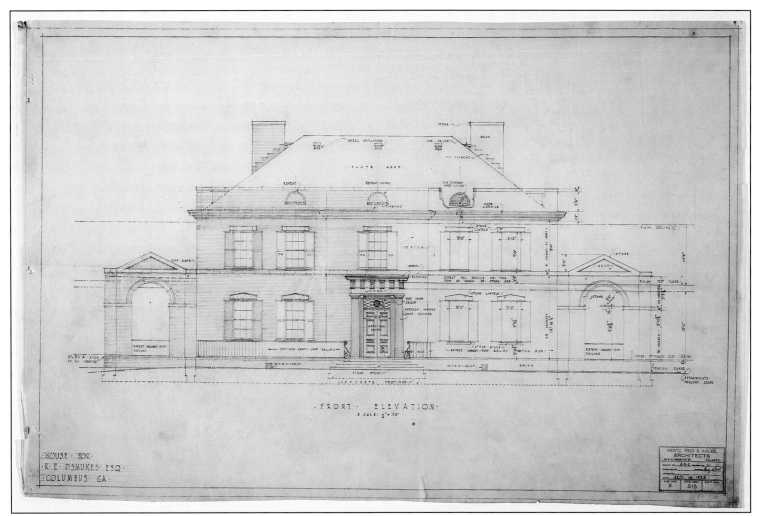

HOUSE FOR H. L. WILLIAMS,
job number 227, 1914, Columbus.

(191.1)

(191.3)

HOUSE FOR ROBERT E. DISMUKES,
job number 513, 1923–24, Columbus. Entrance elevation.

(192.1)

R. E. Dismukes house.
Above: Entrance elevation. Below: Garden view with tea-house gazebo.

(192.2)

(193.1)

R. E. Dismukes house. Above: Stair hall. Below left: Library. Below right: second-floor bedoom.

(193.2)

(193.3)

(194.1)

HOUSE FOR H. W. BARNES,
job number 160, 1912, Griffin.

GRIFFIN, GEORGIA

To the cotton economy of the Old South, the New South added textile manufacturing and railroads, which helped to make possible the growth of Columbus, Macon, and LaGrange. General Lewis L. Griffin laid out and named his railroad depot town in 1840, thirty-five miles south of the junction of railroads that was named Atlanta in 1845. Griffin remained a depot only, became the governmental seat of Spalding County, and continues to be a small, thriving community of homes, churches, and textile mills, which would make its founder proud.

One prominent family, the H. W. Barneses, was the source of three of Neel Reid's works at Griffin. The first of these was their house, job number 160, 1912, at 435 E. College Street, now the home of James R. Fortune Jr.; the second was number 401, the Seaton Grantland Parish House of Saint George's Episcopal Church, 1921–22, 132 N. Tenth Street, and still serving that purpose; the third, number 522, 1922, was a major remodeling of Violet Bank, the Seaton Grantland house, 439 E. College Street, for the H. W. Barneses, who moved across the street in 1923 to Mrs. Barnes's parents' house after the alterations and additions were complete. In this generation, Violet Bank is the home of Mr. and Mrs. John

H. (Jake) Cheatham Jr. Mrs. Cheatham, Leila Barnes, is the daughter of the H. W. Barneses and a granddaughter of Seaton Grantland and Leila Gilliam Grantland.

Neel Reid based the new façade for Violet Bank on the north or entrance elevation of Hansbury Hall, Worcestershire, England, built in 1701, at the close of the reign of William and Mary. Reid used wood to interpret the brick and limestone, somewhat baroque, original; both versions have tall half-columns in the Corinthian order, supporting a pediment over the main doorway. Above this is a central window with a bold frame of console volutes and an oval window in the pediment. Hansbury Hall is illustrated in one of Reid's architectural Bibles, the Late Stuart volume of H. Avray Tipping's *English Homes*, London, 1921, plate 487 (p. 399).

This is Reid's Colonial Revival in a most appealing and appropriate form, since American architecture in the Colonial period was an architecture of stone transposed into an architecture of wood. The Old South was in love with aristocratic Britain, and Neel Reid's New South continued the tradition; contributions such as his remodeling of Violet Bank are a distinct legacy worth preserving.

(195.1)

H. W. Barnes house, stair hall, with view into living room.

(195.2)

GRANTLAND PARISH HOUSE,
SAINT GEORGE'S EPISCOPAL CHURCH,
FOR H. W. BARNES, *job number 401,
1920–21, Griffin. Front view.*

House for *H. W. Barnes, Violet Bank,*
job number 522, 1923–24, Griffin, façade patterned after Hansbury Hall (opposite page).

(197.1)

(197.2)

Left: Hansbury Hall, 1701, Worcestershire, England.
Above: H. W. Barnes house. Below: Barnes dining room.

(197.3)

(198.1)

*HOUSE FOR JOHN G. BOLTON,
job number 598, 1926, Mansfield, Georgia.*

SOCIAL CIRCLE–NEWTON COUNTY, GEORGIA

Hentz, Reid & Adler job number 598 is listed "John G. Bolton, Esq., Mansfield, Georgia." Mansfield, in Newton County, is about seven miles south, down Georgia Highway 11, from this residence's actual location, which is also in that county but considered to be part of Social Circle; the current address is 1504 Alcovy Trestle Road. The explanation for this placement is simple enough: John Gray Bolton Sr. commissioned the firm to design the house on that Social Circle acreage for his son, John G. Bolton Jr., and daughter-in-law, Mollie Legare Reeves Bolton, originally a Charlestonian; Bolton Sr. lived out from Mansfield on the Burge Plantation, where John Jr.'s great-grandmother Dolly Sumner Lunt Burge wrote her Civil War diary published as *A Woman's Wartime Journal* (Macon: J. W. Burke, 1927).

The original amount of the acreage for this Neel Reid Georgia country house was one thousand, which went all the way to the Alcovy River. Planning for the house was begun in 1925, and it was completed in 1926 after Reid's death. The junior Boltons lived there until 1936, when they moved into Covington, the seat of Newton County. Coving-

ton is a sophisticated town with Emory College at adjacent Oxford (where Hal Hentz was graduated in 1904) giving it "tone." The house was closed except for weekends, but the land remained a working farm until the Bolton family sold the place in 1951. In 1972 it was sold again.

The current owners, Richard and Betty Rawlins, bought it in 1975 and completed an extensive restoration-renovation that was already underway. When the Rawlinses bought the place, they did not know the house was designed by Neel Reid. "The woods came up to it, and there were cows on the front porch." After buying it they found in the attic a set of blueprints for the house and called Prof. James Grady, author of *Architecture of Neel Reid in Georgia* (1973). Grady did not know that the house had survived, and he suggested they call Philip Shutze, the last living member of the Hentz, Reid & Adler group of architects. Richard Rawlins went to see Mr. Shutze, who remembered that "Reid had done a house in that area." (The plans show that the draftsman was Mack Tucker.) The Rawlinses have found that Reid had friends in the Covington area before this house was

(199.1)

(199.2)

designed, including Mrs. Thomas Swann of Swanscombe, one of the large, white-columned houses on historic Floyd Street in Covington.

For the Bolton's early twentieth-century plantation house, Reid and his colleagues produced a two-story, white frame, eclectic version of antebellum neoclassicism. In profile, the character is vernacular with its tall and prominent gable-end chimneys in the Southern manner and a grand shed porch supported by square columns (similar to those on George Washington's Potomac River "piazza"). Characteristically, Reid designed handsome woodwork and a formal plan from which balancing French doors open onto a house-long, wide verandah, which Mollie Bolton may have indeed called a piazza because of her Charleston roots.

When Betty and Richard Rawlins first glimpsed the house and site in 1975 as they drove down the long curving driveway, despite the "cows on the front porch," they knew instantly that this was what they had been looking for, "a country plantation house." Clearly, one of Neel Reid's very last houses is appreciated and preserved in loving hands. They see the place as a "responsibility." The large roll of blueprints for Hentz, Reid & Adler job number 598 that they found in the attic has been their ultimate authority in making minor concessions to the needs of the present moment. When they enlarged the kitchen toward the rear, the cabinet work was copied from Reid's classic glass-fronted cabinetry, drawn and specified for the butler's pantry here, as he did for all his houses.

J. G. Bolton house.
Above left: Living room. Above: Dining room.
Below: Stair hall with view into dining room.

(199.3)

EPILOGUE/*Analytique*

Analytique in Beaux-Arts French means a composition analyzing
and summing up fundamental elements.

Hanging in the collection of the University of Georgia's landscape architecture department is a large rendering, or *rendu*, of the elements of the Corinthian order. It is an *analytique*, or "order problem," by J. Neel Reid done when he was a student, c. 1906–7. This large drawing, now framed, a montage study of the proportions and "vocabulary" of the Corinthian order, is a piece of Reid poetry in design, showing artistic individuality while using the conventions of the discipline of a beaux arts composition technique, the *analytique rendu*. It is an example of a "composed sheet," with plan and elevation at small scale and details at larger scale, done in ink with color washes and indications of light and shadow. It is displayed over a mantelpiece in the Garden Club of Georgia's state headquarters house located in the landscape gardens of the school, which is now called environmental design instead of department of landscape architecture as it was when the late dean, Hubert B. Owens, the department's founder, acquired it as part of the program established there in 1946–47 by the Peachtree Garden Club of Atlanta as the Neel Reid Memorial Scholarship.

In 1946, twenty years after Reid's death in the prime of this life and career, he was still considered the patron saint of design in Georgia, the classicist in the old school tradition of the beaux arts. Respect for his legacy and legend was kept alive by such memorials even when modernism was on the rise and land-

(200.1)

*Neel Reid's "Rendered Drawing of Capital"
displayed at the Garden Club of Georgia
headquarters at the University of Georgia
School of Environmental Design.*

scape architecture was becoming environmental design, which evidently had a more contemporary ring to it. Neel Reid had considered it simply garden design, and as a beaux arts man he considered the landscape, the entourage, to be an extension of the architecture, and the smallest detail, inside or out, to be connected to the whole composition, buildings and gardens as one.

Reid's *analytique* rendering was shown at the 1910 Atlanta exhibition as "Number 148, Rendered Drawing of Capital by J. Neel Reid," the exhibition discussed in the Prelude/*Esquisse* of this book. In the center of Reid's composition is a scale figure, as was conventionally required. It appears to be the enshrouded figure of Charon crossing the River Styx, the principal river of the nether world in classical mythology. To this writer, it seems in Reid's design poetry that this necessary scale figure symbolizes the artist's own premonition of an early death from the brain cancer that ferried him to the other world before his forty-first birthday.

There is definitely the romance of Reid's life and work, the mixture of beauty and a young death, that contributes to the legend and legacy of Reid—the romantic classicism aspect in all neoclassicism—in which the artist looks to the past, to classical antiquity, for inspiration to create a timeless contemporary beauty. Thus in the Prelude/*Esquisse* we find the germ for an Epilogue/*Analytique*. Bringing it together are the students who will possibly emulate

Reid's own career as they travel abroad on his memorial scholarship to find sources and wellsprings as he did for his own work, perhaps even to see inspiration in his student beaux arts composition displayed near their own school ateliers at Athens, Georgia.

Writing in his travel diary in England, in his characteristic backhand (not left-handed) scrawl, which is never easy to translate, on Friday, August 25, 1907, Reid, then twenty-two years old, tells us much about himself and the abiding passions of his life and work as his career took form—and we have the actual sketch he made at that moment, compliments of his family, which treasures his legacy as much as, if not more than, we do: "Did a sketch this morning before breakfast of a street in Chichester—the view from our bedroom window. Then I went down to view the garden at the rear of the house. The house is built right on the street—is quite old and has two very fine rooms—the dining and the drawing room. The former runs the full length of the house and has some very nice old china Spode, Chelsea, etc. And some Sheffield silver. The view of the garden was delightful." The young student's interest in architecture, gardens, and the decorative arts is apparent, and he continued: "The garden is not very wide, but it is long and opens onto a square at the end, which contains the vegetable gardens. It is walled as old English gardens are. The wall is over ten feet high. On the South side the fruit trees are trained, the plum trees bearing fruit. This was my first experience, though grandmother has often spoken of fruit grown upon walls." (See sketches, p. 25.)

Neel Reid, the architect who loved and designed gardens, and collected fine arts and antiques for interiors, was training his eye. He closed this entry with a comment on the local cathedral, dozens of cathedrals being an important aspect of his tour: "After breakfast we went at once to the cathedral. It is very interesting and beautiful. The Norman work being particularly good." These diary entries from his 1907 travels, before he and Hal Hentz began their practice together in Georgia, are rare Reid commentary, indeed almost unique; for once he and Hentz began their busy partnership in 1909, the only remaining evidence of his self-expression is from the drawing board and in three dimensions at the building site, including interior decorations and gardens.

An eyewitness account of Reid's last days comes by way of a practicing architect in Atlanta interviewed for this book, who recounted remarks by a mentor of his, George Hall Gibson, who had worked for Hentz, Reid & Adler c. 1920–26. Gibson, who held great admiration for Reid, sometimes went to draw at night in the firm's drafting room in the Candler Building, a seventeen-story skyscraper built in 1906 on Peachtree Street in downtown Atlanta. He recalled, "Reid would be there sitting by a window, practically in the dark, quietly looking out over the city. Not drawing himself, he kept the draftsmen company and was there to answer questions and make suggestions." Gibson had often seen Reid draw a segment of a building free-hand to scale. "He was a genius," Gibson said.

Another account relating to a Reid draftsman appeared in an Albany, Georgia, newspaper January 27, 1952. A columnist for the *Albany Herald*, writing about one of Reid's longest associates, James Means, gives a glimpse into the world of the Georgia architectural classicists. Louise Whiting, known to this author as a sensible witness to the passing southwest Georgia scene, reported: "Mr. Means, who is associated with Edward Vason Jones here, has had a most interesting career. He worked for a long time with the noted architect Neel Reid. Mr Reid was ill for some time before his death and was not able to draw so Mr. Means was his 'hands' and would execute the drawings to his direction. Later, he did design work for Hentz, Adler & Shutze."

In 1949, a generation after Reid's death, well-known Atlanta architect William J. Creighton, of Toombs & Creighton, wrote in a booklet, *Cultural Atlanta, At a Glance*: "Our quick review would not be complete without a grateful remembrance of Neel Reid, the great architect of Atlanta's recent past. He, above all others, enriched the beauty of our community and set a standard of excellence that will challenge the imaginations and abilities of the future" (p. 25). Creighton shows the kind of regard that professional colleagues have had for Reid, even years after his passing from the scene, leaving a legacy of buildings in the classical tradition to appreciate and study.

On Monday afternoon, February 15, 1926, the *Atlanta Journal* published a news account of Reid's funeral held in Macon that day. Accompanied by his family and pallbearers, Reid's remains were taken by train the eighty-five miles south from Atlanta. His

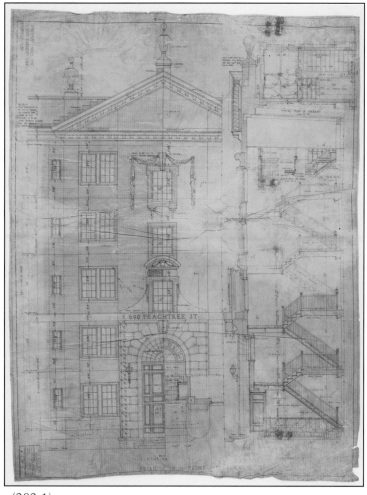

(202.1)

696 Peachtree Apartment (above and below), job number 497, 1922. Detail of entrance was drafted by Rudolph Adler, Philip Shutze, and AEC, and bears the job number 520 for an identical building in Knoxville, Tennessee.

(202.2)

bearers were his partners, Hal Hentz and Rudolph Adler, and friends, each of whom had been a client, Emmett Small, Hunter Perry, Henry Newman, Henry Tompkins, W. F. Manry Jr., and Roy Dorsey. Among the remarks were these: "Mr. Reid had contributed greatly to the architectural beauty of his section. In his painstaking and artistic efforts he left the impress of his life on many beautiful and substantial creations which remain as a tribute to his genius."

The report noted that the Georgia Chapter of the American Institute of Architects had "issued a memorial deploring his death" and then quoted it in full, including this excerpt: "It is natural for architects to give credit to a creative genius and it is a creating architect essentially that we memorialize here. At a time when there was scarcely a trained architect in the South, when buildings were for the most part merely accumulations of materials . . . he had an inspiration of what architecture should be and would mean to the South." The eulogy by his professional colleagues closed in this way: "In his passing he leaves works which may be considered not only monuments to his refined taste and genius of expression, but works which will endure as inspiration to 'lovers of the beautiful,' for generations to come."

Generations to come have arrived as we write, and lovers of the beautiful continue to care for a great percentage of the works he left. There have been some exceptions; some have been demolished or altered badly. Two of the houses pictured in James Grady's 1973 book *Architecture of Neel Reid in Georgia* are gone, the John Whitman house (1914) that stood at 2662 Peachtree Road and the Winship Nunnally house (1923) that was at 1311 West Paces Ferry. Several buildings await restoration, one on Peachtree Street; the 696 Peachtree at Seventh Street in Atlanta's Midtown is boarded up. The Italian Renaissance revival clubhouse of the Atlanta Athletic Club (1925–26), 166 Carnegie Way downtown, was imploded in February 1973 as Grady's book went to press. All around Brookwood Station, as it is called, where Reid's suburban classical railroad depot still stands, much has disappeared, including numerous Hentz, Reid & Adler houses that had stood along Peachtree in the Brookwood neighborhood. In fact, except for this station and the Brookwood Hills residential enclave, the neighborhood has lost its name and identity. At the site where the handsome, Reid-

Above: BUILDING FOR BENJAMIN D. WATKINS, job number 500, 1922. Threatened with demolition in 1997. Below: APARTMENTS FOR J. A. McCORD, job number 491, 1922.

(203.2)

(203.3)

Interior detail of Atlanta Athletic Club, job number 557, 1925; demolished in 1973.

(203.1)

designed Hunter Perry house once stood, there is a newly erected limestone obelisk erroneously marking the Peachtree entrance to Buckhead. Although that new designation is intended to be complimentary, it is historically misleading, if not downright wrong. Perhaps this book can clarify the record and slow down the attrition of a once-upon-a-time more beautiful city, the city before superhighways, that "Neel Reid Made Beautiful."

Research for this book has documented a number of buildings that had been unknown as Reid in recent years, which add to the beauty we will care for, or should. Among these newly identified are the Della Manta Apartments at One South Prado and Piedmont Avenue in Ansley Park and the B. D. Watkins Building at Poplar and Forsyth Streets in downtown Atlanta. On Seventh Street is the elegant red-brick McCord Apartments, hidden much of the year behind Bradford pear trees that have grown like weeds.

(204.1)

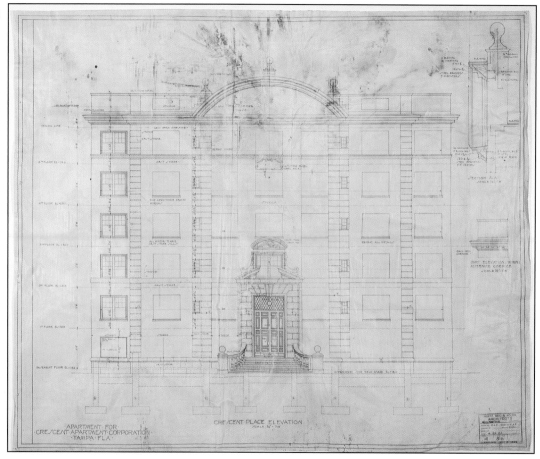

APARTMENT FOR
CRESCENT APARTMENT CORPORATION
TAMPA FLA

CRESCENT PLACE ELEVATION

The Tampa Terrace Hotel (below), job number 535, 1924–25, has been destroyed, but the Tampa Crescent Apartments (above), job number 518, 1923–24, is now a dormitory for the University of Tampa.

(204.2)

Alas, in Tampa, Florida, Reid's robust Florida boom–period Tampa Terrace Hotel (1924–25) was demolished in the 1960s, but this writer found that the six-story Tampa Crescent Apartments in the Hyde Park area near the University of Tampa is now Howell Hall, a college dormitory on the expanding campus of that institution. Its main building is that most appealingly flamboyant Tampa Bay resort hotel (1891) by J. A. Wood, a bizarre contrast, with its minarets, cupolas, domes, and long decorated porches, to Reid's nearby serene and classical Georgian Revival red-brick apartment house with its large-scale limestone frontispiece and arched pediment crowning the top. The two side by side are instant architectural history and historic preservation lessons for the students and community. The Tampa Bay is just the sort of exotic building that challenged, perhaps irritated, American Renaissance figures, such as our much-revered Reid, into becoming architects in the first place. But thankfully we can now love them both: Neel Reid's beaux arts classicism

(205.1)

Atlanta stores for M. RICH AND BROTHERS (above), job number 403, 1921–22, and GEORGE MUSE CLOTHING COMPANY (below), job number 380, 1919–20, have been preserved through adaptive use.

(205.2)

and J. A. Wood's Arabian nights.

It is on this epilogue note we end: to understand the best of Reid's legend and care for his legacy—but not to the neglect of other legends and legacies of our often embattled American culture. Reid is part of a larger legacy and an enriching legend emerging from the American South. The South is New, yes, but even in its late-twentieth-century Sunbelt newness, much that is worthy from its early twentieth-century beaux arts "oldness" must be recognized and preserved.

Let us give J. Neel Reid the last word, however. In England, writing in his travel diary, September 3, 1907, Reid revealed, better than we could ever sum it up for him, his true classicist heart admiring the rare symmetry of a Gothic design: "Stopped in Lichfield for luncheon and a few hours to see the cathedral. It is a beauty, sometimes called the queen of English minsters. Built of red sandstone, with wonderful carving. A beautiful west facade and three beautiful spires. Exquisitely symmetrical."

(206.1)

Above: Neel Reid, age four and one-half years. Below: Neel and John Jr. in the Reid family library, Macon.

(206.2)

1828–30   Joseph Neel Reid's great-grandfather, Judge Samuel Reid (1792–1855), of Troup County, Georgia, laid out LaGrange, the county seat. The Reid plantation of 1830 stands near Interstate 85 on the western edge of LaGrange and is on the National Register of Historic Places.

1858   J. Neel Reid's father, John Whitfield Reid, was born August 12 at the Reid plantation. He married Elizabeth Adams (born 1863) of Jacksonville, Alabama, in 1881.

1879   McKim, Mead & White, a nationally influential architectural partnership, was established in New York City. Partner Charles F. McKim taught at Columbia University, where Neel Reid, Hal Hentz, and Rudolph Adler studied under his guidance.

1881   October. Columbia University School of Architecture was established in New York City. Beaux arts classicism and eclecticism were taught there from the beginning.

1883   May 15. Hal Fitzgerald Hentz was born at City Point, Florida, near the Indian River. Hentz grew up in Quincy, Florida, and married Frances Connally of Atlanta in 1916.

     August 27. Neel Reid's sister, Louise, was born. She never married.

1885   October 23. Joseph Neel Reid, named for family friend Joseph N. Neel, was born in Jacksonville, Alabama, at his maternal grandparents' farm.

1888   April 7. Neel Reid's brother, John Whitfield Jr., was born in Atlanta. He married Susan Marie Birmingham (born 1891) of Baltimore, Maryland, in 1920. They had two children, Elizabeth Meredith Reid (born January 18, 1921) and Neel W. Reid (born December 31, 1921).

1889   Rudolph Sartorius Adler was born in Atlanta.

1890   John and Elizabeth Reid moved their family from Atlanta to Macon, in middle Georgia. A few years after moving to Macon, Reid wrote to his grandmother Adams, "I got a box of blocks and a box of paint and a book to paint in."

     Philip Trammell Shutze was born in Columbus, Georgia. He began working at the office of Neel Reid and Hal Hentz when he was an architectural student at Georgia Tech about 1909.

1901   January 19. John W. Reid Sr. died in Macon.

1904   Hal Hentz was graduated from Emory College at Oxford, Georgia.

       J. Neel Reid began his apprenticeship in Macon and Atlanta with architects Curran Ellis and Willis F. Denny, who practiced in those cities and were informally associated.

       Ansley Park, a planned garden suburb, was established in Atlanta at Fifteenth Street and adjacent streets between Peachtree Street and Piedmont Avenue. Many early Reid designs were built here.

1905–7   J. Neel Reid and Hal F. Hentz became acquainted in Atlanta; they left Atlanta to attend the Columbia University School of Architecture, Reid in the two-year course of special student, Hentz as a post-baccalaureate student.

1906   March 13. The Atlanta Chapter of the American Institute of Architects was established.

1907   Reid journeyed to Europe to study architecture and travel; he attended L'Ecole des Beaux-Arts in Paris. He kept a diary during an August through December sketching tour. Reid returned to New York to work at the end of the year during a financial panic.

1908   Hal Hentz also went to Paris to travel and study. Among Hentz's classmates during his study at L'Ecole des Beaux-Arts was William L. Bottomley of New York, who also studied at Columbia.

       Reid worked for several months with Murphy & Dana, an outstanding firm of architects in New York City, before returning to Georgia.

       Reid designed Hill House for the W. Emmett Smalls of Macon.

1909   Winter. Neel Reid and Hal Hentz established a partnership. By summer they joined Gottfried L. Norrman (1848–1909), a successful older architect, to form Norrman, Hentz & Reid. Norrman died in November, but the short-lived association with the young architects helped establish them in their profession. After Norrman's death the firm's new letterhead read Hentz & Reid, Atlanta and Macon.

(207.1)

Neel Reid, second from left, 1910.

Neel Reid dressed for a costume ball. Of his colleague, Hal Hentz said, "Reid was a genius with beauty dripping from his fingertips."

(207.2)

(208.1)

Above: Neel Reid at the W. Emmett Smalls' house in Macon.

(208.2)

Left: Reid often dressed as a harlequin for Nine O'Clock costume balls at the Piedmont Driving Club in Atlanta.

(208.3)

Neel Reid in Italy in 1922.

1910   May 4–17. The First Annual Exhibition was held by the Architectural Arts League and the Atlanta Chapter of the American Institute of Architects. Hentz & Reid exhibited. Work by Columbia student Rudolph Adler was submitted by the New York Society of Beaux-Arts Architects.

The Georgia Life Building, a ten-story skyscraper on Mulberry Street in Macon, was designed by Hentz & Reid for Reid's friend and client W. Emmett Small, president of Georgia Life Insurance Company.

Hentz & Reid designed a house for Joseph N. Neel in Macon. Reid had made preliminary studies for the job in his 1907 diary.

1911   Rudolph S. Adler returned from Columbia and joined Hentz & Reid as a draftsman.

1913–14   A series of illustrated articles on works by Hentz & Reid in Atlanta, Macon, and Marietta was published in *American Architect*, a national professional journal.

1916   Hentz & Reid job number 233, the Fuller Callaway house, known as Hills and Dales, was completed in LaGrange, Georgia.

Hentz, Reid & Adler was incorporated, with Rudolph Adler joining his former Columbia classmates as a partner. Adler became an important source of clients, especially in the old Jewish community of Atlanta. All three partners drafted working drawings, with Reid (JNR) the principal designer; Hentz (HFH) and Adler (RSA) were also accomplished draftsmen. All the partners were less involved in the actual drafting as time passed.

Reid purchased Mimosa Hall in Roswell, Georgia, nineteen miles north of Atlanta, as his residence. After renovating and landscaping the two-story, c. 1840 classical house, he moved in with his mother and sister in 1917. Reid never drove, so he rode the Roswell jitney to Atlanta. His family lived at Mimosa Hall until 1936.

1919   October. The firm received national notice in the *Architectural Record* issue "The American Country House," by Fiske Kimball. The June and December issues of this still-published journal also had illustrations of the firm's works.

1922 April–July. Neel Reid traveled to Europe with a protégé, Lewis Edmund Crook Jr. (1897–1967), gathering ideas and furnishings for the Andrew Calhoun house, job number 396, in Atlanta, among other projects. Crook later described the trip as a "sketching tour of England, France, and Italy."

1923 May 1. Ivey & Crook was formed by former Hentz and Reid draftsmen Ed Ivey and Lewis Crook. One of their first major jobs was to supervise the building of the Calhoun house for Hentz, Reid & Adler.

1924 Neel Reid was operated on in Boston for a brain tumor by neurosurgeon Dr. Harvey Cushing.

The Garrison Apartments, job number 533, were completed on Peachtree Street in Ansley Park. The building is now called the Reid House Condominiums.

The firm completed the initial design, job number 547, for the E. H. Inmans' grand house in Buckhead.

1925 The firm closed its Tampa, Florida, office as the Florida real estate boom began to fail.

December. Neel Reid took his last trip to Boston to see Dr. Cushing.

The second and third versions of the Inman house drawings were made. Construction on the project, numbered 591, began in 1926 after Reid's death. Called Swan House by its owners, it is now preserved as a house museum by the Atlanta Historical Society.

1926 February 14. Reid died at his home, Mimosa Hall, at ten in the morning. The next day, after extensive front-page coverage of his death, the funeral for Joseph Neel Reid was held at Saint Paul's Episcopal Church in Macon; he was buried in the family plot at Rose Hill Cemetery.

End of Florida real estate boom.

Spring. Hentz, Reid & Adler added "Phil Shutze, Associate" to letterhead. Shutze became the principal designer.

1927 January 1. Shutze was made a partner in the new firm, Hentz, Adler & Shutze.

(209.1)

Above: Neel Reid in his Candler Building office. Below: The monument for Neel Reid's grave in Rose Hill Cemetery in Macon was possibly designed by Philip Shutze.

(209.2)

1928 The April issue of *Southern Architect and Building News* published "The More Recent Country House Architecture of Hentz, Adler & Shutze," by Ernest Ray Denmark, who praised "the late Neel Reid, as the firm's chief designer, [who] was largely responsible for the success of this work."

1943 Hal Hentz retired and moved to Winter Garden, Florida.

1945 January 19. Rudolph Sartorius Adler died and was buried at Oakland Cemetery, Atlanta's oldest graveyard.

1946–47 J. Neel Reid memorial scholarship established at the University of Georgia Landscape Architecture School by the Peachtree Garden Club, of Atlanta, and other Reid admirers. Reid's portrait (left) was presented for that program by Hal Hentz, Hunter Perry, M. A. Ferst, and the Jesse Drapers.

1966 Ernest D. Ivey died.

1967 Lewis E. Crook died. Ivey and Crook were two of the last of the early Reid associates to remain in practice.

1971 A master's thesis by Stephanie A. Kapetanokos, "The Architecture of Neel Reid," was presented at the University of Georgia. It remains an important source of photographs and interviews, especially with Hal Hentz, who died the next year, and James Means, who died in 1979.

1972 February 16. Hal Fitzgerald Hentz died at Winter Haven, Florida, and was buried at Westview Cemetery in Atlanta next to his wife Frances, who died in 1942. Hentz (and subsequently his estate) presented his collection of the firm's drawings and blueprints to the Atlanta Historical Society, which has copied a majority of them on microfilm.

1973 *Architecture of Neel Reid in Georgia* by James Grady was published. It was sponsored by the Peachtree-Cherokee Garden Trust.

1982 October 17. Philip Trammell Shutze died. Among the papers he bequeathed to the Atlanta Historical Society was the list of jobs begun in 1909 by Hentz and Reid and kept through later partnerships as a continuous listing.

1993 The Neel Reid Educational Fund of the Georgia Trust for Historic Preservation was established.

(210.1)

A portrait of Neel Reid by Laurent Tompkins is displayed at the Garden Club of Georgia headquarters in Athens. Standing next to the portrait is one of four cabinets designed by Reid for Mimosa Hall. Two of these were given by Neel W. Reid to the Garden Club of Georgia.

APPENDIX II
J. NEEL REID AND SELECTED GEORGIA CLASSICISTS

J. Neel Reid (1885–1926) and Hal Fitzgerald Hentz (1883–1972) became friends in Atlanta, Georgia, in 1904. Reid was working for Atlanta architect Willis F. Denny (1872–1905), and Hentz, who had just graduated from Emory College, was associated with Asa G. Candler as he and his sons built the Candler Building. In 1905, Reid and Hentz went to Columbia University in New York to study architecture where the influence of Charles F. McKim and his American beaux arts classicism was pervasive. At Columbia, they met Rudolph Sartorius Adler (1889–1945), an Atlanta native, who was also studying architecture. In 1909 after a time in Paris at the Ecole des Beaux-Arts, travel, and short experience with practicing architecture separately, Reid and Hentz formed the partnership Hentz & Reid, centered in Atlanta, with a Macon branch office. (For only part of 1909, the firm was Norrman, Hentz & Reid, but there are a few jobs by that name even after Gottfried L. Norrman died in November 1909.) In 1910, Adler went to work for them, after graduating from Columbia, and became a partner in 1916 in the firm of Hentz, Reid & Adler. This firm lasted until May 1926, soon after Reid's death, until the business of that partnership was settled. All three were excellent draftsmen and architects; Reid was the best designer. Their firm was a sort of Atlanta beaux arts atelier (studio). Some of the other architects who worked with them and were influenced by their approach were Ernest Daniel Ivey (1887–1966) and Lewis Edmund Crook Jr. (1898–1967), who formed Ivey & Crook in 1923; and Philip Trammell Shutze (1890–1982), who became the junior partner of a newly formed partnership, Hentz, Adler & Shutze, in 1927. (Shutze wrote Harvey Smith a letter, dated October 10, 1974, housed in the Smith Collection of the Atlanta Historical Society, stating that "Upon Neel's death, I was appointed his successor.") James Means (1904–79) went to work for Hentz, Reid & Adler in 1917 as an office boy and in time became an expert draftsman and residential designer, Reid's "hands," as he was described in 1952 when he became the partner of Edward Vason Jones (1909–82) of Albany, Georgia, for two years. Jones had worked for Hentz, Adler & Shutze in the 1930s and early '40s. Jones

perhaps defined the Georgia school of classicists best when he said in a lecture in 1973, "Neel Reid, and Philip Shutze, who followed in Reid's footsteps, were convinced that the design of a house or any structure for that matter, could not be successful unless it was correctly landscaped and properly furnished. So I religiously followed this concept."

Some other architects who should be considered part of the Georgia school of classicists, in order of their birth, are Philip Thornton Marye (1872–1935), Atlanta; Francis Palmer Smith (1886–1971), Atlanta; James J. W. Biggers (1893–1992), Columbus; W. Elliott Dunwody Jr. (1893–1986), Macon; Samuel Inman Cooper (1894–1974), Atlanta; Henry J. Toombs (1896–1967), Atlanta; McKendree A. (Mack) Tucker (1896–1972), Atlanta; C. Wilmer Heery (1904–89), Athens; Albert Howell (1904–74), Atlanta; Clement J. Ford (1906–92), Atlanta; and William Frank McCall (1914–91), Moultrie.

When E. D. Ivey was with Hentz, Reid & Adler, he initialed his working drawings EDI; Lewis Crook used LEC. Mack Tucker used MAT and McK. Some other Hentz, Reid & Adler draftsmen that have been identified are Augustine E. Constantine, AEC; George Hall Gibson, GHG; Horace B. Hammond, HBH; and Harry E. Lindley, HEL. Neel Reid usually used the initials JNR, NR, and sometimes R; Hal Hentz, HFH; and Rudolph Adler, RSA. With very few, if any, exceptions, the working drawings these Georgia classicists produced with their talented hands are themselves works of art, as this book demonstrates.

(212.1)

JOB	OWNER	
75	Albemarle Park Co	Ashville, N.C.
76	Armstrong, R.B.	Atlanta, Ga
77	Coca Cola Factory	Atlanta, Ga
78	Willis Timmons	Atlanta, Ga
79	W.C. Ballenger	Atlanta
80	T.H. Hall	Macon, Ga
81	Mrs. Lawson Brown	Macon, Ga
82	W.P. Coleman	Macon, Ga
83	Mrs. Florence Coleman	Macon, Ga
84	C.C. Twitty	Harksville, S.C.
85	Mrs. E.T. Dorsey	Atlanta, Ga
86	Misses Dorsey	Fayetteville, Ga
87	W.S. Duncan	Atlanta, Ga
88	Emory Winship	Macon, Ga
89	Solomon & Smith	Macon, Ga
90	W.C. Manning	Spartanburg, S.C.
90·X	MRS. L. FITZSIMMONS	ATLANTA
90·Y	CENTRAL M.E. CHURCH	SPARTANBURG, S.C

Original index card from the firm's list of jobs.

EXPLANATORY NOTE

This compilation is the result of several years of study of many kinds of original records, largely, but not limited to, drawings, writings, archival photographs, and structures considered as primary sources. It is an annotated index of the commissions of the firms for which Neel Reid was the principal designer, from 1909 until his death, February 14, 1926; first, with Hentz & Reid; then the short-lived Norrman, Hentz & Reid (1909); again as Hentz & Reid (1909–15); and, finally, Hentz, Reid & Adler (1916–26); ending with job number 606. It includes commissions for entire buildings, for additions and alterations, for interior decorating, for gardens, and sometimes for combination of these services. There are a few entries for commissions for which drawings were made but the work was never executed, although the architects assigned a contract or job number.

In all cases, the dates assigned had to be derived from research, usually from working drawings, and these are the dates for designs or commissions, not for construction and completion. An exact address is given when that could be determined from city directories or other sources for the cities of location. Where possible, current addresses are provided, but in some cases the original address must be given from the period of design and construction, especially when a structure no longer stands on a site because a superhighway has obliterated a neighborhood. Atlanta's Brookwood Interchange is almost all that remains of the old Peachtree Street neighborhood, once called Brookwood, where a number of Hentz, Reid & Adler designs stood in the 1920s.

In 1926 the address numbering system for Atlanta streets was changed and took effect on January 1, 1927. As an example, in the 1915 city directory the address for the house in Druid Hills where Neel Reid lived is listed as 52 Fairview Road. That house was job number 249, and the drawings are dated June 26, 1914. The following year's city directory has Reid residing at 56 Fairview Road, which was job number 271, drawings dated 1915. The 1927 directory, however, lists these houses as 1436 and 1454 Fairview Road, respectively. The change in the city's street numbering, coupled with the firm's volume of work at the time and its somewhat spare method of listing jobs, has complicated the task of identifying the firm's surviving commissions. The category "Remarks" on this compilation allows for indications of such things as status, "demolished," and other clarifications.

One of the most important primary sources for this inventory is the list of jobs by contract number (job number) that Neel Reid and Hal Hentz began keeping in 1909. It contained the number, a commission or client's name, and the city, with only a few annotations, such as "not built." These survive in their original form on the blue-green, four-by-six-inch index cards held at the Atlanta Historical Society. That index, if not the actual file of cards, dates from the partnership the young architects formed with Gottfried L. Norrman in 1909. Norrman was more than thirty years their senior and died that same year. Research shows there were at least a dozen jobs attributed to the firm of Norrman, Hentz & Reid, which lasted, in title at least, into 1910. No business records for this partnership have been located; however, the general index of jobs contains works that can be identified, at least in a business or professional sense, as Norrman, Hentz & Reid, because of working drawings and other surviving sources, including the buildings themselves.

The very first item on that index of jobs is the Albemarle Park Company, Asheville, North Carolina, which was assigned number 75. (The drawings are dated 1910.) Evidently, Reid and Hentz considered their new partnership's inaugural work to be worthy of a number that would indicate more experience than the numeral "1," and, indeed, all three men were further along, especially Norrman, who was at the end of a long and successful career. (About the new partnership, an *Atlanta Constitution* article entitled "They Are Well-equipped In Their Profession," June 27, 1909, commented: "Mr. Norrman is too well known to the people of Atlanta to need any introduction," and then it introduced the younger architects in some detail, quite aptly, except for an unfortunate switching of names

beneath the photographic images of their youthful, yet unknown, faces.) The last job in the name of that firm is number 105, in Macon, a house for Joseph Neel. The dozen jobs identified from that partnership are 75, 77, 79, 82, 84, 87, 88, 89, 90, 92, 95, and 105; in Atlanta, Macon, South Carolina, and North Carolina. Other jobs within the numbering range 75–105, but not among the dozen listed above, were apparently outside the agreement with Norrman and were identified on the drawings as from the firm of Hentz & Reid.

The valuable, shop-worn cards in the historical society archives came there in 1982 as part of Philip Trammell Shutze's bequest (Box 40, MSS 498). This working index was in Mr. Shutze's possession as the last associate of the firm of Hentz, Reid & Adler, but further explanation of how it came to Shutze and remained with him until he died is necessary, and it also explains how many of the older working drawings came to the Atlanta Historical Society.

Philip Shutze had first worked as a draftsman for Neel Reid and Hal Hentz when he was studying architecture at Georgia Tech, and he had continued as an associate, on and off, for many years. After Reid's death and the settlement and closing out of the business aspects of Hentz, Reid & Adler, the surviving partners, Hentz and Adler, on January 1, 1927, made Shutze a junior partner in a new corporation, Hentz, Adler & Shutze. This partnership continued to use the card file as a running index until number 717 in 1935, after which it adopted the year as the first two digits of the job number; thus 3601 indicated the first job of 1936.

After Hentz's retirement in 1942–43 and Adler's death in 1945, Shutze became the senior man and fell heir to the professional papers that remained in the large Candler Building office. In 1950 Shutze left that office for a smaller space in the venerable building. At that time, Shutze wrote Hal Hentz that he could no longer store the older working drawings and blueprints. This letter survives in the historical society's extensive Shutze collection, as does Hal Hentz's reply, in which he encouraged Shutze to pack up those invaluable documents at Hentz's expense and send them to him at Winter Haven, Florida, for safekeeping. Mr. Shutze retained the old index file, which included cards for the contract numbers of Hentz, Adler & Shutze and other items

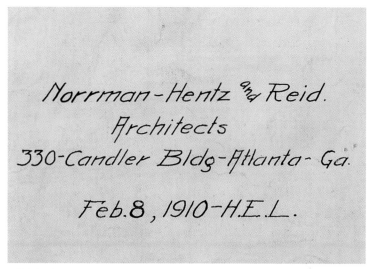

(214.1)

Norrman-Hentz ⅋ Reid.
Architects
330-Candler Bldg-Atlanta-Ga.

Feb.8, 1910-H.E.L.

HENTZ & REID,
ARCHITECTS
ATLANTA & MACON GA.

DRAWN BY *Neel Reid* TRACED BY *Neel Reid*
CHECKED BY *Rhodes* REVISED
APPROVED
DATE *September 4-1915*

DR. NO.	JOB NO.	SET NO.
5	266	

(214.2)

(214.3)

HENTZ, REID & ADLER,
ARCHITECTS
82-88 CANDLER BLDG. ATLANTA.

DRAWN BY *N.R.* TRACED BY *N.R.*
CHECKED BY *IVEY* REVISED
APPROVED
DATE *5-3-1919*

DR. NO.	JOB. NO.	SET NO.
4	357	

Above: Drawings were titled by hand, with additional
information provided within the ink block, usually
stamped in the lower right corner.

dating from the early days of the practice, and sent drawings and blueprints to Hentz.

For her thesis "The Architecture of Neel Reid" (Athens, Georgia, 1971), Stephanie A. Kapetanakos visited and interviewed Hal Hentz at Winter Haven. When she learned he had a large collection of the firm's drawings and blueprints, she encouraged him to find them a permanent home. Hentz did this, making them available just before he died in 1972. He left the Atlanta Historical Society (identified on the list herein as AHS) the drawings and prints (accession number 72–226) for works in Atlanta, which the society subsequently had copied onto microfilm. The repository for works in other locations is the Georgia Tech (GT) architecture library, which has also committed reproductions of its collection to microfilm. In that form, the large drawings are much more conveniently studied in sequence, allowing a chronological overview, c. 1909–26. For some jobs, the only record of drawings that survived is in the form of tracings or blueprints in private hands.

Basic to compiling an annotated list of works for this publication are those two primary sources, the index of jobs and the drawings. One has to compare these two records to begin preparing a completed list of works. (Not all of the jobs have surviving drawings or blueprints, as this list indicates under "Remarks.") One of the main sources of dates for the jobs, of course, is the identification, or title, block, usually stamped on the lower right corner of the drawings. Normally, this block has spaces for date(s), job number, drawing number, and draftsman's initials. Sometimes two sets of initials are found, and on occasion there appeared all three of the principals' initials: HFH, JNR, and RSA—all of whom were expert and prolific draftsmen. Additionally, there are spots for "traced by" and "checked by," which are not always filled. In the early days of the practice, before the ink-stamped block was used, the information was hand-lettered, and on the preliminary drawings, only a few of which survive, attribution is often absent.

This annotated list is a synopsis of what had to be studied and known to compile an authentic list of what could be included in such a book—a "catalogue raisonné." It is, as indicated, a result of scholarly research, not the annotation of an existing list found intact in an archive. This fruition could not be assembled as an appendix until the end of the study.

Among other sources used to prepare this compilation were city directories; building permits; deed, mortgage, and other business records; old maps; newspapers; magazines; archival photographs; letters; interviews; and previous research, such as the files created by the Peachtree-Cherokee Garden Trust Committee for the 1973 James Grady book and the papers of the late Mr. and Mrs. Calder Payne of Macon, which are housed at the Middle Georgia Historical Society.

Last, there is the invaluable Neel Reid family archive in Baltimore, Maryland, in the hands of Neel Reid's niece and nephew, which in old scrapbooks and photographic albums includes copies of business, professional, and estate records and family mementos related to Reid's career. In that collection are snapshots taken by Reid of Hill House, which he designed for the W. Emmett Small family in Macon. This design from 1908 predates his first Hentz & Reid partnership and therefore is not on this annotated list of works, but it is shown and discussed in the Macon section of this book. It was his first executed residential design, but it no longer exists. Mrs. Ethel Small wrote Louise Reid, Neel's sister, in 1946: "Neel loved the house he was building; it was incomplete until the grounds had become an integral part, and a garden was for him a necessity. I remember Hill House and how he toiled there. It was Neel's first house and he loved doing it for it was a long cherished dream coming true." This letter from the Reid family collection describes the true Neel Reid job number 1, the first "Neel Reid house," designed and completed when he was twenty-three years of age.

NOTE:

The annotated list of jobs following is a fundamental index to be used when job numbers appear in the text to ascertain current addresses, locations of working drawings, either at Georgia Tech (GT) or the Atlanta Historical Society (AHS), and other data. Firms are identified by initials: Norrman, Hentz & Reid (NHR); Hentz & Reid (HR); and Hentz, Reid & Adler (HRA). Illustrations throughout the book can be cross-referenced from the architectural index and the index of jobs. Identifying numbers locate each illustration by page number and position.

The images that follow illustrate the broad variety of design, type, scale, and location of projects represented in the list of jobs identified with Reid and his practice.

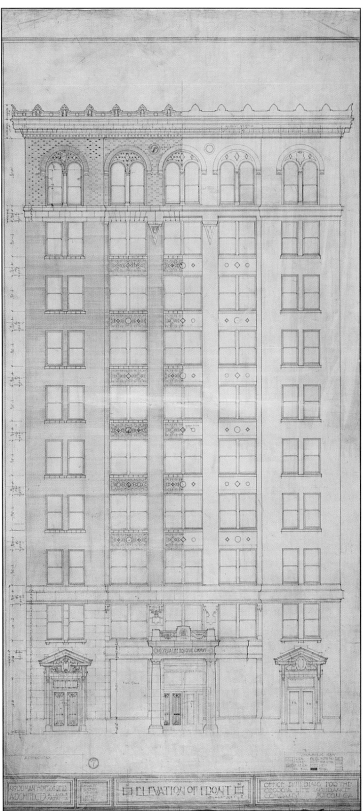

(215.1)

Above: GEORGIA LIFE INSURANCE COMPANY, *job number 101, 1910–11, Macon.*

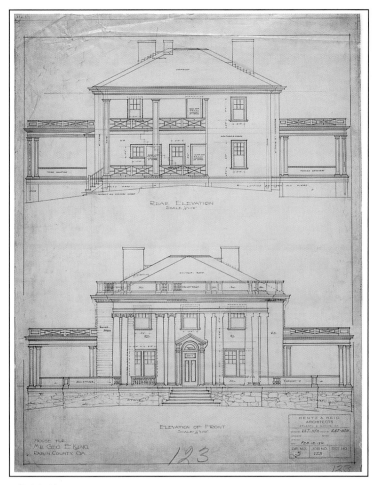

(216.1)

(216.2)

Left: HOUSE FOR GEORGE E. KING,
job number 123, c. 1911, Rabun County, Georgia.
Above: HOUSE FOR BEN Z. PHILLIPS,
job number 195, 1913, Druid Hills, Atlanta.

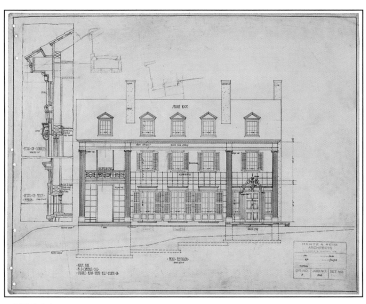

(216.3)

HOUSE FOR W. J. CAMPBELL,
job number 200, 1913–14, Druid Hills, Atlanta.

(216.4)

A. K. HAWKES LIBRARY,
job number 262, 1915, Griffin, Georgia.

(217.1)

Scottish Rite Hospital for Crippled Children, job number 339, 1918–19, Decatur, Georgia.
The elevation and floor plan (below) were drawn by Hal Hentz, who, along with Atlantan Forrest Adair,
was instrumental in the construction of hospitals for crippled children throughout the United States.

(217.2)

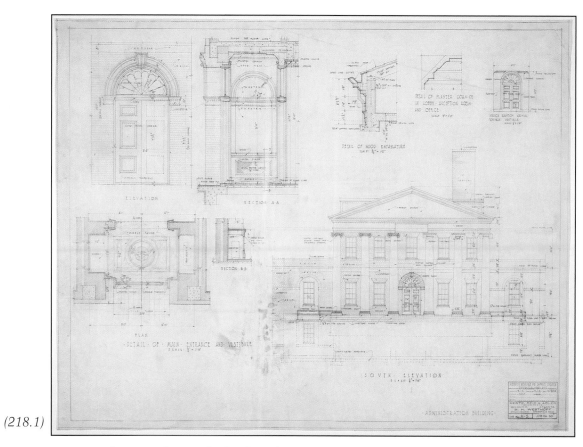

(218.1)

Among the many hospitals the firm designed were the SHRINER'S HOSPITAL FOR CRIPPLED CHILDREN (above), job number 531, 1923–24, Springfield, Massachusetts, and the SHRINER'S HOSPITAL FOR CRIPPLED CHILDREN, job number 550, 1925, Chicago, Illinois (below).

(218.2)

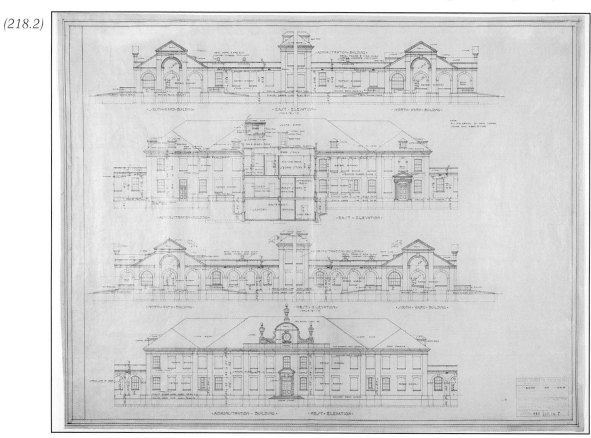

(219.1)

Left: MICHAEL BROTHERS STORE, *job number 411, 1921–22, Athens, Georgia.*

In LaGrange, Georgia, the firm designed several projects with connections to the Callaways, who commissioned the design for Hills and Dales, job number 233. Job numbers 485 and 486 (from left, below) were adjacent houses for H. S. WOODING *and* MRS. EUGENE C. FARMER *in LaGrange. Mr. Wooding was a Callaway Mills vice-president, and his wife was Mrs. Farmer's sister.*

(219.2)

The house designed for JAMES WHITE (right and below), job number 530, 1923–24, in Athens, Georgia, shares certain characteristics with the rear of the E. H. Inman house, job numbers 547 and 591, in Atlanta.

(220.2)

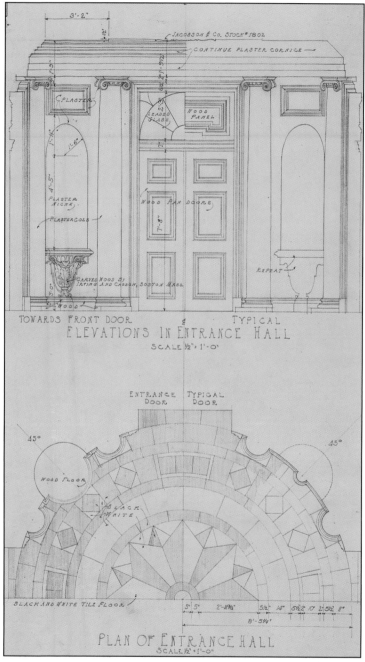

(220.1)

Above: HOUSE FOR ROBERT GOLDBERG, job number 532, 1923–24, Gastonia, North Carolina.

Right: HOUSE FOR CHARLES SHELTON, job number 572, 1925–26, Peachtree Heights Park, Atlanta.

(220.4)

JOB	DATE	CLIENT / COMMISSION	LOCATION	REMARKS
75	1910	Albermarle Park Co., cottage	Asheville, N.C.	NHR. GT.
76	1910	R. Blair Armstrong, building	Houston St., Atlanta.	HR. AHS.
77	1909	Coca-Cola, factory	Magnolia St., Atlanta.	Photographs HR. AHS. Demolished.
78	1911	Willis Timmons, house	1639 Peachtree Rd., NE, Brookwood, Atlanta.	HR. AHS. Stood where Brookwood Interchange was built. Demolished.
79	1910	Dr. E. G. Ballenger, house	Druid Hills, Atlanta.	NHR. AHS. Evidence of construction unclear.
80	1909	T. H. Hall, house	155 Oak Haven Ave., Macon.	HR. GT. Grady, pp. 2–7.
81	1910	Mrs. Robert Lawson Brown, house alterations	College St., Macon.	NHR and HR. GT.
82	1910	W. P. Coleman, house	596 College St., Macon.	NHR. GT. Grady, pp. 14–15.
83	c. 1910	Mrs. Everett Coleman, house	1116 Bond St., Coleman Hill, Macon.	No other data.
84	1909	C. C. Twitty, casino	Hartsville, S.C.	NHR. GT.
85		Mrs. R. T. Dorsey, houses	Clarke St., Atlanta.	Rental houses.
86		Misses Dorsey, house alterations	Fayetteville, Ga.	GT. No firm name listed; no other data.
87	1909	W. S. Duncan, house	East 14th St., Atlanta.	NHR. AHS. Destroyed.
88	1910	Emory Winship, house	Georgia Ave., Macon.	NHR. GT. Destroyed.
89	1910	W. G. Solomon and Northrup Smith, house	Forsyth St., Macon.	NHR. GT. Old photograph. Burned down.
90	c. 1909	W. S. Manning, house	Spartanburg, S. C.	NHR. GT.
90–x		Mrs. L. Fitzsimmons	Atlanta	No other data.
90–y		Central M.E. Church	Spartanburg, S.C.	No other data.
91	1908	Mrs. Helen Logan, house	1962 Forsyth St. at College St., Macon.	Neel Reid. Called Redding in Grady, pp. 12–13. Old photograph.
92	1909	J. W. Bates, house	Macon.	NHR. GT.
93		H. F. Hentz	Atlanta.	No other data.
94		E. P. Roberts	Atlanta.	No other data.
95		Dr. S. R. Roberts, house	Atlanta.	NHR. AHS.
96		T. C. Johnson	Atlanta.	No other data.
97		Miss Alice Hentz, house	Winter Park, Fla.	AHS. The sister of Hal Hentz.
98	1908	Miss Alice Hentz, house	Atlanta.	AHS. Drawings show H. F. Hentz, Architect, 103 Park Avenue, NYC.
99	1912	Gadsden County Courthouse	Quincy, Fla.	GT.
100	1910	L. P. Hillyer, house	2715 Cherokee Ave., Macon.	HR. Old photographs; also see job no. 334.
101	1910–11	Georgia Life Insurance Co. Office Building	544 Mulberry St., Macon.	HR. GT. Now American Federal Building.

JOB	DATE	CLIENT / COMMISSION	LOCATION	REMARKS
102	1911	Hillyer Trust Co. Office Building	140 Peachtree St., Atlanta.	HR. AHS. Top stories removed.
103	c. 1910	Roland Hall	Atlanta.	HR. AHS.
104	c. 1910	Miller and Barnett	Atlanta.	No other data.
105	1910	Joseph Neel, house	730 College St., Macon.	HR. Grady, pp. 8–11. Now Macon Garden Center.
106	c. 1910	Piedmont Driving Club, remodeling	1215 Piedmont Ave., Atlanta.	No other data, but this was the first of many Piedmont Driving Club commissions.
107	c. 1910	Jewish Educational Alliance	Capitol Ave., Atlanta.	HR. Destroyed after organization moved away and changed its name to Jewish Community Center.
108	1910	Neel Reid, alterations and interior decorations	Forsyth St. at Arlington Place, Macon.	HR. Old photographs of Reid's remodeling of his mother's home; house demolished.
109				No data.
110	1910–11	Walter T. Johnson, house	1238 Jefferson Terrace at Forsyth St., Macon.	HR. Grady, pp. 16–17.
111	1911	Dr. H. W. Walker, house	2540 Vineville Ave., Macon.	HR. GT.
112	1910–11	Mrs. R. T. Dorsey, house	262 The Prado, NE, Ansley Park, Atlanta.	HR. AHS. Mrs. Dorsey was widowed here; she commissioned a new house, job no. 156.
113	1911	Ronald Ransom, house	Juniper St., near Ponce de Leon Ave., Atlanta.	HR. AHS. Destroyed
114	1911	W. M. Haynes, house	218 15th St., Ansley Park, Atlanta.	HR. AHS.
114-a	1913	Dan Harris, house alterations	218 15th St., Ansley Park, Atlanta.	HR. AHS. Harris evidently acquired the house from Haynes.
115	c. 1911	Dr. Thompson Frazier		No other data.
116	1911	A. A. Christy, bungalows	658 Killian St., SE , Grant Park, Atlanta.	HR. GT. Six of these rental houses survive.
117	1912	Oglesby Hotel	Quitman, Ga.	HR. GT.
118	1911	Lee Branch	Quitman, Ga.	No other data.
119				No data.
120	1911	E. W. Stetson	2749 Cherokee Ave., Macon.	HR. GT. Grady, pp. 24–25. Sold in 1911 to James Stetson; see also job no. 141.
121	c. 1911	National Cash Register Co.	Atlanta.	No other data.
122	1910	S. S. Kresge	Whitehall St., Atlanta.	HR. AHS.
123	c. 1911	George E. King	Rabun Gap, Ga.	No other data.
124	1911	Charles Roberts		No other data.
125				No data.
126		Southern School Book Depository	Auburn Ave., Atlanta.	HR. AHS.
127				No data.

JOB	DATE	CLIENT / COMMISSION	LOCATION	REMARKS
128		Cole Book Co.	Atlanta.	HR. AHS. No other data.
129		J. E. Wilson	Macon.	No other data.
130				No data.
131		Mrs. C. B. Walker		No other data.
132	1911	Edwin and Leonard Haas, house	140 Waverly Way, NE, Inman Park, Atlanta.	HR. AHS.
133	1911	George Forrester, house	Peachtree St., Ansley Park, Atlanta.	HR. AHS. Stood north of "Reid House," job no. 533. Illustrated in *American Architect*, May 1916. Destroyed.
134	1911	Misses Nagle, house	132 Peachtree Cir., Ansley Park, Atlanta.	HR. AHS.
135		D. I. McIntyre, alterations	Atlanta.	No other data.
136	1911	Frank Adair, house	1341 South Ponce de Leon Ave., Druid Hills, Atlanta.	HR. AHS. Grady pp. 20–23. Illustrated in *American Architect*, March 1914.
137	1911	Benjamin D. Watkins, house	798 Oakdale Rd., Druid Hills, Atlanta.	HR. AHS. Also see job nos. 239 and 500. House illustrated in *American Architect*, November 1913.
138		J. C. McMichael, house	Peachtree Rd., Atlanta.	HR. AHS.
139		Mrs. Walter Beeks, house	Oak Haven Dr., near Vineville Ave., Macon.	HR. AHS. Mistakenly filed at AHS instead of at GT.
140	1911	Steve Solomon, house	196 Oak Haven Dr., Macon.	HR.
141	1911	Eugene Stetson, house	2733 Cherokee Ave., Macon.	HR. Grady, pp. 24–25. See also job no. 120. Designed for Eugene Stetson, who sold it immediately to John Pate Stetson.
142		Sam Schoen	Washington St., Atlanta.	HR. AHS.
143		Leon Dure		No other data. Probably a Macon project.
144	1911	Mr. Huguenin, house	1278 Jefferson Terr., Macon.	HR. GT.
145	1911	T. D. Tinsley, house alterations	505 College St., Macon.	HR. GT. College Hill.
146	1911	Mrs. J. W. Shinholser, house alterations	397 College St., Macon.	HR. GT. Grady, pp. 18–19.
147	1911	J. W. Boston, house	Marietta, Ga.	Illustrated in *American Architect*, Oct. 1913.
148	1911	Herbert Sage, house	Atlanta.	HR. AHS. Was it built?
149	1911	C. E. Roberts, house	718 College St., Macon.	HR. GT. Still occupied by a Roberts in 1997.
150	1911	Thurston Hatcher, house	Macon.	HR. GT. May not have been built.
151	1911	Dr. Charles W. Pepper	Oxford, Ga.	No other data.
152	1911	Mrs. Buford Davis, house alterations	Vineville Ave., Macon.	HR. GT.
153		J. D. Fleming, apt. house	Atlanta.	No other data.
154		Herbert Sage, stores	Atlanta.	No other data.
155		Leon Dure, hotel	Macon.	No other data.

JOB	DATE	CLIENT / COMMISSION	LOCATION	REMARKS
156	1912	Mrs. R. T. Dorsey, house	West 16th St., NE, Ansley Park, Atlanta.	HR. AHS. Stood behind First Presbyterian Church. Destroyed. See job no. 112
157		Atlanta Free Kindergarten	Atlanta.	No other data.
158		J. T. Dargan	Atlanta.	No other data.
159	1912	Louis Moss, house	Inman Park, Atlanta.	AHS. R. S. Adler, Hentz & Reid, Associated Architects.
160	1912	H. W. Barnes, house	435 E. College St., Griffin, Ga.	HR. GT. For second Barnes commission see job no. 522.
161	1912	Thurston Hatcher, house	Macon.	HR. GT. Was this built?
162	1912	Mrs. H[unter] P. Cooper, house	1798 Peachtree Rd., NW Brookwood, Atlanta.	HR. Illustrated in *Architectural Record*, Dec. 1917. Destroyed.
163	1912	Winship Nunnally, house	Peachtree Rd., NW, Brookwood, Atlanta.	HR. AHS. Destroyed, c. 1950.
164	1912	H. Mendel, warehouse	Atlanta.	HR. AHS.
165	1912	Locomobile Co., building	Atlanta.	No other data.
166	1912	O. M. Grady	Macon.	No other data.
167	1912	S. S. Selig Jr., house	Atlanta.	HR. GT (instead of AHS).
168	1912	J. P. Stevens Engraving Co.	Atlanta.	No other data.
169	1912	S. C. Porter, house	2612 Parkside Dr., NE, Peachtree Heights East, Atlanta.	HR. AHS. Mrs. Porter was of the firm of Porter & Porter, interior decorators.
170	1912	Girls High School		No other data.
171	1912	Steven T. Marett, house alterations	Druid Hills, Atlanta.	HR. AHS.
172	1912	Emory College Domitory	Oxford, Ga.	HR. GT. Building burned.
173	1912	D. I. McIntyre, house	Peachtree Rd. at Brookhaven Dr., Atlanta.	HR. AHS. Destroyed.
174	1912	George Derry, house	Vista Cir. at Osborne Place, Macon.	HR. GT.
175	1912	T. C. Parker Jr., house	3955 Vista Cir., Macon.	HR. GT. See also job no. 179.
176	1912	M. Y. Manley, stores	Macon.	HR. GT.
177	1912–13	C. H. Langford, house	2990 Orchard Rd., Conyers, Ga.	HR. GT. Now the Langford–Elliott Hall Cultural Center.
178	1913	Monticello High School	Monticello, Fla.	No other data. See also job no. 250.
179	1912	T. C. Parker, servants' qtrs.	3955 Vista Cir., Macon.	HR. GT. See also job no. 175.
180	1912	Mrs. I. N. McNair, house	On Jefferson Terr. at Georgia Ave. and College St., Macon.	HR. GT.
181		W. W. MacKenzie	Atlanta.	No other data.
182	1912–13	Frank Inman, house	Lake Toxaway, N.C.	No other data.
183	1912	Hugh M. Dorsey	West 16th St. at Lombardy Way, NE, Atlanta.	HR. AHS. Destroyed.

JOB	DATE	CLIENT / COMMISSION	LOCATION	REMARKS
184		Adair, remodeling offices	Broad and Alabama Streets, Atlanta.	No other data.
185		Dr. H. L. Reynolds	West Peachtree St., Atlanta.	No other data.
186		Mrs. C. F. Breeden, house	Spartanburg, S.C.	No other data.
187	1912–13	Albermarle Park Co., cottage	Asheville, N.C.	HR. GT. See job no. 75.
188	1912	T. T. Turnbull, house	Monticello, Fla.	HR. GT.
189		Mrs. Cora W. Nunnally	Lake Toxaway, N.C.	No other data.
190		Louis B. Magid	Tallulah Falls, Ga.	No other data.
191	1913	Mrs. George Armstrong, house, "Hillmont"	West side of Lake Toxaway, N.C.	HR. GT. Now Greystone Inn; on National Register of Historic Places.
192		West End Church	Atlanta.	No other data.
193		M. L. Cannon	Concord, S.C.	No other data.
194		J. Hall Miller, cottage	Flat Shoals Rd., East Lake, Ga.	HR. AHS.
195	1913	Ben Z. Phillips, house	1246 Ponce de Leon Ave., Druid Hills, Atlanta.	HR. AHS. Now the Howard School.
196	1913	Wallace Miller, house	773 North Ave., Macon.	HR. North Highlands Historic District.
197	1913	William White, house	Atlanta.	HR. AHS.
198	1913	Victor R. Smith, house	1800 Ponce de Leon Ave., Druid Hills, Atlanta.	HR. AHS. Old photograph; now part of Fernbank Science Center.
199	1913	Harold Hirsch, house addition	Euclid Ave. and Waverly Way, Inman Park, Atlanta.	HR. AHS.
200	1913–14	W. J. Campbell, house	888 Oakdale Rd., Druid Hills, Atlanta.	HR. AHS. Grady, pp. 32–33.
201		Edward Inman, house	Lake Toxaway, N.C.	No other data.
202	1913	Arthur Howell, house	1308 Fairview Rd., Druid Hills, Atlanta.	HR. AHS.
203		Forrest Adair	Atlanta.	No other data.
204	1913	Eugene V. Haynes, house	Whitehall St., Atlanta.	HR. AHS.
205	1913	W. S. Witham	Atlanta.	No other data.
206	1913	E. Lee Worsham, house	North Highland, Atlanta.	HR. AHS. Was it built?
207	1913	Mrs. Richard Johnson	Atlanta.	No other data.
208	1913	E. L. Henderson	Cedartown, Ga.	No other data.
209	1913	Edgar Dunlap	Atlanta.	No other data.
210	1913	Arthur Coddington, house	2510 Vineville Ave., Macon.	HR. GT.
211		Hatcher Studio	Atlanta.	No other data.
212		Shepard Bryan	Atlanta.	No other data.
213	1913	Milton Klein, apt. house	Piedmont Ave., Atlanta.	HR. AHS. Was it built?

JOB	DATE	CLIENT / COMMISSION	LOCATION	REMARKS
214	1913	City of Atlanta Pavilion Grant Park	Grant Park grounds, Atlanta.	HR. AHS. Destroyed.
215		(Bishop)		No other data.
216		(Stone)		No other data.
217	1913	Mrs. M. L. Underwood	Atlanta.	No other data.
218	1913	J. Frank Meador, house	West 14th St., Atlanta.	HR. AHS. Destroyed.
219	1913	Frank Adair, house	1337 Fairview Rd., Druid Hills, Atlanta.	HR. AHS. Built for sale by Adair and Weinmeister. Being restored in 1997.
220		Home for Incurables	Atlanta.	No other data.
221		Adair, stores alterations	Whitehall St., Atlanta.	HR. AHS.
222	1914	Edward Alsop, house alterations and additions	490 West Paces Ferry Rd., NW, Atlanta.	HR. AHS.
223	1914	D. H. Strauss, house alterations and additions	Washington St., SW, Atlanta.	HR. AHS.
224		Adler Building	Atlanta.	No other data.
225	1914	D. M. Morgan, house	East Lake Dr. near Memorial Dr., Atlanta.	HR. AHS. Unrestored in 1997.
226		Russell Show	Quitman, Ga.	No other data.
227	1914	H. L. Williams, house	Wynnton Rd. at 18th St., St., Columbus, Ga.	HR. GT. Old photograph. Destroyed.
228		A. K. Hawkes	Atlanta.	No other data.
229		Norris Candy Factory	Atlanta.	No other data.
230	1914			No data.
231	1914	Druid Hills Club	Atlanta.	No other data.
232	1914	W. D. Luckie Lodge	West End, Atlanta.	HR. AHS. Destroyed.
233	1914	Fuller E. Callaway, house	1200 Vernon Rd., LaGrange, Ga.	HR. GT. Grady, pp. 44–61. Old photographs.
234	1914	W. I. Middleton, store	122 Whitehall St., Atlanta.	HR. GT. Drawings filed at GT by mistake, instead of AHS.
235	1914	Charles N. Dannals, house	2662 Peachtree Rd., NE, Peachtree Heights Park, Atlanta.	HR. AHS. Grady, pp. 34–36. Drawings show J. B. Whitman, Dannals's father-in-law. Destroyed.
236	1914	Donald A. Loyless, house	Atlanta.	HR. AHS. Not built.
237	1914	Oglethorpe University Competition	Atlanta.	HR.
238	1914	Adair and Weinmeister, house	1315 Fairview Rd., NE, Druid Hills, Atlanta.	HR. Building permit. Built for sale.
239	1914	Benjamin D. Watkins, house		HR. No other data.
240	1914	Adair and Weinmeister, house	1444 Fairview Rd., NE, Druid Hills, Atlanta.	HR. Built for sale.

JOB	DATE	CLIENT / COMMISSION	LOCATION	REMARKS
241	1914	East Lake Club, clubhouse	2575 Alston Dr., SE, East Lake, Atlanta.	HR. AHS. Clubhouse remodeled after a fire in 1926, but exterior remained much the same.
242	1914	Robert Kelly	Jacksonville, Fla.	HR.
243	1914	W. L. Burwell	Sparta, Ga.	No other data.
244	1914	Iner Trousdall	Savannah, Ga.	No other data.
245	1914	Jacobs Pharmacy, remodeling	Atlanta.	No other data.
246	1914	Robert Woodruff	Atlanta.	No other data.
247	1914	George Woodruff	Atlanta.	No other data.
248	1914	Adair and Weinmeister, stable	Atlanta.	No other data.
249	1914	Neel Reid, house	1436 Fairview Rd., NE, Druid Hills, Atlanta.	HR. AHS. Grady, pp. 38–39. Building permit. Completed September 2, 1914. In 1915 City Directory Reid lived here. He sold it in 1915 to L. C. Matthews when Reid moved to 1454 Fairview, job no. 271.
250	1914	Monticello High School, alterations and additions	Monticello, Fla.	HR. GT.
251	1914–15	James L. Dickey Jr., house	456 West Paces Ferry Rd., NW, Atlanta.	HR. AHS. Old photographs.
252	1914	Oscar Pappenheimer, house alterations	144 Ponce de Leon Ave., NE, Atlanta.	HR. AHS. Columns added to alter front entrance.
253	1914	Will Miller, house alterations	638 College St., Macon.	HR. GT.
254	1915	Charles Shelton, house	827 Oakdale Rd., NE, Druid Hills, Atlanta.	HR, GT. Se job no. 572.
255	1915	Adair and Weinmeister, house	1464 Fairview Rd., NE, Druid Hills, Atlanta.	HR. AHS. Built for sale. Not built exactly as drawn.
256	1915	E. B. Bromhead, store building remodeling	35 South Broad St., Atlanta.	HR. AHS. Original address given here.
257	1915	Sid H. Phelan Co., apartments	Peachtree St. and Peachtree Place, NE, Atlanta.	HR. AHS. Known as the Palmer House, for Phelan's wife.
258	1914–15	Jesse Draper and A. C. Newell (1915), house	779 Clifton Rd., NE, Druid Hills, Atlanta.	HR. AHS. Grady pp. 42–43. Newell purchased in 1915 and made changes. Jobs list says Draper; drawings say Newell. See job no. 586.
259	1915	Sigmund Montag, house	850 Oakdale Rd., NE, Druid Hills, Atlanta.	HR. AHS. Grady, pp. 40–41.
260	1915	E. P. Dismukes, house	Third Ave., Columbus, Ga.	HR. GT. Old photograph. Destroyed.
261	1915	Dan Carey	Atlanta.	No other data.
262	1915	A. K. Hawkes Library	210 South 6th St., Griffin, Ga.	HR. AHS. Now offices for school system; on National Register of Historic Places.
263	1915	L. C. Adler	Atlanta.	No other data.
264	1915	E. R. Gunby, garage and servant house	Atlanta.	HR. AHS.
265	1915	William Candler, house	940 Springdale Rd., NE, Druid Hills, Atlanta.	HR. AHS.

JOB	DATE	CLIENT / COMMISSION	LOCATION	REMARKS
266	1915	Albert Bach, house	114 Buford Place, at Vineville Ave., Macon.	HR. GT. Grady, pp. 62–63. Two versions were drawn.
267	1915	Max Morris, house	2082 Vineville Ave., Macon.	HR. GT. In 1997 Panther Classics, Inc.
268	1915	Robert M. Crumley, house	17 Inman Cir., NE, Ansley Park, Atlanta.	HR. AHS. Grady, pp. 64–67.
269	1915	Southeastern Fair	Atlanta.	No other data.
270	1915	Herbert Stubbs, house	Quitman, Ga.	HR. GT.
271	1915	Neel Reid, house	1454 Fairview Rd., NE, Druid Hills, Atlanta.	HR. Built for sale. According to 1916 City Directory Reid lived here before moving to Roswell.
272	1915	Methodist Church	Griffin, Ga.	No other data.
273	1916	YMCA Colored Branch Building (Butler St. YMCA)	22 Butler St., SE, Atlanta.	HRA. AHS. One of the first for Hentz, Reid & Adler. Now East Central Branch.
274	1915	National Straw Hat Co., Albert and Emanuel Kaufmann	Trinity Ave., Atlanta.	HR. AHS.
275	1915	William R. Prescott, house	799 Clifton Rd., Druid Hills, Atlanta.	HR. AHS. Grady, p. 37.
276	1915	Mrs. Ida Cramer	Atlanta.	No other data.
277	1916	Ingleside Country Club, clubhouse	Avondale Estates, Ga.	HRA. GT. See job no. 573.
278	1916	W. L. Cleveland, house	LaGrange, Ga.	No other data.
279	1916	George A. Bland	Atlanta.	No other data.
280	1916	Mrs. Lettie Whitehead	Atlanta.	No other data.
281	1916	Emory University Out-patient's (J. J. Gray) Clinic	46 Armstrong St., SE, at Grady Hospital, Atlanta.	HRA. AHS. Now Woodruff Memorial Research, Henry Woodruff Extension.
282	1916–17	Southern Railway Passenger Station	1688 Peachtree St., NW, Brookwood, Atlanta.	HRA. AHS. Grady, pp. 166–67. Old photographs. Usually called Brookwood Station. Served by Amtrak in 1997. On National Register of Historic Places.
283		Store	170 Peachtreet St., Atlanta.	HRA.
284		Nunnally Co.	Atlanta.	HRA.
285		Charles Case, house	69 W. Muscogee Ave., NW, Atlanta.	HRA. A set of blueprints survives in private hands. Case sold this house in 1919. See job no. 372.
286	1916	Forrest Adair Jr., house	857 Oakdale Rd., NE, Druid Hills, Atlanta.	HRA. AHS.
287		Julian Prade	Atlanta.	HRA.
288	1916	Walter Rich, house	1348 Fairview Rd., NE, Druid Hills, Atlanta.	HRA. Grady, pp. 26–28 (gives wrong date).
289		Mrs. John T. Moody	Atlanta.	HRA.
290	1916	J. T. Holleman, house	1744 Ponce de Leon Ave., NE, Druid Hills, Atlanta.	HRA. AHS. Destroyed.
291		J. W. Royster	Griffin, Ga.	HRA.

JOB	DATE	CLIENT / COMMISSION	LOCATION	REMARKS
292	1917	O. R. Strauss, house	1372 Fairview Rd., NE, Druid Hills, Atlanta.	HRA. AHS. Grady, pp. 68–70.
293		Albert Howell	Atlanta.	HRA. *No drawings survive from this number through job no. 309.*
294		Nunnally Tea Room	Peachtree St., Atlanta.	HRA. Was in the Erlanger Theater.
295	1917	Louis Regenstein, house	848 Springdale Rd., NE, Druid Hills, Atlanta.	HRA. Grady, p. 71.
296	1917	Lowenstein Investment Co.	Atlanta.	HRA.
297	1917	Dr. J. C. Williams	Atlanta.	HRA.
298	1917	Howard Muse	Atlanta.	HRA.
299	1917	Mrs. S. W. Pickett	Atlanta.	HRA.
300	1917	Hon. John M. Slaton	Atlanta.	HRA.
301	1917	Lee Ashcraft	Atlanta.	HRA.
302	1917	C. T. Dunham	Atlanta.	HRA.
303	1917	Piedmont Driving Club, remodeling	1215 Piedmont Ave., NE, Ansley Park, Atlanta.	HRA. Photographs of clubhouse as remodeled in *Architectural Record*, June 1917. See job no. 106.
304	1917	Edward C. Peters	Atlanta.	HRA.
305	1917	Misses Culpepper	Atlanta.	HRA.
306	1917	James L. Dickey Jr., store	Atlanta.	HRA.
307	1917	Dunbar and Sewell, apartment building	1268 Piedmont Ave., NE, at 1 South Prado, Ansley Park, Atlanta.	HRA. Della Manta Apartments. On National Register of Historic Places, because Margaret Mitchell lived here in the 1930s and '40s.
308	1917	E. R. Hood	Atlanta.	HRA.
309	1917	Methodist Church	Quincy, Fla.	HRA.
310	1917	Fulton Bag and Cotton, YMCA Building	Fair and Chastain, Atlanta.	HRA. AHS.
311	1917	Willard Storage Battery	Atlanta.	HRA.
312	1917	Nurses Home, Spelman College	Atlanta.	HRA.
313	1917	Mrs. Kelly Evans	Hot Springs, Va.	HRA.
314	1917	Patrick Lyons	Atlanta.	HRA.
315	1917	Domestic Science Building, Spelman College	Atlanta.	HRA.
316	1917	Fulton Bag and Cotton, cottages	Atlanta.	HRA.
317	1917	B. E. Thrasher	Watkinsville, Ga.	HRA.
318	1917	Eagle Cafe	Atlanta.	HRA.
319	1917	John R. White	Athens, Ga.	HRA.

JOB	DATE	CLIENT / COMMISSION	LOCATION	REMARKS
320	1917	F. O. Stone Bakery	Highland Ave. and Dunlap St., Atlanta.	HRA. AHS. Destroyed.
321	1917	Presbyterian Church, remodeling	Covington, Ga.	HRA. GT. Burned, 1926.
322	1917	Mrs. J. L. Hand, house decorating	Pelham, Ga.	HRA. GT. Destroyed.
323	1917	Atlantic Steel Co.	Atlanta.	HRA.
324	1917–18	LaGrange YMCA	LaGrange, Ga.	HRA. GT. Old photographs. Destroyed.
325	1917	Fulton Bag and Cotton Mills, fireproof houses	Atlanta.	HRA.
326	1917	Louis Elsas	Atlanta.	HRA.
327	1917	Exposition Cotton Mills, day nursery–kindergarten	Marietta St., NW, Atlanta.	HRA.
328	1917	Judge Lamar, Marietta Hotel	Atlanta.	HRA.
329	1917	Richard Willingham	Macon.	HRA.
330	1917	Miss E. C. Johnson	Clarkesville, Ga.	HRA.
331	1917	Brooks Morgan, house	Atlanta.	HRA. AHS.
332		Railroad YMCA	Atlanta.	HRA.
333		LeRoy Myers	Savannah.	HRA.
334	1917	Oscar Kinney, house alterations and additions	2715 Cherokee Ave., Macon.	HRA. Remodeling of job no. 100 after it was sold to the Kinney family.
335	1917	Mrs. T. C. Burke, house alterations	1085 Georgia Ave., Macon.	HRA. First of two Reid commissions for this 1887 house. Also see job no. 385.
336	1917	Dr. Michael Hoke	Atlanta.	HRA.
337	1917	Hirsch Brothers, alterations	44 Whitehall St. (old address), Atlanta.	HRA. AHS.
338	1917	David Woodward, house	Atlanta.	HRA. AHS. Elevation sketches only.
339	1918–19	Scottish Rite Hospital for Crippled Children	321 West Hill St. at East Lake Dr., Decatur, Ga.	HRA. AHS. Now Community Center of South Decatur. On National Register of Historic Places. This was the model for many such hospitals around the U.S., an effort lead by Atlantans Forrest Adair and Hal Hentz.
340	1918	A. McDonald Wilson, house	945 Hawick Dr., NW, Atlanta.	HRA. AHS. Later additions and alterations. Original address was Howell Mill Road.
341	1918	Willis Timmons	Atlanta.	HRA.
342	1918	Electric Retail Co.	Atlanta.	HRA.
343	1918	Mrs. J. B. McCurry	Hartwell, Ga.	HRA.
344	1918	Piedmont Sanatorium	Atlanta.	HRA.
345	1918	Mason's Annuity	Atlanta.	HRA.
346	1918	H. S. Weaver, house remodeling	479 Atlanta St., Roswell, Ga.	HRA. Palladian entrance porch added to old house.

JOB	DATE	CLIENT / COMMISSION	LOCATION	REMARKS
347	1918	Harry Silverman	Atlanta.	HRA.
348	1918	Sam T. Weyman	Atlanta.	HRA.
349	1918	Forrest and George Adair	Atlanta.	HRA.
350	1918	Arthur Harris, house	South Ponce de Leon Ave., Druid Hills, Atlanta.	HRA. AHS. Evidently not built as designed.
351	1918	Dan Horgan	Rivoli, Ga. (Macon).	HRA. Horgan was a longtime client.
352	1918			No data.
353	1918	J. W. Woodruff	Columbus, Ga.	HRA.
354	1918	Judge William B. Lamar	Monticello, Fla.	HRA.
355	1918	Hand Memorial (Pelham) Methodist Church	Pelham. Ga.	HRA. GT. Has been altered by addition of a steeple.
356		W. T. Knox	Social Circle, Ga.	HRA.
357		Mrs. George L. Snowden	Spartanburg, S.C.	HRA.
358		Carter Electric Co., warehouse	Atlanta.	HRA.
359	1918	Mrs. J. L. Brooks, house	1226 Springdale Rd., NE, Druid Hills, Atlanta.	HRA. AHS.
360	1918	W. E. Browne Decorating Co.	Atlanta.	HRA. Possibly was the Browne building at 443 Peachtree St. Destroyed.
361	1918–19	D. H. Brantley, house	836 Mimosa Blvd., Roswell.	HRA. AHS. Reid designed this for the jitney driver with whom he rode.
362	1919	George S. Cobb, house	611 Ave. C, West Point, Ga.	HRA. GT.
363	1919	A. S. Hines, house	Bowling Green, Ky.	HRA. GT.
364	1919	Nunnally Co.	Atlanta.	HRA.
365	1919	Mrs. Benjamin Ohlman, house	Springdale Rd., Druid Hills, Atlanta.	HRA. AHS. Evidently not built as designed.
366	1919	I. Stiles Hopkins, house	1202 Springdale Rd., Druid Hills, Atlanta.	HRA. Drawings have not survived.
367	1919	Dunbar and Sewell	Atlanta.	HRA. No drawings. Dunbar and Sewell built apartments; also see job no. 307.
368	1919	Edward Inman, house alterations	238 East 15th St., NE, Ansley Park, Atlanta.	HRA. One blueprint sheet of this job survives in the author's collection, a library detail drafted by Lewis E. Crook, dated June 30, 1920. See job nos. 547 and 591; parts of this remodeled library were re-used in the Inman house on Andrews Drive.
369	1919–20	George Troup Howard, Howard Theater, later Paramount	163–165 Peachtree St., NE, Atlanta.	HRA. AHS. Interior decoration by W. E. Browne Co. Destroyed in 1960. Elements of the façade were taken to Moultrie, Ga., and reassembled as the façade of a house.
370	1919	J. Abe Perry	Ben Hill St., LaGrange, Ga.	HRA. Decorating for a Callaway associate.
371	1919	Williams Hospital, remodeling and additions	downtown, Macon.	HRA. GT. Now part of Middle Georgia Hospital. Dr. Charles Richardson, client.

JOB	DATE	CLIENT / COMMISSION	LOCATION	REMARKS
372	1919–21	Charles C. Case, house	2624 Habersham Rd., NW, Peachtree Heights Park, Atlanta.	HRA. AHS. Grady, pp. 72–75. The current owner has the original working drawings on architect's linen and other original data.
373	1919	W. E. Small, house alterations and additions	Riverside Dr., Macon.	HRA. GT. Remodeling of original 1908 house, Reid's first. Main house burned, December 25, 1949.
374	1919	Charles B. Lewis	Macon.	HRA.
375	1919	Tennessee Coal and Iron R.R. Co., school house	Birmingham, Ala.	HRA. GT..
376	1919	J. K. Orr Jr.	Atlanta.	HRA.
377	1919	R. L. Reed, house	Atlanta.	HRA.
378	1919	Mrs. George McKenzie	Atlanta.	HRA.
379	1919	W. A. Florence and G. W. Blair, store front	Marietta, Ga.	HRA. AHS.
380	1919–20	George Muse Clothing Co. (Muse's)	52 Peachtree St., NW, downtown, at Walton St., Atlanta.	HRA. This main Muse's store opened in 1921; closed in 1991; renovated in 1995–96 as loft apartments.
381	1919	Basil Emory Brooks Sr., house	1196 Springdale Rd., NE, Druid Hills, Atlanta.	HRA. AHS. Robert W. Woodruff, Coca-Cola magnate, purchased the house in 1926 and lived here until 1935.
382	1919	Hawkes Library	North College St., Cedartown, Ga.	HRA. GT. Now Polk County Historical Society building. On National Register of Historic Places.
383	1919	Mrs. Evie Wright	Atlanta.	HRA.
384	1919	Hatton Lovejoy	LaGrange, Ga.	HRA. Possibly decorating?
385	1920	Mrs. T. C. Burke, house	1085 Georgia Ave., Macon.	HRA. The Burkes were friends of Reid and twice made alterations outside and inside their 1887 Queen-Anne style house. On the National Register of Historic Places. Also see job no. 335.
386	1920	Junius Oglesby	Atlanta.	HRA.
387	1920–21	Stephan A. Lynch, house	109 Peachtree Cir., NE, Ansley Park, Atlanta.	HRA. AHS. Grady, pp. 80–83. Walter H. Rich bought in 1926 and HRA made a bedroom suite addition.
388	1920	Emory University, Wesley Memorial Hospital	1364 Clifton Rd., NE, Atlanta.	HRA. Old photograph. With Henry Hornbostel's firm as consulting architects.
389	1920	Cedartown Cotton and Export Co., cottage	Cedartown, Ga.	HRA.
390	1920	Haskell Bass	Griffin, Ga.	HRA.
391	1920	Cedartown Cotton and Export Co. (Oil Station)	Cedartown, Ga.	HRA.
392	1920	Southern Mortgage Co.	Atlanta.	HRA.
393	1920	Davison-Paxon-Stokes Tea Room	Atlanta.	HRA.
394	1920	Mrs. J. H. Hicks	Atlanta.	HRA.

JOB	DATE	CLIENT / COMMISSION	LOCATION	REMARKS
395	1920	Forrest Adair Store, building	Atlanta.	HRA. AHS.
396	1921–22	Andrew Calhoun, house	1140 West Paces Ferry Rd., NW, now 3418 Pinestream Rd., NW, Atlanta.	HRA. AHS. Grady, pp. 112–22. Completed in 1923, this was a major project requiring the combined talents of the entire firm. The grounds and gardens are now much reduced.
397	1919–20	Mrs. James H. Porter, house alterations and additions	562 College St., Macon.	HRA. AHS.
398	1920	C. W. Lane Co.	Atlanta.	HRA.
399	1920	Miss Mary Davis	Macon.	HRA.
400	1920	Haas-Howell Building	NW corner of Poplar and Forsyth Streets, Atlanta.	HRA. AHS. Designed as an eight-floor high-rise in a simplified Renaissance style. Details not executed as drawn.
401	1920–21	H. W. Barnes; Grantland Parish house, Saint George's Episcopal Church	132 North 10th St., at Broad St., Griffin, Ga.	HRA. A surviving copy of blueprints for this job is in the church's collection. On National Register of Historic Places
402	1921	Robert Barnes	Macon.	HRA. *From the preceding job, through job no. 454, with only a few exceptions, drawings or blueprints do not survive.*
403	1921–22	M. Rich and Brothers, store (Main Rich's store.)	45 Broad St., SW, Atlanta.	HRA. Opened in March 1924. Closed in 1991, now preserved as part of the Federal Center.
404	1921	Mrs. Jennings Adams	Macon.	HRA.
405	1921	Morehouse College	Atlanta.	HRA.
406	1921	J. Regenstein and Co.	Atlanta.	HRA.
407	1921	Cason Callaway Sr.	1106 Vernon Rd., LaGrange, Ga.	HRA. Cason was a son of Fuller Callaway Sr. of nearby Hills and Dales, job no. 233. Antique furnishings selected by Reid for this house survive in the Callaway family.
408	1921	David H. Strauss, house additions, guest house	1348 Fairview Rd., NE, Atlanta.	HRA. Strauss purchased the main house, job no. 288, from his relative, Walter Rich in 1921.
409	1921	YMCA Swimming Pool	LaGrange, Ga.	HRA. Destroyed.
410	1921	Auburn Street Carnegie Library	Atlanta.	HRA.
411	1921–22	Michael Brothers Store	320 East Clayton St., Athens, Ga.	HRA. Grady, pp. 168–69. No longer a department store.
412	1921	Hampton Cotton Mills	Hampton, Ga.	HRA.
413	1921	Collier Mills	Barnesville, Ga.	HRA.
414	1921	J. H. Hilsman	Atlanta.	HRA.
415	1921	Piedmont Driving Club, additions and alterations	1215 Piedmont Ave., NE, Ansley Park, Atlanta.	HRA. This is for the replacement of the 1917 ballroom (job no. 303) burned in October 1920. In style, this new ballroom survives in a larger, rebuilt form from 1964.
416	1921	LaGrange Female College	LaGrange, Ga.	HRA.
417	1921	W. L. Dumas	Atlanta.	HRA.
418	1921	J. S. and C. R. Collins, apartment	Atlanta.	HRA.

JOB	DATE	CLIENT / COMMISSION	LOCATION	REMARKS
419	1921	L. J. Elsas	Atlanta.	HRA.
420	1921	J. W. Patterson	Atlanta.	HRA.
421	1920–21	Walter J. Grace, house	Macon.	HRA. Not built. Mary Grace (Mrs. Sewell) Elliot has a copy of the blueprints.
422	1921	Cornelia Moore Day Nursery	Atlanta.	HRA.
423	1921	Nunnally Factory	Atlanta.	HRA.
424	1921	Thornton's Cafeteria	Atlanta.	HRA.
425	1921	G. Troup Howard	Atlanta.	HRA.
426	1921	Mitchell King	Atlanta.	HRA.
427	1921	Greek Cemetery	Atlanta.	HRA.
428	1921	Cason Callaway	LaGrange, Ga.	HRA. Also see job no. 407.
429	1921	Winship Nunnally	Atlanta.	HRA. See job nos. 163 and 517. This house at Lakemont in Rabun County, Ga., replaced the original that burned.
430	1921	J. Hall Miller	Atlanta.	HRA.
431	1921	D. C. Horgan, Idle Hour Nursery	Macon.	HRA. Job no. 622, 1926, is also Horgan.
432	1921	Alfred C. Newell, house alterations	Atlanta.	HRA. AHS. This is a remodeling of job no. 258 after a fire.
433	1921	Lee Ashcraft	Atlanta.	HRA.
434	1921	Piedmont Driving Club, extra wiring contract for new ballroom	1215 Piedmont Ave., Atlanta.	HRA. Surviving letters and receipts in the Reid family collection, dated April 1921. Also see job no. 415.
435	1921	T. C. McHatton	Athens, Ga.	HRA.
436	1921	J. D. Anderson	Marietta, Ga.	HRA.
437	1921	R. H. White	Atlanta.	HRA.
438	1921	Mrs. Sanders Walker, house alterations	935 High St., Macon.	HRA. Remodeling of the house now called the Sidney Lanier Cottage.
439	1921	Alfred R. Swann	Dandridge, Tenn.	HRA.
440	1921	Joel Hunt Jr.	Murfreesboro, Tenn.	HRA.
441	1921	H. M. Dorsey	Atlanta.	HRA.
442	1921	Jacobs Pharmacy	Atlanta.	HRA.
443	1921	W. B. Lamar	Washington, D. C.	HRA.
444	1921	Mahoney and Manry	Atlanta.	HRA.
445	1921	Montag Brothers	Athens, Ga.	HRA.
446	1921	L. E. Scott	Athens, Ga.	HRA.
447	1921	J. W. Grant	Atlanta.	HRA.
448	1921	Judge Hilliard	Decatur, Ga.	HRA.

JOB	DATE	CLIENT / COMMISSION	LOCATION	REMARKS
449	1921	T. M. C. Bram	Atlanta.	HRA.
450	1921	Hunter Perry, house	1719 Peachtree St., NE, Brookwood, Atlanta.	HRA. AHS. Stood diagonally across Peachtree St. from Brookwood Station. Moved to Charlottesville, Va., 1930s, recomposed, and named "Brookwood."
451	1921	Oliver Hotel	Atlanta.	HRA.
452	1921	J. M. Slaton	Atlanta.	HRA.
453	1921	Elks Club, clubhouse	LaGrange, Ga.	HRA. Demolished.
454	1921	Adair and Senter	Atlanta.	HRA.
455	1922	J. Bulow and Laura Campbell, house	164 Andrews Dr., NW, at Habersham Way, Atlanta.	HRA. AHS. Demolished. Chatham Hill development built on the site.
456	1921–22	David C. Black, house	186 15th St., NE, Ansley Park, Atlanta.	HRA. Grady, pp. 84–85. Large side porch based on the Miles Brewton house portico, Charleston, S.C.
457	1921–22	Willis Jones, house	1753 Peachtree St., NE, at Huntington Rd., Brookwood, Atlanta.	HRA. AHS. Preliminary plans dated 1921. Moved to 520 West Paces Ferry Road, NW, and renovated.
458	1921	Carrollton School	Carrollton, Ga.	HRA.
459	1921	R. L. Pitts	Calhoun, Ga.	HRA.
460	1921	William F. Manry Jr., house	2804 Habersham Rd., NW, Peachtree Heights Park, Atlanta.	HRA. AHS. Grady, pp. 76–77. Neel Reid was often a house guest here.
461	1921–24	Shriners Hospital for Crippled Children	Shreveport, La.	HRA. AHS. See job no. 339.
462	1922	W. A. McCullough	Atlanta.	HRA.
463	1922	Mrs. Echols	Staunton, Va.	HRA.
464	1922	W. H. Kiser, stores	Atlanta.	HRA.
465	1922	J. D. Godfrey	Madison, Ga.	HRA.
466	1922	Adair and Senter, cottage	Atlanta.	HRA.
467	1922	P. C. McDuffie, house	7 Cherokee Rd., NW, Peachtree Heights Park, Atlanta.	HRA. AHS. Grady, pp. 88–93. Also see job no. 605 for classical gazebo.
468	1922	Jesse Draper, house	3 Cherokee Rd., N.W., Peachtree Heights Park, Atlanta.	HRA. AHS. Grady, pp. 94–97. A large rear wing has been added, hidden from the street.
469	1921–22	Henry Newman, house	1 Cherokee Rd., NW, Peachtree Heights Park, Atlanta.	HRA. AHS. Grady, pp. 78–79. Neel Reid drafted the garden layout, formal parterres, 9/13/22.
470	1922	Asa W. Candler, house	1820 Ponce de Leon Ave., NE, Druid Hills, Atlanta.	HRA. Old photographs. Now part of Fernbank Science Center.
471	1922	Marlboro Apartments	Atlanta.	HRA.
472	1922	J. Carroll Payne, house	1756 Peachtree Rd., NW, at 25th St., Brookwood, Atlanta.	HRA. Old photographs. Demolished; a paneled room was saved by antique dealer Kenneth Garcia.

JOB	DATE	CLIENT / COMMISSION	LOCATION	REMARKS
473	1922	Willis Timmons	Atlanta.	HRA. See Timmons, job no. 78; addition?
474	1922	S. A. Lynch, house remodeling	109 Peachtree Cir., NE, Ansley Park, Atlanta.	HRA. Also see job no. 387.
475	1922	Mrs. J. M. High	Atlanta.	HRA. Mrs. High founded the High Museum of Art.
476	1922	Dunson Hospital	LaGrange, Ga.	HRA. Reportedly destroyed.
477	1922	Druid Hills Methodist Church	Atlanta.	HRA.
478	1922	Winship Nunnally	Atlanta.	HRA. Also see job no. 163 and job no. 517.
479	1922	George Muse	798 Spring St., Atlanta.	HRA. Address given on the firm's job index.
480	1922	A. L. Wilson	Quincy, Fla.	HRA.
481	1922	Dr. Stewart R. Roberts	Atlanta.	HRA. Also see job no. 95.
482	1922	Atlanta Athletic Club, caddie house	Atlanta.	HRA. Also see job no. 241, East Lake Club, 1914, but no other data.
483	1922	C. E. Freeman	Atlanta.	HRA.
484	1922	Highland Country Club, clubhouse	LaGrange, Ga.	HRA. Old photograph. Replaced by present Highland clubhouse.
485	1922	H. S. Wooding, house	1004 Broad St., LaGrange, Ga.	HRA. Wooding was a Callaway Mills vice president. See below.
486	1922	Mrs. Eugene C. Farmer,	1002 Broad St., LaGrange, Ga.	HRA. Mrs. Wooding and Mrs. Farmer were sisters. See above.
487	1922–23	Albert Steiner Memorial Hospital	68 Armstrong St., SE, at Butler St., Atlanta.	HRA. Grady, pp. 170–71. This clinic is part of the Henry Grady Hospital complex.
488	1922	Boys Senior High School	Atlanta.	HRA.
489	1922	L. F. Montgomery	Atlanta.	HRA. For this client, see job no. 640 of Hentz, Adler & Shutze, but no other data.
490	1922	Logan Clarke, house	14 Palisades Dr., NE, Brookwood Hills, Atlanta.	HRA. Blueprints survive with the 1997 owners of this house, the only identified Hentz, Reid & Adler design in Brookwood Hills or remaining in Brookwood.
491	1922	J. A. McCord Apartment	109 Seventh St., NE, Midtown, Atlanta.	HRA. Rumor that this was a Reid design proved correct. First occupied in 1923.
492	1922	Prince Webster	Atlanta.	HRA.
493	1922	Otis A. Brumby, house	Cherokee St., Marietta, Ga.	HRA.
494	1922	Piedmont Hotel, alterations	Peachtree St., NW, Atlanta.	HRA. Demolished.
495	1922	M. G. Michael	Athens, Ga.	HRA. See job no. 411.
496	1922–23	George P. Street, house	165 West Wesley Rd., NW, Peachtree Heights Park, Atlanta.	HRA. AHS. Grady, pp. 130–31.
497	1922	696 Peachtree Apartment (Adair)	826 Peachtreet St., NW, at Sixth St., Atlanta.	HRA. GT. Drawings were reused for the Arnold Apartments in Knoxville, Tenn.; see job no. 520.
498	1922	Prof. E. H. Johnson	Atlanta.	HRA.

JOB	DATE	CLIENT / COMMISSION	LOCATION	REMARKS
499	1922	Mrs. O. G. Watson	Atlanta.	HRA.
500	1922	Benjamin D. Watkins, building, shops, and offices	Poplar St. at Forsyth St., downtown, Atlanta.	HRA. AHS. In 1997, abandoned and threatened by demolition. See job no. 137.
501	1922	W. R. Prescott, house	799 Clifton Rd., NE, Druid Hills, Atlanta.	HRA. Grady, p. 37; incorrect date of 1915 given in Grady.
502	1922	Grady Hospital	Atlanta.	HRA.
503	1922–23	Robert Alston, house	2890 Andrews Dr., NW, Peachtree Heights Park, Atlanta.	HRA. AHS. Grady, pp. 135–41.
504	1922–24	Henry Tompkins, house	125 West Wesley Rd., NW, Peachtree Heights Park, Atlanta.	HRA. AHS. Grady, pp. 102–11. On National Register of Historic Places because of the formal yet practical Neel Reid design of this suburban villa.
505	1923	Jacksonville Apartment, building for Adair Realty Co.	310 West Church St., Jacksonville, Fla.	HRA. GT. In 1997 a hotel, with alterations, called the Ambassador.
506	1923	Atlanta Childs Home	Atlanta.	HRA.
507	1923	J. H. Nunnally	Atlanta.	HRA. J. H. Nunnally home, Brookwood, alterations?
508	1923	Spelman Seminary, Science Building	Spelman College campus, West End, Atlanta.	HRA. AHS. Grady, p. 172.
509	1923	Stuart Witham, house	2922 Andrews Dr., NW, Peachtree Heights Park, Atlanta.	HRA. AHS. Grady, pp. 150–51. Grady dates it 1926. Neel Reid drafted some of these drawings, June 18, 1923. On National Register of Historic Places because of Reid's design.
510	1923	James Livingston Wright, house	2820 Habersham Rd., NW, Peachtree Heights Park, Atlanta.	HRA. AHS. Grady, pp. 98–99; he dates it 1922.
511	1923	Frank Adair, beach cottage	Jacksonville, Fla.	HRA. GT. Drawings dated January 27, 1923. Drafted by James Means.
512	1923	Eiseman Building	Atlanta.	HRA. AHS.
513	1923–24	Robert E. Dismukes, house	1617 Summit Dr., Peacock Woods, Columbus, Ga.	HRA. GT. Grady, pp. 142–45. Drawings include garden plan with tea house. On National Register of Historic Places.
514	1923–24	Lakeland Terrace Hotel	Main St. and Massachusetts Ave., Lakeland, Fla.	HRA. GT. Plans in 1997 were to renovate this building as apartments.
515	1924	Mrs. Claude P. Noble	Atlanta.	HRA.
516	1924	Thomas Glenn	Atlanta.	HRA.
517	1923–24	Winship Nunnally, house	1311 West Paces Ferry Rd., NW, Atlanta.	HRA. AHS. Grady, pp. 123–29. Demolished 1970s after it was sold to a developer. See job no. 163, also destroyed.
518	1923–24	Tampa Crescent Apartments (Adair)	102 Crescent Place, Tampa, Fla.	HRA. GT. Now a dormitory, Howell Hall of the University of Tampa.
519	1923–24	Spelman Seminary, chapel	Spelman College campus, West End, Atlanta.	HRA. AHS. Grady, pp. 173–75. Sisters' Chapel.
520	1923–24	Arnold, or Knoxville Apartments	Church St. and Locust Ave., Knoxville, Tenn.	HRA. GT. Demolished. Also see job no. 497, the 696 Peachtree Street apartments.

JOB	DATE	CLIENT / COMMISSION	LOCATION	REMARKS
521	1923–24	Saint Luke Methodist Church	Pearl St. and Kirkwood Ave., Atlanta.	This is job no. 94 of Ivey & Crook, which evidently took over this project.
522	1923–24	H. W. Barnes, house alterations and additions	439 East College St., Griffin, Ga.	HRA. GT. "Violet Bank." This is the second job for H. W. Barnes; also see job no. 160.
523	1923–24	Alhambra Arcade	22 Sixth St. and First Ave., North, St. Petersburg, Fla.	HRA. GT.
524	1923	Dixie Terrace Apartments	Atlanta.	HRA. AHS. Evidently not built.
525	1923	Walter Brooks, house	Palm Beach, Fla.	HRA. GT. May not have been built. Drawings show Palm Beach; jobs index shows Atlanta, where the Brookses lived.
526	1923	W. W. Orr, house	Peachtree Rd., Atlanta.	HRA. AHS. Evidently not built.
527	1923–24	Cam Dorsey, house	2 Vernon Rd., NW, Peachtree Heights Park, Atlanta.	HRA. Grady, pp. 146–49; old photographs. Garden side faces Habersham Road. In 1997 a new Habersham entrance driveway was built at 2789.
528	1923	Mrs. Albert Howell	Atlanta.	HRA.
529	1923	Cedartown Hospital	Cedartown, Ga.	HRA.
530	1923–24	James White, house	1084 Prince Ave., Athens, Ga.	HRA. GT. Grady, pp. 132–34. Now a fraternity house. Drafted by MAT (Mack Tucker).
531	1923–24	Shriners Hospital	Springfield, Mass.	HRA. GT. Also see job no. 461.
532	1923–24	Robert Goldberg, house	1211 East Franklin Blvd., Gastonia, N.C.	HRA. GT. Long considered Gastonia's finest Georgian Revival style house.
533	1923–24	Garrison Apartments	1325–27 Peachtree St., NE Ansley Park, Atlanta.	HRA. Dated construction photographs document construction by the Foundation Company and Adair Realty & Trust Company in 1924; completed September 1924. Now Reid House Condominiums.
534	1924	W. J. and O. J. Massee Apartment Hotel	347 College St., Macon.	HRA. GT. Grady, pp. 176–79.
535	1924–25	Tampa Terrace Hotel	Lafayette and Florida Avenues, Tampa, Fla.	HRA. GT. Well illustrated in *Southern Architect and Building News*, May 1927. Demolished in late 1960s.
536	1925	Keily Apartments	Atlanta.	HRA. AHS. For P. C. McDuffie. Was it built?
537	1924	Charles L. Gately, house	1216 West Paces Ferry Rd., NW, Atlanta.	HRA. AHS. Now part of Pace Academy.
538	1924	Roy Collier	Atlanta.	HRA.
539	1924	Addison Palmer, house	1880 Shadowlawn Avnue, Jacksonville, Fla.	HRA. GT. The front elevation of this stucco house is similar to job no. 249.
540	1924	Antuono Office Building	Tampa and Lafayette Streets, Tampa, Fla.	HRA. GT. This sixteen-story Italian Renaissance eclectic high-rise was demolished.
541	1924	Masur Brothers Store	Monroe, La.	HRA.
542	1924	Joseph D. Rhodes, house	541 West Paces Ferry Rd., NW, Tuxedo Park, Atlanta.	HRA. Grady, pp. 152–54, incorrectly dated 1926. Blueprints have survived in private hands. Drafting by Mack Tucker.
543	1924	Shaw University Science Building	Raleigh, N.C.	HRA. GT.

JOB	DATE	CLIENT / COMMISSION	LOCATION	REMARKS
544	1924	Benedict College Science Building	Columbia, S.C.	HRA.
545	1924	Alexander National Bank	687 Central Ave., St. Petersburg, Fla.	HRA.
546	1924	Walter G. Mitchell	Atlanta.	HRA.
547	1925	E. H. Inman, house (preliminary version)	3099 Andrews Dr., NW, Atlanta.	HRA. AHS. The topographical map for this Inman property dates March 1925. The HRA 547 contract with Inman dates June 1925. Ultimately, a smaller, slightly different version of job no. 547 was redesigned as job no. 591, dated July 1926, and was built here.
548	1924	Covington School	Covington, Ga.	HRA.
549	1924	Charles Hopkins, house addition	Atlanta.	HRA.
550	1925	Chicago Unit, Shriners Hospital	Chicago, Ill.	HRA. GT. See other Shriners hospital jobs, nos. 461, 521, etc.
551	1924	Shreveport Shriners Unit, additions	Shreveport, La.	HRA. GT. Also see job no. 461.
552	1924	Roy Dorsey	Atlanta.	HRA.
553	1924	Hawkes Library	Jackson, Ga.	HRA. GT.
554	1924	Contagious Hospital	Atlanta.	HRA. AHS.
555	1925	Vaughn Nixon, house	3080 Andrews Dr., NW, Atlanta.	HRA. Grady, pp. 155–62. Blueprints with 1997 owner, Mrs. Wayne Watson.
556	1925	Fulton County High School	Atlanta.	HRA. AHS.
557	1925	Atlanta Athletic Club	166 Carnegie Way, NW, Atlanta.	HRA. AHS. Grady, pp. 180–83. Opened in 1926; demolished in 1973.
558	1925	Blackman Terrace, sanitarium	1824 Peachtree Rd., NW, Atlanta.	HRA. AHS. Became the Colonial Terrace Hotel. Demolished c. 1975.
559	1925	R. B. Wilby Theater (Cameo)	61 Peachtree St., NE, Atlanta.	HRA. AHS. Demolished c. 1970.
560	1925	Fuller E. Callaway	LaGrange, Ga.	HRA. Also see job no. 233, Hills and Dales.
561	1925	Alexander W. Smith, house	3407 Tuxedo Rd., NW, Tuxedo Park, Atlanta.	HRA. AHS. Drawings dated 1925; drafted by James Means and Mack Tucker.
562	1925	Dr. Lawson Thornton, house	2570 Habersham Rd., NW, Peachtree Heights Park, Atlanta.	HRA. AHS. Drawings dated 1925.
563	1925	Hollywood Realty Co., office	Atlanta.	HRA.
564	1925	Twin Cities Unit, Shriners Hospital		HRA.
565	1925	Macy Store and Capitol Theater	180 Peachtree St., NW, Atlanta.	HRA. Starrett and Van Vleck, New York, architects. In 1997 Macy's is still there; theater is gone.
566	1925	McBride & Associates, hotel	St. Petersburg, Fla.	HRA. GT.

JOB	DATE	CLIENT / COMMISSION	LOCATION	REMARKS
567	1925	Nurses Home, Scottish Rite Hospital	321 West Hill St. at East Lake Dr., SE, Atlanta.	HRA. GT. Also see job no. 339.
568	1925	Hunter Cooper, house	Rivers Rd., NW, Atlanta.	HRA. AHS. Not built.
569	1925	Shriners Hospital	Lexington, Ky.	HRA. GT. Drawing dated 1925.
570	1925	Coca-Cola Co., office	Atlanta.	HRA.
571	1925	A. W. Stubbs, alterations	Cedartown, Ga.	HRA. GT.
572	1925–26	Charles Shelton, house	2740 Habersham Rd., NW, Peachtree Heights Park, Atlanta.	HRA. AHS. First Shelton house, job no. 254, 1915. Drawings dated March 1926, MAT (Mack Tucker).
573	1925	Ingleside Country Club, swimming pool and terrace	Avondale Estates, Ga.	HRA. AHS. Also see job no. 277. Adler drafted working drawings June 1925.
574	1925	Henry H. Cole	Tampa, Fla.	HRA. Destroyed.
575	1925	Mack International Motor Truck Corporation	Tampa, Fla.	HRA. GT. Completely altered.
576	1925	J. B. Clark	Ridgeland, S.C.	HRA.
577	1925	Key West Apartments, Inc.	Key West, Fla.	HRA.
578	1925	Key West Kindergarten	Key West, Fla.	HRA.
579	1925	Key West Gymnasium	Key West, Fla.	HRA. Not built.
580	1925	Shriners Hospital, Isolation Ward	Portland, Ore.	HRA. GT.
581	1926	Cator Woolford, house	Ponce de Leon Ave., Atlanta.	HRA. AHS. Not built as designed.
582	1926–27	University of Georgia, School of Commerce and Journalism	Athens, Ga.	HRA. GT.
583	1926	Greenville Shriners Hospital	Greenville, S.C.	HRA. GT.
584	c. 1925	John W. Grant, garden	155 West Paces Ferry Rd., NW, Atlanta.	HRA. Garden has disappeared since this property became the Cherokee Town Club.
585	1925	Mother Murphy, Inc., restaurant	Atlanta.	HRA. AHS.
586	1925	A. C. Newell, house alterations	779 Clifton Rd., NE, Druid Hills, Atlanta.	HRA. AHS. Grady, pp. 42–43; also see job no. 258. Post-fire alterations and remodeling.
587	1926	East Lake Country Club, alterations	2575 Alston Dr., SE, Atlanta.	HRA. AHS. Remodeling after a major fire, especially interiors; drawings dated February 1926. See job no. 241.
588	1925–26	Piedmont Park Open Air Theater	Atlanta.	HRA.
589	1925–26	W. L. Dumas, house alterations	Talladega, Ala.	HRA. GT.
590	1925	Howard Theater, remodeling	163–165 Peachtreet St., NE, Atlanta.	HRA. AHS. Also see job no. 369, 1919–20.
591	1925–26	Edward H. Inman, "Swan House"	3099 Andrews Dr., NW, Atlanta.	HRA, with Philip Shutze, associate. AHS. Design process for this commission began with job number 547 in 1925. Now a house museum at the Atlanta History Center.

JOB	DATE	CLIENT / COMMISSION	LOCATION	REMARKS
592	1926	Maison Maurice, store	Whitehall St., SW, Atlanta.	HRA. AHS.
593	1925–26	Hyde Park Presbyterian Church	Swann Ave. at Orleans St., Tampa, Fla.	HRA. Demolished and building replaced in 1952. See cornerstone.
594	1926–27	Marion Smith School	Pennsylvania Ave., East Point, Ga.	HRA. AHS.
595	1926	Beach Drive Holding Co., store building	St. Petersburg, Fla.	HRA. GT.
596	1926	Nunnally's Store front	Atlanta.	HRA. AHS.
597	1926	David H. Strauss, swimming pool and pool house	1348 Fairview Rd., NE, Druid Hills, Atlanta.	HRA. Grady, pp. 26–28. Also see job no. 288, Walter Rich house, 1916–17.
598	1926	John G. Bolton, house	1504 Alcovy Trestle Rd., Social Circle, Ga.	HRA. GT. Blueprints show "Hentz, Reid, & Adler, Phil Shutze, Associate." See text.
599	1926	Adair, Hunter Perry Stores at Peachtree Station	1687, 1689, 1691, 1693, 1695 Peachtree St., NE, Brookwood, Atlanta.	HRA. AHS. Row of store fronts with Corinthian pilasters, but without original classical doorways, stands diagonally across from station. In 1997, the Beer Mug.
600	1926	Jacobs Store	Peachtree St., Atlanta.	HRA. AHS.
601	1926–27	Wesleyan College Library	Wesleyan Campus, Macon.	HRA. Completed after Neel Reid's death.
602	1926	James Watt & Brothers	Thomasville, Ga.	HRA.
603	1926	Adair Realty Co.	Atlanta.	HRA.
604	1926	American Legion Building	Atlanta.	HRA.
605	1926	P. C. McDuffie, house, garden addition	7 Cherokee Rd., NW, Peachtree Heights Park, Atlanta.	HRA. Gazebo at job no. 467; see gazebo elevation with those drawings.
606	1923–26	Martin Dunbar, Cooperative Apartments	200 Montgomery Ferry Dr., NE, Ansley Park, Atlanta.	HRA. A cooperative apartment project originally called the Italian Villa apartments; land purchase and planning began in 1921, the design process, around 1923, and construction in 1926. Now the Villa Condominiums.

APPENDIX IV: SOURCES

PRIMARY SOURCES

Buildings by Hentz, Reid & Adler in my native Atlanta inspired an early interest in American beaux arts architecture and led to graduate study that gave me perspective on my hometown classicists. My experience with researching and writing about the Reid era is a kind of primary source on which I have depended in this project.

I based my 1967 master's thesis on the Philadelphia T Square Club, an intriguing beaux arts atelier founded in 1883, which spawned a Philadelphia school of architecture in the late nineteenth and early twentieth centuries. I found the T Square minute books and other original records lost in the attic of a Philadelphia rowhouse where the organization had moved from its original clubhouse and was struggling to survive the modernist 1960s. The 1910 catalogue of the Atlanta Architectural Arts League, discussed in the introduction, followed a pattern the annual architectural catalogues of the T Square Club had set earlier. My 1984 History Business publication *Lewis Edmund Crook, Jr., Architect, 1898–1967*, about a protege of Neel Reid, contributed primary experience and sources, including a rare Hentz, Reid & Adler business card and the frontispiece photograph of Neel Reid in Italy in 1922 when he and Crook made an April–July grand tour, Reid's second and Crook's first.

Similarly, I undertook this book because of my discovery of formerly unresearched original materials, primary sources both private and public. I wanted to answer questions I had had since high school about what I have now identified as a Georgia school of classicists. These sources were not available when a University of Georgia thesis on the residential architecture of Neel Reid, a very helpful document, was completed in 1971, nor in 1973 when James Grady and the Peachtree-Cherokee Trust published *Architecture of Neel Reid in Georgia*, a scarce and now expensive book. These new sources were not available when I wrote *Landmark Homes of Georgia* in 1981–82.

First is the Reid family archive with Neel Reid's niece and nephew in Baltimore, Maryland. The late Richard A. Truitt Jr. of Georgia had first tracked this down about 1992 and revealed it to me because he had read *Classic Atlanta* and *Landmark Homes*, books that he appreciated because of the way I presented Hentz, Reid & Adler buildings. Annie (Mrs. Frank) Jones, a Peachtree Garden Club member, of Atlanta and Macon, and I flew to Baltimore for the day in July 1994 to meet the Reids, Neel W. and his sister, Meredith, to see what had survived with them that would shed light on Reid's life and career. In our short visit I saw that the Reids were preserving extraordinary things that had hardly seen the light since their uncle died in 1926.

In Atlanta, I had already met a cousin of Neel Reid on his mother's side, Charles Taylor and his wife, Vesta, when I was writing *Classic Atlanta* in 1988; they lent me their copy of the guidebook to villa gardens of Italy that Reid used in 1907 on his student tour of England and Europe. It has his bookplate and signature, and I have used it as a source in this text.

The Reids have the diary that their uncle kept on that trip and sketches that he made and referred to in his diary. They have business records from the practice, scrapbooks and photograph albums and architectural books, as well as other volumes from his library, and furnishings, including furniture and other objects that he designed, all from Mimosa Hall where their uncle had lived and died and which they had visited when they were children. They had the Columbia University annual from their uncle's second year there when he was art editor and illustrator.

From Jared Paul, a student in my Evening at Emory course, "Atlanta Architecture, Preservation, and Society," I was able to borrow some unique Neel Reid mementos, three of Reid's scrapbooks of magazine clippings of favorite buildings, interiors, and gardens, evidently begun when he was a student at Columbia University. Those had survived in the basement of Atlanta's Candler Building. Mr. Paul's aunt and uncle, Mr. and Mrs. Charles W. Harrison of Atlanta, fell heir to these because a custodian, who recognized that the old volumes had value, saved them from the trash and gave them to the Harrison family to preserve. In one of the dusty volumes that is signed in Reid's handwriting in the front, "Joseph Neel Reid," are some of his rare student architectural studies, *esquisses*, on tracing paper. With this "find" is a large collection of photographs dated 1924 of the step-by-step construction of the Garrison Apartments (Reid House) on Peachtree Street in Atlanta, job number 533. These relics have given me a glimpse into Reid's actual world, just as his diary has. The Baltimore Reids have photographs of Reid in his Candler Building office, surrounded by his reference library containing scrapbooks such as those the Harrisons lent me. These are the only ones known to have survived, other than a few in the Reid family archive.

In public hands, now, are things that had not been available until after Philip Shutze's bequest to the Atlanta Historical Society in 1982. These included the working jobs list kept by Reid and Hentz beginning in 1909–10, a primary source, indeed. (See my annotated version of this in Appendix 3.) In 1972, Hal Hentz left the historical society his trove of working drawings and blueprints, through about 1927, that he was preserving in his garage at Winter Haven, Florida. Hentz had requested Shutze to ship these to him in the 1950s. (See explanatory note to jobs appendix.) Jim Grady had access to those when he was preparing his text of his book in 1972, and I was also blessed with additional drawings and other items that Shutze left to the Atlanta Historical Society in 1982.

It was this myriad of original sources that made the book possible: the jobs list, working drawings and blueprints, business records, Reid's diary and sketches, old photographs, magazines, and newspaper articles, old city directories and maps, building permits, knowledge of and visits to existing buildings, and interviews with individuals such as Ellen Newell Bryan, Wright Bryan's widow, who grew up in a Neel Reid house, job number 258, in Atlanta's Druid Hills. Additional were the research files produced by the Peachtree-Cherokee Trust for James Grady's book, most of which are preserved at the Atlanta Historical Society, placed there by Laura W. Dorsey of Atlanta, who was chairman of that trust. The research files that were produced for the Macon buildings are housed there at the Middle Georgia Historical Society, which the late Mr. and Mrs. Calder W. Payne made the repository of their files.

The explanatory note for the jobs appendix should also be consulted for a discussion of sources used in its preparation. That annotated jobs list reveals the wide assortment of building types and locales for the firm's works; I visited many of these buildings during the long course of research and photography, among them buildings in towns throughout Georgia and some in Florida.

In addition to E. Meredith Reid and Neel W. Reid, here are some of the people whom I interviewed during research or who were particularly helpful during that aspect of the preparation of the manuscript.

INDIVIDUALS:

Michael A. Anderson, Norman D. Askins, William E. Baird, Ph.D., Jean B. Bergmark, Jane Hailey Boyd, Ellen Newell Bryan, Mr. Robert F. Bryan Jr., James C. Bryant, Ph.D., David R. Byers III, Mrs. C. Merrell Calhoun, Mrs. Cason Callaway Jr., Mrs. Fuller Callaway Jr., Mrs. Charles F. Causey, Mr. and Mrs. John H. Cheatham Jr., Dr. and Mrs. James C. Clark, Mrs. Thomas Hal Clarke, F. H. Boyd Coons, Mary Jane Crayton, Lois Crook Crossley, Lawrence B. Custer, Ms. Carol Ann Daniel, Edward L. Daugherty, Mrs. Jarrett L. Davis III, Mrs. Arthur Foreman Dismukes, Laura W. Dorsey, Olga T. Duffey, Mr. and Mrs. J. Sewell Elliott, Harriet W. Ellis, Mrs. Henry Florance, Mrs. Betty Hitz Foreman, James R. Fortune Jr., Richard D. Funderburke, Franklin M. Garrett, Mrs. R. Irving Gresham Jr., Mrs. C. Edward Hansell, Mr. and Mrs. Charles W. Harrison, Dr. and Mrs. Jasper T. Hogan, Henry L. Howell, Mr. and Mrs. Leland Jackson, Mr. and Mrs. Austin P. Kelley, Mrs. E. Buford King Jr., F. Clason Kyle, John W. Linley, Elaine G. Luxemburger, Harold F. McCart Jr., Mrs. Michael A. McDowell, Mrs. Katie Cox Dickey Marbut, Mrs. William H. Martin, Claire Strauss Miller, Joseph H. H. Moore, Harryet Pape Nash, Mr. and Mrs. McKee Nunnally Sr., Lisa L. Parks, Jared M. Paul, Mr. and Mrs. E. Fay Pierce Jr., Mrs. Cecil M. Phillips, Mrs. Frank A. Player, Mr. and Mrs. Richard Rawlins, Charles E. Roberts Jr., Ms. Doris Robinson, Bernard B. Rothschild, FAIA, Mrs. Greg Rush, James F. Speake, Jane G. Syme, Kenneth H. Thomas Jr., Mrs. McKendree A. Tucker Jr., Michael Vanderwerf, Mr. and Mrs. Wayne Watson, Margaret Strauss Weiller, John C. Waters, James P. Watkins, Mrs. Louis Wells, Mrs. John C. Wilson, Charlton H. Williams, Mrs. Susan B. Withers, Mrs. Bernard P. Wolff.

ORGANIZATIONS:

Atlanta Historical Society, Staff, Anne Salter, Director, Library and Archives; Emory University, Woodruff Library, Special Collections and other Staff, Linda Matthews, Director of Special Collections; Georgia Institute of Technology, Architecture Library, Staff, Kathryn Brackney, Librarian; Middle Georgia Historical Society, Staff, Macon, Georgia, Katherine Oliver, Director; State of Florida, Division of Archives and History, Staff, Tallahassee, Florida, Joan Morris, Walt Marder, Architect; Troup County Archives, Staff, LaGrange, Georgia, Kaye L. Minchew, Director; Washington Memorial Library, Genealogical Room, Macon, Georgia, Willard L. Rocker, Librarian.

SECONDARY SOURCES

*Asterisk indicates books and periodicals Neel Reid owned as of August 19, 1924, February 24 and February 28, 1926, from inventories of his library in possession of Neel W. Reid.

BOOKS

Adam, Robert. *Classical Architecture: A Comprehensive Handbook*. New York: Harry N. Abrams, 1990.

Art Work of Northern Central Georgia. Published in Nine Parts. Chicago: Gravure Illustration Co., 1919.

Barnard, Susan Kessler. *Buckhead: A Place for All Time*. Marietta, Ga. 1996.

*Bolton, Arthur T., ed. *The Gardens of Italy*. London: Country Life, 1919.

Brengle, Kim Withers. *The Architectural Heritage of Gaston County, North Carolina*. Gastonia, N.C., 1982.

Bryant, James C. *Capital City Club: 1883–1983*. Atlanta, 1991.

Catalogue of the First Annual Exhibition, Architectural Arts League of Atlanta and the Atlanta Chapter of the American Institute of Architects. Atlanta, 1910.

*Crane, Edward A., and E. E. Soderholtz. *Examples of Colonial Architecture in South Carolina and Georgia*. Boston: Boston Architectural Club, 1985.

Craven, Wayne. *American Art, History and Culture*. New York: Harry N. Abrams, 1994.

*Coffin, Lewis A. Jr., and Arthur C. Holden. *Brick Architecture of the Colonial Period in Maryland and Virginia*. New York: Architectural Book Publishing Co., 1919.

Crook, Lewis Edmund Jr. Foreword to *Southern Architecture Illustrated*. Atlanta: Harmon Publishing Company, 1931.

Current, Richard N., Frank Freidel, and T. Harry Williams. *American History, A Survey*. New York: Alfred A. Knopf, 1961.

Davidson, William H. *Pine Log and Greek Revival*. Alexander City, Ala., 1964.

Dowling, Elizabeth Meredith. *American Classicist: The Architecture of Philip Trammell Shutze*. New York: Rizzoli International, 1989.

Drexler, Arthur, ed. *The Architecture of the Ecole des Beaux-Arts*. New York: MIT Press, 1977.

*Eberlein, Harold D. *Villas of Florence and Tuscany*. New York: Architectural Record Co., 1922.

Efird, Mrs. J. Ray, ed. *The Houses of James Means*. Atlanta, 1979.

Elliott, Charles. *East Lake Country Club History*. Atlanta: Cherokee Publishing Co., 1984.

Frary, I. T. *Thomas Jefferson: Architect and Builder*. Richmond: Garrett and Massie, 1931.

Garrett, Franklin M. *Atlanta and Environs: A Chronicle of Its People and Events*. 2 vols. New York: Lewis Historical Publishing Co., 1954; Athens: University of Georgia Press, 1969.

Grady, James. *Architecture of Neel Reid in Georgia*. Athens: University of Georgia Press, 1973.

*Field, Horace, and Michael Binney. *English Domestic Architecture of the XVII and XVIII Centuries*. London, 1905.

Griswold, Mac, and Eleanor Weller. *The Golden Age of American Gardens, 1890–1940*. New York: Harry N. Abrams, 1991.

Harbeson, John F. *The Study of Architectural Design*. New York: Pencil Points Press, 1929.

Hatton, Hap. *Tropical Splendor: An Architectural History of Florida*. New York: Alfred A. Knopf, 1987.

Hewett, Mark Alan. *The Architect & the American Country House, 1890–1940*. New Haven: Yale University Press, 1990.

*Horton, Mrs. Corinne Ruth Stocker. "Savannah and Parts of the Far South," in *The Georgian Period*, Part 12, 1902.

*Kimball, Fiske. *Domestic Architecture of the American Colonies and of the Early Republic*. New York: Charles Scribner's Sons, 1922.

Kidney, Walter C. *Eclecticism in America, 1880–1830*. New York: George Braziller, 1974.

*LeBlond, Mrs. Aubrey. *The Old Gardens of Italy*. London: B. T. Batsford, 1907.

Lyon, Elizabeth A. *Atlanta Architecture: The Victorian Heritage, 1837–1918*. Atlanta, 1976.

Matthews, Antoinette Johnson. *Oakdale Road, Atlanta, Ga., DeKalb County: Its History and Its People*. Atlanta, 1972.

McGill, Ralph. "Southern Exposure." In *Vogue's First Reader*, edited by Frank Crowninshield, 300–305. New York: Julian Messner, 1942.

Miller, Paul W., ed. *Atlanta: Capital of the South*. New York: Oliver Durrell, 1949.

Mitchell, The Rev. Donald G. Jr. *History of St. Paul's Episcopal Church in Macon, Georgia*. Macon, 1970.

Mitchell, William R. Jr. *Gardens of Georgia*. Atlanta: Peachtree Publishers and Garden Club of Georgia, 1989.

———. *Lewis Edmund Crook, Jr., Architect, 1898–1967*. Atlanta: History Business, 1984.

Mitchell, William R. Jr., and Van Jones Martin. *Classic Atlanta*. Savannah: Golden Coast Publishing Co., 1991.

———. *Landmark Homes of Georgia, 1733–1983*. Savannah: Golden Coast Publishing Co., 1982.

Monograph of the Works of Charles A. Platt. With an Introduction by Royal Cortissoz. New York: Architectural Book Publishing Co., 1913.

Morgan, Keith N. *Charles A. Platt: The Artist as Architect*. New York: Architectural History Foundation, 1985.

Morgan, Keith N., ed. *Shaping an American Landscape: The Art and Architecture of Charles A. Platt*. Hanover, N.H.: University Press of New England, 1995.

Morris, Charles. *The Old South and the New, from the Earliest Times to the Jamestown Exposition*. Washington, D.C., 1907.

Nichols, Fredrick Doveton, and Frances Benjamin Johnston. *The Early Architecture of Georgia*. Chapel Hill: University of North Carolina Press, 1957.

Noffsinger, James Phillip. *The Influence of the Ecole des Beaux-Arts of the Architects of the United States*. Washington, D.C.: Catholic University Press, 1955.

Oliver, Richard. *The Making of an Architect, 1881–1981, Columbia University*. New York: Rizzoli, 1981.

Perkerson, Medora Field. *White Columns in Georgia*. New York: Rinehart, 1952.

Piedmont Driving Club, 1887–1987, the First Hundred Years. Atlanta: The Centennial Book Committee, 1987.

Platt, Charles A. *Italian Gardens*. New York, 1894.

Rainwater, Hattie C., ed. *Garden History of Georgia*. Atlanta: Peachtree Garden Club, 1933.

Roth, Leland M. *McKim, Mead & White, Architects*. New Haven: Yale University Press, 1983.

———. *The Architecture of McKim, Mead & White, 1870–1920: A Building List*. New York: Garland Publishing Co., 1978.

*Scott, Geoffrey. *The Architecture of Humanism*. New York: W. W. Norton & Co., 1974. Reprint of 1914 original edition.

*Tipping, H. Avray. *English Homes, Late Stuart, 1649–1714*. London: Country Life, 1921.

Tintinhull House, Somerset. The National Trust, 1986.

*Triggs, H. Inigo, and Henry Tanner Jr. *Some Architectural Works of Inigo Jones*. London: B. T. Batsford, 1901.

*Ware, William Rotch. *The Georgian Period: Measured Drawings of Colonial Work*. New York: American Architect, 1902.

*Weaver, Lawrence. *Houses and Gardens by E. L. Lutyens*. London: Country Life, 1913.

Wharton, Edith, and Ogden Codman Jr. *The Decoration of Houses*. New York, 1902.

Williford, William Bailey. *Peachtree Street, Atlanta*. Athens: University of Georgia Press, 1962.

Wilson, Richard Guy, et al. *The American Renaissance, 1876–1917*. New York: Brooklyn Museum, 1979.

Wood, Wayne W. *Jacksonville's Architectural Heritage*. Jacksonville: University of North Florida Press, 1989.

Wright, Richardson, ed. *House & Garden's Second Book of Houses*. New York: Conde Nast Publications, 1925.

UNPUBLISHED WORKS

Coons, F. H. Boyd. "The Cotton States and International Exposition in the New South, Architecture and Implications." Master's thesis, University of Virginia, 1976.

Heffernan, Paul M. "A History of the School of Architecture." Manuscript, Georgia Institute of Technology, 1975.

Kapetanakos, Stephanie A. "The Architecture of Neel Reid: A Study of the Architecture of Neel Reid in Atlanta." Master's thesis, University of Georgia, 1971. Plates.

Mitchell, William R. Jr. "The T Square Club, Philadelphia, 1883–1938." Master's thesis, University of Delaware, 1967.

National Register of Historic Places, Inventory—Nomination Forms. Atlanta, 1969–.

Tunnell, Spencer II. "Stylistic Progression Versus Site Planning Methodology." Master's thesis, University of Virginia, 1989.

PERIODICALS

American Architect. In 1913 and 1914 works by Hentz & Reid began to be published in this national architectural journal.

Annual Review, Department of Architecture, Georgia School of Technology. The first edition of this bulletin was published in October 1910; Neel Reid and Hal Hentz were listed in it as design critics for the department and in the 1911–12 and 1915–16 editions.

Architectural Record. In 1917 works by Hentz, Reid & Adler began to appear in this national publication. The October 1919 issue, 46, illustrates three of the firm's Druid Hills houses in a country house article written by Fiske Kimball.

The Atlanta Historical Bulletin. Neel Reid is mentioned in articles in this journal, but especially see: Lewis Paul, "Neel Reid, 1885–1926" (Spring 1971), 9–30. Some of Mr. Paul's data and details have been superceded by new research. Also see Thomas Morgan, "The Georgia Chapter of the American Institute of Architects" (September 1943), 89–167. (Neel Reid and Hal Hentz were incorporators of the Georgia Chapter of the AIA in 1913.)

Atlanta Journal Magazine. The Atlanta newspapers are a source of articles on Reid and his colleagues. See especially Medora Field Perkerson, "He Made Atlanta Beautiful" (October 20, 1946, 6–7).

House & Garden. This national magazine began including Neel Reid designs in the 1920s. See the March 1949 "Southern Houses" issue, pages 94–97, with this statement: "The late Neel Reid, architect of some of the best contemporary houses in Atlanta, Georgia, was never more successful than when he

built this house for Mr. and Mrs. Henry B. Tompkins." Also see volume 1, 1901, and other early editions when it was published in Philadelphia and featured early works by Charles A. Platt.

Life. See "Atlanta Homes," 24, no. 23 (June 7, 1948), 75–82, in which Neel Reid's houses are praised.

Southern Accents. Beginning in the 1970s, articles about Neel Reid houses and gardens were published, and through the present moment.

Southern Architect and Building News. A professional journal published in Atlanta from the late nineteenth century until the 1930s. The Woodruff Library of Emory University, the Atlanta History Center, and the author have issues, but no complete run has been located. Features about Hentz, Reid & Adler designs culminated in the April 1928 issue, 54, no. 4, after Neel Reid died, with a country house issue by editor Ernest Ray Denmark, in which he wrote on page 29, "The late Neel Reid, as the firm's chief designer, was largely responsible for the success of this work." Illustrations from various issues have been used in this book; see picture credits.

White Pine Series of Architectural Monographs. Boston, 1915–1920s. Neel Reid owned copies of this national series containing measured drawings of Colonial and Federal architectural precedents.

ARCHITECTURAL INDEX

INDEX OF JOBS

This alphabetical list of jobs by clients identifies job numbers in parentheses, followed,
where applicable, by text page numbers and/or italicized illustration numbers.